THE COMMON SECRET

SEXUAL ABUSE OF
CHILDREN AND ADOLESCENTS

A series of books in psychology

Editors
Richard C. Atkinson
Gardner Lindzey
Richard F. Thompson

THE COMMON SECRET

SEXUAL ABUSE OF CHILDREN AND ADOLESCENTS

Ruth S. and C. Henry Kempe
The C. Henry Kempe National Center
for the Prevention and Treatment of Child Abuse and Neglect,
Department of Pediatrics,
University of Colorado School of Medicine,
Denver, Colorado

W. H. Freeman and Company
New York

Ruth S. Kempe is Associate Professor of Pediatrics and Psychiatry (Child Psychiatry) at the University of Colorado School of Medicine in Denver, Colorado.

C. Henry Kempe is Professor of Pediatrics and Microbiology at the same institution and is Editor-in-Chief of *Child Abuse & Neglect, The International Journal.* The University Regents have recently renamed Denver's National Center as the C. Henry Kempe National Center for the Prevention and Treatment of Child Abuse and Neglect, of which he is now Director-Emeritus.

Library of Congress Cataloging in Publication Data

Kempe, Ruth S.
    The common secret.

    (A Series of books in psychology)
    Bibliography: p.
    Includes index.
    1. Sexually abused children.   2. Incest victims.

I. Kempe, C. Henry, 1922–   . II. Title. III. Series.
RJ507.S49K45   1984   362.7'044   84-4093
ISBN 0-7167-1624-0
ISBN 0-7167-1625-9 (pbk.)

Printed in the United States of America

234567890 KP 210898765

Dedication

We respectfully and affectionately dedicate this volume
to the memory of Anna Freud (1896–1982)
who for many years enlightened and inspired
all persons, lay and professional,
who wish to understand, comfort, and protect children
through the vicissitudes and the opportunities
of their early years.

Acknowledgements

Our work has had warm and long term encouragement from many. We have received support from the William T. Grant Foundation, The Piton Foundation, the Henry J. Kaiser Family Foundation and the Friends of the C. Henry Kempe National Center for the Prevention and Treatment of Child Abuse and Neglect, Denver, Colorado, U.S.A.

We appreciate the constant professionally shared relationships with all our colleagues of the C. Henry Kempe Center. We are grateful to Gay Dietrich, Candace Grosz and Gail Ryan for their assistance in assembling material for Appendices III through V and their critique of films and publications. We were also helped by critical suggestions received from readers of an early draft: Don Bross, Ph.D., J.D., lawyer, George T. Cherryhomes, M.Div., minister, Allison Kempe, M.D., pediatric resident; Jennifer Kempe, college student, Karin Kempe, M.D., family physician, Clifford K. Kobayashi, M.D., pediatrician, Cathy Kobayashi, R.N., nurse, Mitsuo Tottori, M.D., pediatrician, Jane Tottori, M.A., teacher.

Finally, we are most grateful for the encouragement given this book by Eric Wanner of the Alfred P. Sloan Foundation from its first draft, to W. Hayward Rogers and James F. Maurer of W. H. Freeman and Company, our publishers, and to Mrs. Margaret Cherryhomes, our loyal and devoted friend who saw this book through many changes and unfailingly added her own good suggestions in preparing the manuscript.

TABLE OF CONTENTS

Part I

Introduction   3

CHAPTER ONE
Definitions and Incidence   9

CHAPTER TWO
The Nature of   22
Extrafamilial Sexual Abuse

CHAPTER THREE
The Nature of   47
Intrafamilial Sexual Abuse: Incest

Part II

CHAPTER FOUR
Legal Aspects   82

CHAPTER FIVE
Comprehensive First Aid after Childhood Sexual Abuse 92

Part III

CHAPTER SIX
Evaluation and Treatment of Extrafamilial Abuse   112

CHAPTER SEVEN
Evaluation and Treatment of Intrafamilial Abuse: Incest 144

CHAPTER EIGHT
What Happens to Child and Adolescent Victims   188

CHAPTER NINE
Prediction and Prevention   197

Epilogue:
Vindicating the Rights of Children   205

**Part IV
Appendices**

APPENDIX ONE
A Model   211
Criminal Diversion Program

APPENDIX TWO
Forms for Evaluation   220
and Case Records

APPENDIX THREE
Educational Materials   263
on Child Sexual Abuse

Index   282

THE COMMON SECRET

SEXUAL ABUSE OF
CHILDREN AND ADOLESCENTS

PART I

INTRODUCTION

A discussion of incest and other forms of sexual abuse of children is likely to bring forth feelings of revulsion or disbelief. These same feelings have caused professionals to shy away from the problem of sexual abuse and to underestimate its severity and extent. Difficulties in coping with personal feelings about the very occurrence of child sexual abuse face all who have to deal with it: social workers, police, physicians, nurses, psychologists, teachers, clergymen, lawyers, judges, and the lay public, including former victims.

In order to give these problems more reality and to indicate how they may be dealt with, a number of case examples are included in this book. The rapid progress made in understanding physical abuse, which seemed at one time just as abhorrent, has led us to feel that this problem must be dealt with just as openly.

While the many types of physical, emotional, and sexual abuse and neglect in childhood have been widely studied and discussed in the past twenty-five years, there has recently been much more attention paid to sexually abused children and their families. This is in part due to the fact that in the 1950s the immediate life-and-death decisions involved in serious physical abuse required accurate and prompt diagnosis and treatment, both of the victims and the perpetrators. Attention could then shift slowly to less dramatic instances of child abuse, such as the nonorganic "failure-to-thrive" syndrome due to maternal emotional deprivation and bonding difficulties during infancy. Next, chronic neglect came to the fore, and this very difficult and ill-defined area came to be seen as perhaps the most common and obvious form of long-term child abuse. In the past ten years, the plight of sexually abused children is receiving a rather complete reevaluation.

Social changes over the last one hundred years have increasingly accorded children rights as individuals. Children are no longer regarded as chattel, wholly owned by their fathers as property. Although much is now made of the gradually improving changes in regard to sexual practices involving children, there is a failure to appreciate the remaining widespread and pervasive continuance of childhood sexual abuse over large parts of the world. Boy prostitution, for example, flourishes in areas as far apart as Sri Lanka, the United States, and much of the Moslem world, despite stern condemnation by clergy and governments alike. Child pornography exposes young children of both sexes to the practice of blatant and particularly deviant sexual abuse, often accompanied by threats or bribes, with the cooperation of the parents.

Before the Judeo-Christian era, history was filled with descriptions of sexual abuse of children. Anal intercourse by adult males (often within the family) and by teachers was imposed on young boys and routinely accepted in both Greece and Rome. Early castration of male children helped to preserve a more feminine appearance for enhancement of their beauty as male prostitutes. Some of them became great favorites of men in power and occupied the same kind of position as the royal mistresses of more recent centuries. Well into Christian times, castration of young boys before adolescence to preserve their soprano voices for church choirs was accepted by a series of popes and members of the highest level of the church hierarchy.

Incest and all other forms of child sexual abuse go back to antiquity. Some royal castes routinely practiced incest to preserve the purity of the royal line. As the Incas of Peru and the Pharaohs of Egypt, so, as late as the early nineteenth century, did the Hawaiian nobility of the top rank still insist on incest as a usual and highly regarded practice. With the establishment of the Hawaiian Kingdom in 1810, the ruling Kamahameha family retained this geneological right until the inroads of missionary zeal brought forth a general abandonment of the ancient tradition in the middle of the nineteenth century. From ancient times, royalty (*alii*) routinely expected offspring of brother-sister incest as a duty and in formal marriage. Father-daughter and son-mother incest were, again, accepted until widespread conversions from their own faith occurred and the concept of "sin" became current. A living part-Hawaiian may boast of the fact that his or her grandmother was the product of some fourteen generations of brother-sister marriages, and in many groups a cousin was only considered eligible for marriage if a closer relative was unavailable. Gradually, incest became a criminal offense in many parts of the world (as late as 1908 in England). But it is still not punished at all, for example, in Portugal, Turkey, or Luxembourg.

Currently, we encounter incest at all levels of society with a tilt toward higher rather than lower economic and educational levels. Pedophilia, exhibitionism, and childhood sexual abuse by friends and strangers, which victimize boys as well as girls, are increasingly recognized.

The recent growth in child pornography and child prostitution suggests that little has changed over the centuries except the degree of social recognition of the problem by the public at large and gradual development of laws which reflect these communal concerns.

One of the authors, Ruth S. Kempe, has worked in pediatrics and adult and child psychiatry for twenty-five years. The other, C. Henry Kempe, a pediatrician, started an early adolescent unit in the United States in 1956, gaining experience with the medical and psychological problems of that underserved age group while also getting involved in the field of child abuse at all ages. In retrospect, both of us look back on a number of patients under our care in whose cases we simply did not consider sexual abuse as a major or the single cause of the youngsters' problems. This is particularly disturbing now when the matter seems so very obvious and when competent physicians include sexual abuse in their differential diagnoses in virtually all psychosomatic illnesses involving children and adolescents.

Many psychiatrists still think that incest reports by their patients, some of whom are in hospital for emotional problems which include suicide attempts, are fantasies. Many of our patients report that they have tried again and again to tell social workers and psychiatrists about their incest history but are cut off and obviously not believed. This phenomenon is so commonly observed that it suggests extreme discomfort on the part of therapists in facing the issue, either because of their own background experiences, their training, or their fear of legal implications and confidentiality concerns should they report their findings to the mandated agency.

A number of expert colleagues at our Center are working in this field and many have shared our experiences; we certainly consult with each other a good deal. But we wish to stress that, with two exceptions, all the examples in this book come from our personal clinical experience. Clearly when we concentrate on one individual in such vignettes we are aware that the rest of the family members also have needs, as do the offenders.

In our companion book, *Child Abuse*, Kempe and Kempe, Harvard University Press, The Developing Child Series, 1978 (also Fontana/Open Books, UK) we did discuss sexual abuse, particularly incest, as a part of the whole spectrum of child abuse. This present small volume is also written for students, nurses, physicians, teachers, ministers and priests, lawyers, legislators, and all concerned laypeople who have a desire to be briefly introduced to the subject. It is not written as a scholarly text nor is it meant for experts in the field. For them we recommend *Sexually Abused Children and their Families*, Mrazek & Kempe, eds. Pergamon Press, Oxford and New York, 1981. That rather comprehensive and multidisciplinary book has an extensive bibliography and references with selected annotations, for those who wish for scholarly accounts as well as for more detailed information.

This book, on the other hand, has a brief reading list and visual aids in Appendices III to VI. Specific quotes are made in areas of incidence estimates and others are found at the end of Chapters 2, 6, and Appendix VI as well. Additional references are found in the publications described above. The rest of this book represents the authors' own experiences and views. It is therefore highly personal and there is no attempt to do justice to what is by now a huge literature in the field, with many very different points of view based on each worker's own special experience. We feel that both approaches are needed; and our present brief book is quite deliberately not comprehensive, is not a survey, and is non-technical in the sense that its language is meant to be understandable to all readers.

It is our hope that this book will advance the understanding of those who know little about the subject of sexually abused children and adolescents, an important subject that for too long has been regarded as a "family affair," or the "last taboo."

CHAPTER ONE

DEFINITIONS AND INCIDENCE

Sexual abuse is defined as the involvement of dependent, developmentally immature children and adolescents in sexual activities that they do not fully comprehend and to which they are unable to give informed consent or that violate the social taboos of family roles (Schechter and Roberge, 1976).

Two other definitions may be useful: "The sexual use of a child by an adult for his or her sexual gratification without consideration of the child's psychosocial sexual development" (Mrazek & Mrazek, 1981). This formulation assumes a degree of sophisticated judgment not made by perpetrators and lay people but rather by those experts who deal in retrospect with the discovered problem. It also fails to define "child." Generally, for this purpose, the term "child" covers those ranging from birth through adolescence. A second definition includes "(1) the battered child whose injuries are primarily in the genital area; (2) the child who has experienced attempted or actual intercourse or other inappropriate genital contact with an adult; (3) the child who has been inappropriately involved with an adult in sexual activities not covered by 1 or 2" (Mrazek, Lynch, & Bentovim, 1981). This definition also has problems. A catch-all definition, perhaps more useful in legal settings, it is handicapped by the words "child" (defined by what age range?) and "inappropriate" which is too vague.

The National Center on Child Abuse and Neglect (NCCAN) prefers still another definition: "Contacts or interactions between a child and an adult when the child is being used for the sexual stimulation of that adult or another person. (Sexual abuse may also be committed by a person under age 18.)"

All definitions emphasize that the abuse occurs for purposes desired by adult offenders, usually their own sexual gratification but sometimes for profit, as in pornography. Whatever the response of the child, the activity does show at least disregard of the child's developmental and emotional needs, and often his or her physical safety as well. These definitions must be broad because the kinds of abuse vary enormously in the degree of physical intrusion and in the significance of the perpetrator as a figure in the child's life, from the distantly viewed exhibitionist stranger who is never seen again to the natural father who may be the central person in the child's life.

The categories of sexual abuse which will be described include incest, pedophilia, exhibitionism, molestation, statutory rape and rape, child prostitution, and child pornography. Each category of sexual abuse is described, although our state of knowledge of some, even as to incidence, is sometimes meager.

CATEGORIES OF SEXUAL ABUSE

Incest is defined as any physical sexual activity between family members. Blood relationship is not required: the term "family" is used in its broad social connotation as well as to describe the actual living arrangement of the involved persons. Thus, stepfathers or stepmothers and nonrelated siblings living together, often as a result of their parents' previous marriages, are included in the definition of incest. So are other relatives who do not permanently live with the child—uncles, aunts, and grandparents, for example. Incest, as we define it, has occurred from age 6 months through adulthood, but we have limited our concern to those ages up through adolescence.

Pedophilia (literally, "love of child") denotes the preference of an adult for prepubertal children as the means of achieving sexual excitement. Either girls or boys may be the sexual object, with some variations in the patterns of preference for each. The range of actual activity may include any of the forms of sexual abuse, since the term "pedophilia" really indicates not a kind of activity but the fact that a child must be the participant-object in the activity.

Exhibitionism (indecent exposure) involves the exposure of the genitals by an adult male to girls, boys, and women. The purpose for the exhibitionist is to experience sexual excitement from the encounter (he may masturbate as well as expose himself) and to register the shock or surprise of the onlooker. Although he may talk or call attention to himself, he does not usually make any other approach.

Molestation is a rather vague term which usually includes other vague terms such as "indecent liberties." Molestation includes such behaviors as touching, fondling, or kissing the child, especially in the breast or genital areas, engaging in masturbation of the child, or urging the child to fondle or masturbate the adult. These activities may progress to mutual masturbation or to oral-genital contact. It is an unsatisfactory term because its limits are not defined.

Sexual intercourse (statutory rape) with a child of either sex, including fellatio (oral-genital contact), sodomy (anal-genital contact), or penile-vaginal intercourse, may occur without physical violence through seduction, persuasion, bribes, use of authority, or other threats. The lowest limit at which a child is presumed to be able to give legal consent to intercourse varies from state to state from ages 12 to 18. Except for legal consequences, age of consent is of much less significance than the meaning of the individual experience for the child or adolescent involved.

Rape is defined as sexual intercourse or attempted intercourse without consent of the victim. Even very young children (under 6 months) have been objects of rape, but the majority of victims are over 5 years of age. The perpetrators are generally younger men under 35 years of age. Rapists tend to approach child victims because they are less threatening to the rapist's self-confidence and are unlikely to have the strength to resist.

Alcoholic intoxication is often blamed for the occurrence of rape, and certainly the incidence of intoxication or being "under the influence" is high. Alcohol merely acts as a trigger, reducing inhibition against impulses which are present but which might not be indulged so readily without alcohol. Alcohol does not "cause" rape: it makes its commission easier.

Rape often occurs with deliberation and planning when the perpetrator is not under the influence of alcohol or drugs, and repetition of rapes, as a pattern of aggressive behavior towards females, is a common finding. Nor is forcible rape confined to female victims. Male children and adolescents, in their own neighborhoods and especially in penal institutions, are often subjected to forced oral sex and sodomy. In the former setting, the victim may be assaulted once; in a closed environment, forced rapes may continue over years and involve many partners.

A significant number of child rapists have also practiced exhibitionism, and it is this fact that has led many to reexamine long-held beliefs that divided violent from nonviolent offenders. Further, many children under age 15 who have been involved in incest or childhood rape are also victims of intrafamilial physical abuse which may have gone undetected in the past and which is brought to light only when sexual abuse is discovered.

Sexual sadism is the inflicting of bodily injury on another as a means of obtaining sexual excitement. Fortunately it is rare that this deviation occurs with a child as the object. Depiction of sexual sadism is sometimes part of child pornography, however, and the scenes are not always "faked."

Child pornography is the arranging, photographing by still, video, or film production of any material involving minors in sexual acts including other children, adults, or animals, regardless of consent given by the child's legal guardian, and the distribution

of such material in any form with or without profit, and the exhibition of such material, with or without profit. The 1982 landmark decision of the Supreme Court held that the twenty states
with laws outlawing child pornography did not infringe on First
Amendment rights of freedom of the press. Thus any state can
now take the steps needed under criminal law to ban and prosecute all those involved in the child pornography industry, from
producer to buyer. It may require time to evaluate the effect of
this ruling, but, importantly, the court held that acts need not be
"obscene," a vague term, but that all materials depicting sexual
activities involving children are unlawful.

The estimate of American children involved in prostitution
and pornography is 300,000. The majority of older youngsters involved in prostitution and pornography do so to provide themselves with money for food, clothing, drugs and liquor. Actually
they may turn over most of their money to a pimp. In either case,
they feel no hope of changing their life-style. Testimony at one
congressional hearing revealed that in Los Angeles a 12-year-old
boy can earn as much as $1,000 a day in prostitution.

Child prostitution involves children in sex acts for profit and,
generally, with frequently changing partners. This widespread
practice involves boys as well as girls. Although the children are
sometimes acting on their own, adults (and parents) often manage
their activities and receive the profits.

INCIDENCE AND DISTRIBUTION OF SEXUAL ABUSE

When one looks at each of the different kinds of sexual abuse,
estimates become even less accurate than they are for the problem
as a whole. It is presently impossible to give accurate estimates
of the total incidence of sexual abuse in the United States; they
vary enormously, depending upon how the information has been
obtained. Early estimates were very low. In 1969, a study of the
American Humane Society estimated a yearly incidence of 40 per

million. In 1981, NCCAN estimated an annual incest incidence of over 100,000 cases per year, based on extrapolation of reporting, while another national incest estimate is 250,000 cases per year (Giaretto 1982), based on incidence in one county. A questionnaire of college students revealed nearly 1 in 5 of girls and 1 in 11 of boys reporting had had a sexual experience of some kind with a much older person during childhood (Finkelhor 1979). Figures for officially reported cases are usually much smaller than those obtained from questionnaires, but the likelihood is that questionnaires give a closer approximation of the true total incidence of sexually abusive incidents.

Only a fraction of these are reported. Another study bears out the finding that only a minority of children (1 in 2 girls and 1 in 10 boys) report episodes of sexual abuse, even to their parents. Even so, 9 percent of adults questioned were aware of sexual abuse attempted or completed with their child, but only a fraction of these episodes were then reported to an official agency.

The definition of "any sexual experience" would probably include episodes of exhibitionism, but in many statistical studies, particularly when official reporting by hospitals or protective services agencies is the data base, these less serious episodes may not be counted at all. For example, two superficially similar studies of sexual abuse were reported, one from police department records over three years in Minneapolis, and the other from one year's records of a hospital-based sexual-assault crisis center. In each series, 33 percent of the total cases reported were children under 16 years of age. In the Minneapolis police report, however, 46 percent of the cases were listed as "indecent exposure" (exhibitionism), a category not even included in the second study which reported only on children who were seen for diagnosis and treatment. Thus the former study gave a picture of the total spectrum of sexual abuse, including large numbers of minor incidents, and the latter, a picture primarily of cases involving intimate contact with the child.

Sexual abuse of children and adolescents may be even more common than physical abuse and may occur in a reported sex ratio (4 female to 1 male) markedly different from other forms of child abuse such as maternal deprivation (nonorganic failure-to-thrive in infancy), physical abuse, and neglect.

In a Denver study (Cantwell 1981) of all reported cases of sexual abuse to children under 18 years, the reported incidence for that year was 1 in 1,000 total population. If one considers that much abuse continues for years, the total number of children concerned in sexual abuse is very high, indeed. Further, in the Denver study 45 percent of sexually abused children are under 12 years of age and 16 percent are under 6. Finally, the percentage of perpetrators who are "family members" (fathers, stepfathers, mothers' boyfriends) was 54 percent, and, if one adds to that group other relatives, family friends, and babysitters, the numbers go much higher yet. When the perpetrator was a stranger, the average age of victims was around 12. Sexual play with a trusted adult may not be frightening or perceived as inappropriate by the child under age 6. The average age of onset of all forms of incest, in our personal experience has been eight to nine years, and its duration, about five years.

There has been a 200 percent increase in *reported* cases of sexual child abuse since 1976. The federal government's National Incidence Study (1981) is based on a probability sample using a questionnaire sent to 26 counties in 10 states (out of 3,041 counties in 50 states). It deals with all child abuse cases *reported*, not true incidence. To know the true incidence is not possible in a democratic society where official access to families is generally limited. Even among these *reported* cases, only 33 percent of the children were reported from child protective service agencies. Including some overlap, 86 percent were reported from all other sources combined: families, neighbors, daycare facilities, babysitters, schools, police, physicians, and hospitals. Incidence rates were higher for Caucasian than non-Caucasian children, but *reporting* was higher for lower income groups of all races. As in all forms of child abuse, middle- and upper-middle-class families are more likely to be in a financial position to avoid reporting at all levels.

In the area of sexual abuse, the age incidence rates among male victims were constant across age groups from 6 to 16, and 50 percent of female sexual abuse victims were 11 years of age or younger. Sexual abuse was proportionally more common in rural counties than elsewhere. Demonstrable injury was not at all uncommon. Although the rate of fatalities was very low, there were proportionately more serious injuries associated with sexual exploitation than with all reported physical abuse. Many violent rapes include sodomy (rectal intercourse), and this may not infrequently lead to rectal (as well as vaginal) tears which are very painful; massive blood loss can also sometimes result. The chief cause of death of sexually abused infants and children in New York City each year is rectal hemorrhage.

Among perpetrators, one-third of reported cases involved natural fathers, or, at times, mothers; one-third, nonrelated parent substitutes (stepfathers or mothers' live-in men friends); and the remaining one-third, nonparental perpetrators. Except for exhibitionism and rape assaults by strangers, the perpetrator of sexual abuse tends to be someone the child knows and trusts: a family member, relative, friend or babysitter. Biological mothers were thought to be clearly accessories to their daughters' involvement in incest in at least 43 percent of reported cases, at least to the extent that they knew about the problem and allowed it to continue, often for many years.

But even the very careful National Incidence sample study, done at great cost, failed to enlist needed information from some important protective groups other than social service departments. For example, one large urban hospital, which has an active sexual and physical child abuse team, and one large metropolitan police department in a major city failed to respond to the questionnaire. Also, denial of sexual abuse, even among social service departments and some psychiatrists, mirrors that of the community at large, especially in the case of incest. Further, this study was highly restrictive in that actual penile penetration was required for a "yes" answer in the "intrusion" subcategory, while molestation, child pornography with parental consent, attempted sexual contact, exhibitionism, and pedophilia were not included at all. In all areas, the burden of proof in this study was on the respondent to show that the child had been "*significantly* traumatized or injured." The study estimated an incidence of only 0.2 percent (perhaps 10 percent of actual in-family sexual abuse and 5 percent of all childhood sexual abuse).

This vast discrepancy is based on the differences of reports received from population studies and adult patients about childhood experiences compared to what professionals now know to be minimal reporting from all sources. This may change as the subject of sexually abused children loses some of its taboo. In 1970, the state of Florida had an overall incidence of seventeen reports for *all* child abuse combined. In 1971, when a public education program was launched following the passage of a reporting law, 19,120 reports were made, totally overloading the existing diagnostic and treatment systems. In a 1979 Denver survey of 2,000 cases of child abuse for that year, 327, or 16 percent, were reported as sexual abuse (Cantwell 1981). Between 1967 and 1972, the number of sexually abused children and adolescents increased tenfold in our Center, and from 1973 to 1983 it increased by the same proportion again.

Two million children run away from home each year, and up to half of them do so because they have been abused, primarily sexually. The average age of a runaway child is now 12 years, whereas ten years ago it was 15.

The lowest estimates based on official reports suggest that at least one of every one hundred women has been a victim of incestuous sexual abuse by her father or step-father before she reached adulthood. It is more likely that the number is 2 percent or higher. This would mean that between 1 and 2 million women in the United States have been victimized by incest. Additional

abuse due to other perpetrators, such as exhibitionists, child molesters, and rapists, many of them familiar to the child, bring the
total numbers of women who have experienced some forms of
sexual abuse in childhood to well over 4 percent, or at least 4
million women in the United States. In fact, however, even these
estimates are far below the actual incidence in both sexes, since
most cases of sexual victimization are never reported to anyone.

A far larger incidence figure is obtained if one approaches
these questions through painstaking interviews of adults looking
back on their life experience in a carefully conducted set of interviews. In one such study directed to a population of eastern
United States college students, 19 percent of the women and 8
percent of the men admitted to childhood sexual victimization.
In a most recent landmark study of a large randomized group of
skillfully interviewed female adults, (Russell 1983) 16 percent of
women reported at least one incidence of intrafamilial sexual
abuse before age 18; 12 percent reported at least one experience
before age 14; 32 percent reported at least one experience of extrafamilial sexual abuse before the age of 18; and 20 percent reported at least one such experience before age of 14. When both
categories of sexual abuse are combined, 38 percent report at least
one experience before the age of 18, and 28 percent report such
an experience before the age of 14 years. Only 2 percent of these
cases of intrafamilial sexual abuse and 6 percent of extrafamilial
sexual abuse of female victims were ever reported to the police.

In two recent studies of children or adolescents admitted to
psychiatric wards for other reasons, 14 percent and 37 percent of
the girls and 8 percent of the boys (in one of the studies) had an
unsuspected history of incest.

RELATION OF SOCIOECONOMIC STATUS, INTELLIGENCE, AND RACE TO INCEST

Sexual abuse is now far more often reported than it was just a
few years ago, while the reporting level for all other forms of child

abuse has risen more slowly. Reports of physical abuse, neglect, and nonorganic failure-to-thrive in infancy have not increased dramatically of late. We feel that increased concern has been helped along by the women's movement in this country and the willingness of teachers, mothers of the victims' friends, and the police to intervene, especially if the adolescent victim goes directly to a school counselor or the police. For this reason, criminal action, also, is now initiated far more often than in cases of physical abuse. More recently reported cases and their disposition seem to be much more free of bias against any racial and economic groups when compared with those who are Caucasian and/or more affluent. This is an important change in the past ten years.

The importance in evaluating the representativeness of *all* studies is readily shown by comparing two incest studies: one, completed twenty years ago, showed that, of those coming to official attention in New York City, 67 percent were poor, 64 percent of the incestuous fathers had a low IQ, and a disproportionate number of blacks were found in the sample. In a California sample done ten years later, on the other hand, among three hundred families constituting a fair cross-section of the area with a population of 1.1 million, the families represented the precise racial composition of their community. The make-up of the work force represented in the incest group leaned toward the professional, semiprofessional, and skilled workers, with an average income, in 1972, of $13,413 per household, and a median educational level of 12.5 years. In our experience (1977) with a small sample, which included a number of professional wage earners, the *average* income was about $28,000, and the families could be regarded as in the higher educational and financial groups of our society. In fact, it seemed probable that, as opposed to families involved in physical abuse, families involved in sexual abuse seemed to be materially better off. In our experience, black and Hispanic families were proportionally less represented than Caucasian, but only slightly so. This corresponds with the Giaretto experience in Santa Clara County, California, and it is hardly the sterotypical picture commonly assumed in the past when incest was thought to occur mainly in poor, isolated, remote rural parts of the United States, such as Appalachia. Even older studies, done fifty years ago, of the intelligence of victims had suggested that among sexually abused 8- to 14-year-old girls, 30 percent were mentally retarded. While we have seen sexually exploited children who were retarded and had little judgment about such exploitation, they are a minority of about 5 percent when one includes incest in the total definition of exploitation. The older finding by Williams and Hall that of sixty-eight persons convicted of incest and imprisoned, twenty-four were of low or subnormal intelligence may simply mean, as we feel is common, that less intelligent people are more likely to be found out, charged, and convicted. Thus such conclusions are merely artifacts of a highly selective system of medical and criminal management. This situation has now changed or is rapidly changing in many states.

Is the therapist ever justified in bypassing the "system" and not reporting sexual abuse while still providing the needed care to all members of family and also effectively putting an end to the sexual exploitation? The answer could be yes in rare circumstances if as a condition of being asked to help a deeply troubled adolescent, confidentiality is demanded and if the public sector of that community deals with the problem in a destructive and nontherapeutic way. But the idea that the physician could do better on his or her own than by using the local authorities to deal with physical abuse led to physicians objecting to mandated reporting laws and to their poor utilization by private physicians even to this day. Still, the evidence mounts that the public services responding to child abuse are gradually improving, while effective and humane treatment of each member of a family involved in incest is still in its very infancy and should improve rapidly. Each case differs, and the decision should clearly be to give help skillfully and at once, without regard to the economic level of the family, using a multidisciplinary approach. In the field of sexual exploitation, we are twenty years behind physical abuse, and this difference must be quickly made up.

REFERENCES

Cantwell, H. B. Sexual abuse of children in Denver, 1979; Reviewed with implications for pediatric intervention and possible prevention. *Child Abuse & Neglect* 5:75–85, 1981.

DeFrancis, V. *Protecting the Child Victims of Sex Crimes Committed by Adults*. American Humane Association, Children's Division, Denver, 1969.

Finkelhor, D. *Sexually Victimized Children*. The Free Press, New York, 1979.

House Hearing before the Subcommittee on Crime. House of Representatives, Serial #12, 95th Congress, 1st session. U.S. Government Printing Office, Washington, D.C., 1977.

Mrazek, P. B., and C. H. Kempe (Eds.). *Sexually Abused Children and Their Families*. Pergamon Press, Oxford and New York, 1981.

National Center on Child Abuse and Neglect. *Study Findings: National Study of the Incidence and Severity of Child Abuse and Neglect*. U.S. Department of Health and Human Services, No. (OHDS) 81-30325. U.S. Government Printing Office, Washington, D.C., 1981.

Russell, D. E. H. The incidence and prevalence of intrafamilial and extrafamilial sexual abuse of female children. *Child Abuse & Neglect* 7:2, 133–146, 1983.

Schechter, M. D., and Roberge, L. Sexual Exploitation in Helfer, R. E. and Kempe, C. H. (ed). *Child Abuse and Neglect: The Family and the Community*. Ballinger, Cambridge, Mass 1976.

United States Congress, Senate Judiciary Committee Subcommittee on Juvenile Justice. Exploitation of Children, Hearing, 97th Congress, 1st Session, November 5, 1981, pp. 1–165. U.S. Government Printing Office, Washington D.C., 1981.

CHAPTER TWO

THE NATURE OF EXTRAFAMILIAL SEXUAL ABUSE

In this chapter, we describe sexual abuse in which the offender is someone outside the immediate family of the child; in the following chapter, sexual abuse in which the offender is within the family, or incest. The sexual activities themselves are essentially the same, but because the circumstances and the relationship with the offender can be so different in incest, we prefer to consider it separately. Even such a division must take into account the fact that many of the offenders in repeated extrafamilial abuse are known to the child and family and may sometimes be in the position of surrogate caretaker (as a babysitter) or a position of authority or trust (as a teacher).

Several variables must be considered when talking of the results of sexual abuse of children, variables which make important differences in their effect upon the child immediately or over time. Other variables relate to the degree of pathology in the offender and therefore to the potential for treatment and future protection of child victims. Variables which relate to the effect upon the child are:

1. The character of the act itself and how it is perceived by the child—as confusing, frightening, painful, pleasant, or exciting.

2. The nature of the nonsexual relationship between child and offender, whether or not it is an ongoing contact with the potential betrayal of trust and continuing fear, for example, or even the awakening of impulses of bargaining and greediness in the child.
3. The age and developmental level of the child and his/her ability to understand the significance of the points listed above.
4. The response of the child's family and others to the sexual abuse if the child reports it or if it is discovered.

If one were to look at those factors which might make a child more vulnerable to sexual abuse, one would be obliged to look first at the quality of the child's relationships, especially with his/her parents. This is relevant not only to the reaction of the child to the abusive episode and the response of the family in protecting the child afterward, it may also be implicated in the vulnerability of potential exposure to sexual abuse. If the child is emotionally deprived at home, with rejection or little or no attention and affection from the parents or siblings because the parents are overwhelmed with other problems, the child may be prone to seek attention and affection in an indiscriminate way wherever he/she finds it. In the neglectful family where there is inadequate supervision, the child may be allowed to roam about at odd hours without any protection or anyone noticing an absence. In the abusive family, the child may avoid being home at times and deliberately prefer inappropriate places to being at home.

This by no means implies that most children who are sexually abused have neglectful or inattentive parents, but that when adequate affection and supervision are absent the child may be exposed to greater risk of being available to abuse. Such a history may also make the child more vulnerable to the acceptance of companionship and affection very inappropriately offered by an adult outside the family and more interested in continuing a relationship which soon involves activities which must be kept secret from his/her family.

Many families, because of economic necessity, live in neighborhoods where the streets are unsafe, and yet, because the parents must work, they are unable to be at home to provide adequate supervision for their children. The lack of money for good daycare may place their children at increased risk through no fault of their own. It must also be remembered that well-off families can be equally inattentive or neglectful, particularly when their children become older and rebel against the babysitting which they can afford.

Inattentive parents may be more overwhelmed by other problems or may not recognize their children's needs. Poor intelligence with poor judgment, lack of knowledge about children, a cultural background which does not place a high priority on child development, large family size with little if any time to pay attention to the individual child—all may prevent the parents from noticing their child's behavior or from responding to tentative efforts to confide.

The legal intervention and treatment processes which follow sexual abuse may have profound effects on all participants. Variables relating to the degree of pathology in the offender are discussed with each kind of abuse. It is of great importance, however, to keep in mind that the present state of knowledge concerning sexual offenders is still very limited, particularly with regard to their capacity to respond to treatment. It is also useful to know that sexual offenders do not always remain fixed in a given pattern but may engage in more than one kind of sexual activity. Some may progress from less serious to more dangerous kinds of abuse. Some—exhibitionists, for example—may become disinterested and less active as they grow older. Clearly we need to learn more, not only about each individual offender's history and pathology, but also about how to evaluate his potential for future criminal activity.

EXHIBITIONISM

Exhibitionism (indecent exposure) involves the exposure of the genitals (or buttocks) by an adult male, mostly to girls and women. It is probably the most frequent kind of sexual abuse episode in numbers of occurrences and of victims. A single exhibitionist may continue to perform for many years before he is apprehended, and the chances are great that he will feel the compulsion to resume the activity as soon as he is free again to do so.

Exhibitionists are usually younger men, late adolescents through those in their 20s and 30s. Their numbers decline after the age of 40. Such men usually have normal intelligence, a good work history, and may appear socially intact on superficial view. Often described as shy and immature, they are or have usually been married and may have one or two children.

A frequent explanation for exhibitionistic behavior is that it is based on castration fear and the exhibitionist finds reassurance about his masculinity through seeing the surprise, shock, and fear on the face of his female victim. He may prefer younger girls to women because of their more frightened response.

Usually the exposure takes place in a public place, a public building or a car, or, more often, out of doors, as in a park or school playground after hours. After he has removed part of his clothing, the offender may simply place himself so he will be seen or may call out to the girl to attract attention, or, if seated in a car, he may ask road directions in order to have her come close enough to see him. Some exhibitionists masturbate during the exposure. They may make suggestive sexual comments or ask about the girls' response—"Do you know what this is?"—but usually they do not reach out to make any contact.

For young children who have experienced exhibitionism, these experiences may in themselves not necessarily be very traumatic, though they can upset the family a great deal. The child's response may be fairly transient if the incident occurs in a comparatively safe situation, such as a city street where the exhibitionist is seated in a car or standing in a window, and the child is not approached in any other way except perhaps by a few words to get her attention. Often, what the exhibitionist awaits is the look of astonishment and then fear or shock. Having thus made his impression, he is content with no further action and the child is free to run away.

More frightening, and sometimes appropriately so, is the exhibitionist who chooses an isolated spot in which he and the child are alone. Although usually said to be harmless, a small number of exhibitionists also molest or rape their victims, and a rare few are murderers. When isolated the child is, and feels herself or himself to be, more vulnerable, and the fear is prolonged until she/he has made an escape. If the man also makes an attempt to reach or touch the child, he may well intend to go on to molestation, or even rape and sodomy.

Children should be warned about isolated walks and careless exploration. This may mean "walking a tight rope" between reasonable caution and instilling unnecessary fear. Advice about reasonable coping behavior, here quietly walking away, may be helpful.

Sometimes children are frightened by an exhibitionist because they really do not understand what they have seen, and a calm explanation, perhaps with some anatomical detail, may serve to rob the experience of its unreal and bizarre qualities. It is important with children to be fairly matter-of-fact about such explanations, letting them know that some adults have sick ideas and that, while such people are not necessarily dangerous, they should be avoided.

Of course episodes of indecent exposure should be reported to the police and, if they occurred in proximity to a school, to the school principal as well. With repeated and overt exhibitionism as the beginning symptom, more flagrant sexual abuse can escalate to molestation, then to attempted rape, and even to murder, either because of sadistic impulses or the wish to escape identification, detection, and punishment. Sometimes the body of a murdered child does not show evidence of sexual molestation because preliminary exhibitionism led to a response which caused so much fear that murder occurred first, but the sexual motive should be kept in mind as possible in searching for the perpetrator.

The great majority of exhibitionists never become violent, and even though they may go to prison for a time, they do come out of prison and are apt to repeat their offense, regardless of punishment. These repeat offenders are less likely to be active after around age 40. It is likely that onset of exhibitionism after that age is due to organic causes and is a symptom of disease (brain tumors, advanced alcoholism, brain injuries, and senility).

PEDOPHILIA

Pedophilia is a term which is often used in a confusing way, most frequently as a synonym for "child molester." Strictly used, the term describes not a kind of sexual activity but the kind of object necessary to provide the sexual excitement and therefore to share the activity. For the pedophiliac, this object is a prepubertal child, usually 4 to 12 years old, of either sex. The nature of the sexual activity could vary from simple exposure to violent rape, with the victim a totally strange child or a biological son or daughter. Even in those men who correspond most closely to what is usually meant by the term "pedophile," there may be variations in reasons for the preference for children. A superb and insightful description of pedophilia without any actual contact—or even communication—between adult and youngster appears in Thomas Mann's famous short story, "Death in Venice."

Pedophilia, literally meaning "love of child," was historically sanctioned in ancient Greece and Rome, and it has some stout defenders to this day. The Society for Pedophilia is an above-ground organization that idealizes the love, emotional and physical, between adult males and boys, although it is an offense under law to have physical contact.

Recently, more and more groups for the promotion of homosexual pedophilia have surfaced. The North American Man-Boy Love Association (NAMBLA) was founded in Boston in 1978. The society, with many members in other states, puts itself forward as a lobbying organization with a "libertarian, humanistic outlook on sexuality." It argues that adult society has no right to limit a child's right to a sexual partner. By contrast, for example, a similar Los Angeles based group, the René Guyon Society, has as its motto "Sex by 8 is too late." The British Pedophilic Information Exchange (P.I.E.) which has a longer history wants to lower the age of consent to as low as 4. How many boys are held under direct or indirect constraint is not clear, but from time to time some "disappeared child" is found by authorities living with or fleeing from among such pedophilic individuals.

Such new forms of openly publicized activity are defended by members as rational extensions of recent changes in sexual permissiveness and the "sexual revolution." They liken their preferences to those of adult homosexuals and demand the same openness. Many of these men appear to come from the higher economic and social strata; one recent set of arrests included a physician, a teacher, a politician, and a physicist.

It is generally thought that many offenders may have themselves been victims in childhood. One characteristic such pedophiles seem to share is the need to control a child sexually, perhaps in order to convince themselves that their own past personal experiences can be rendered harmless and idealized through repetition. For others the "movement" is simply a way to try to legitimize what they know to be socially unacceptable acts and to put them into some acceptable relationship with other recent social changes which have affected sexual behavior.

Some sexual exploration between preadolescent boys and girls and younger boys and boys is common and normal in the developing child ("playing house"). With adolescence, a gradual change occurs in the majority of young people. They tend to become more shy about exposing their bodies to anyone, and while adolescents fantasize a great deal about various sexual objects and acts, they tend to develop sexual preferences of a permanent type during the period between ages 12 to 20. Most clearly seem headed for heterosexual lives; others are drawn to persons of their own sex almost exclusively; and a third group are either bisexual or asexual by preference. While literally thousands of studies about these developmental traits and changes have been done, we have no actual factual knowledge of these choices at this time to explain the development of preferences. To what extent the social millieu, life experience, hormonal differences, cultural custom, or even genetic differences play a role, nobody knows as yet.

In pedophilia less is known about causation than in any other form of sexual abuse of children. At times pedophilia may not be accompanied by overt sexual activity but rather may express itself through socially very acceptable behavior (such as giving genuine and suitable gifts and by companionship, such as taking a child to a circus), all totally approved by the parents or the divorced mother who wants her child to have male models for identification. Other pedophiles write poetry or devote their lives to working for children in socially approved settings. Some of these adults feel no conscious sexual attraction; others keep the sexual attraction carefully hidden in personal fantasies. At other times, however, temptations to cross over into forbidden activities may be irresistible, to the dismay of the offender, the victim, and his trusting family or social group. Thus, from time to time, choirmasters, Boy Scout leaders, Little League Baseball coaches, and teachers are found to be suffering from pedophilia. While prompt disruption of the contact is needed, it is not clear that all of these first-time borderline offenders, often legal nonrepeaters, should be criminally prosecuted, especially as there is evidence that self-punishment in the perpetrator is great and the loss of esteem and often of employment are in themselves punishment of great magnitude. Often child molestors are brutally assaulted in prison by fellow inmates. Long-term psychotherapy has, with this limited group been, at times, successful, but it must involve the spouse if there is one, and it must not be cursory.

Pedophilia has been studied in varying circumstances—some subjects have been in private or clinic psychiatric treatment and some in mental hospitals or penitentiaries—so findings are not always easy to correlate. In general, these men have normal intelligence, they tend to have unremarkable work histories, and many have lives which are otherwise successful and unexceptional. There is a real probability that three groups can be differentiated from one another on the basis of victim choice. One group (heterosexual) prefers contact with little girls; another (homosexual), with boys; and a third small group (undifferentiated) is equally interested in both boys and girls. There is no study as yet which has given a convincing explanation of how these groups have developed, just as we do not yet have convincing evidence as to why many individuals are homosexual. One factor which seems to be of real significance is that many of these men are or have been married, and there is some evidence that when the marriage is frustrating or has failed or the spouse is no longer available, these men then may turn to a child for sexual activity rather than to another woman.

Regardless of object choice, pedophiles are more active at certain peaks in age. The first of these occurs in late adolescence and the early 20s and probably represents a delay in sexual maturation, with immature sexual exploration with a younger child as the substitute for genital activity with a girl of the same age. A second age peak occurs in the 30s and probably represents the largest group, both homosexual and heterosexual. There are men in this group, many of whom have married, who found their marriages unsuccessful and then, instead of looking for an adult partner, have regressed to choosing a prepubertal girl for sexual activity. In keeping with this kind of retreat from competition in the adult social and sexual spheres, these men are often described as passive-aggressive personalities who frequently have wives who are dominant-dependent and demanding but ungiving within the marital relationship. In the same age group, the other homosexual half of the pedophile group also seems to retreat from adult sexual competition. They are less often married. They may often be engaged in voluntary jobs which serve children's groups in addition to their usual work. This does not necessarily mean that their victims are found in their jobs but that they spend their time with boys.

The older age group of pedophiles is smaller than usually thought. These men have often had a moderately satisfactory family life but now find themselves alone, without any relationships. In looking for closeness, they choose inappropriately young children and, if sexual impulses break through, become offenders.

The undifferentiated group has not been well segregated in most studies thus far, but they seem to include a smaller number of pedophiles who are indiscriminate as to choice of boys or girls and whose sexual development is poorly organized, perhaps in conjunction with more pervasive sexual and personality pathology. They tend to be more consistent throughout life in their sexual interests, less dependent than the others on happenstance in initiating sexual acts, and probably are more resistant to treatment.

Alcohol plays an important role in pedophilia as it does in much of child sexual abuse. It appears that in more than half the cases of pedophilia the offender has been drinking alcohol, and this may well have been sufficient to lower weak inhibitions against impulses which could otherwise be resisted. Deliberate use of alcohol when temptation is mounting is one self-deceptive way of denying responsibility.

The sexual activity usually described when speaking of pedophiles is a fairly immature form of sexual gratification and reveals a desire to dominate the sexual activity. It consists primarily of undressing and looking at the child, touching and fondling and kissing, especially the genital areas, and perhaps masturbation of the child. At the same time, the adult pedophile may request the child to do these same things to him. Such activities are often initiated very slowly, over several episodes. The lack of more mature sexual activity raises the probability of a fixation at an early stage of psychosexual development as a major factor in the offender. The domination of the child has been described as a possible attempt to feel in control, to master the feelings associated with a simular episode in the offender's childhood.

The child molester is often at least vaguely known to the child or may be within the family's social circle. He does not usually threaten but ingratiates himself by playing games with the child, offering candy, or providing activities and treats which may be approved or encouraged by the parents who do not recognize the danger. Only gradually does he introduce a sexual aspect to his activities with the child. The behavior of the molester may not seem strange to the child, and he may often not be frightening, because any element of coercion is clothed in seduction.

The threats concerning exposure may come later and may be phrased so as to make the child a partner who is also fearful of exposure. If molestations take place over a period of time, and they often do, the child is gradually exposed to more explicit sexual activity, and this may go beyond fondling of the genitals or mutual masturbation to actual intercourse. In more recent studies, hand or genital contact with the genitals of the child is frequently reported.

A good ten-year outcome may be seen in the case of *Mr. T.*, a brilliant young lawyer and father of two. On several occasions he engaged in genital fondling of 6- to 8-year-old girls, friends of his daughter who were in his house visiting his children. The neighbors contacted us with a view to stopping this behavior, wanting at the same time to prevent the ruin of this attractive family and to obtain psychiatric help for the patient. Their compassionate and nonpunitive view was largely the result of their affection for the lawyer's young wife, whom they greatly liked. They insisted, however, that the family leave the neighborhood promptly. The patient moved to a distant city where he entered psychotherapy and has had a long-term cure of his addictive pedophilia. His professional and family life have remained stable.

A less happy outcome occurred for *Dr. A.*, a 53-year-old physician, who was accused of fondling the genitalia of his pre-adolescent boy patients. A hearing before the medical board confirmed that he regularly measured the penis of each of his boy patients, much as he would record their weight. His defense was that measurements like these are part of comprehensive care, but the board held that the procedure was not routine anywhere, except when the specific medical problem concerned the size of the penis, as is the case in some hormonal disorders. He voluntarily resigned his license to practice but refused offers of help.

There is considerable disagreement in the literature about the long-term effects of extrafamilial sexual abuse and incest, and clearly a lack of adequate information upon which to base conclusions. Because so few studies have been completed in the past and attempts at follow-up have not adequately studied many variables, it is difficult to do more than draw tentative conclusions. Before 1970 there were few attempts to study the psychological characteristics of sexual abuse victims, and almost no effort was made to learn about their different responses at different ages, in different family situations, and in reaction to different kinds of sexual assault. Currently several major centers are doing good work in sexual abuse, and with time, the knowledge concerning both victim and offender should be greatly expanded.

One distinction which is of importance is whether or not the victim was specifically known to the offender and specifically chosen, or whether the abuse was more the result of seizing an opportunity which was more or less accidental. The more complete the separation between the offender and the victim, the easier it is for the victim to see himself/herself as totally innocent of provoking the encounter. The tendency of so many people to retain the old attitude toward sexual abuse or rape, epitomized by the phrase "she asked for it," is evident in the kind of questions asked of the victim: "What kind of clothes were you wearing? What were you doing in that place at that time? Didn't you know it would be dangerous to speak to a stranger? Couldn't you have run away?"

SEXUAL INTERCOURSE BETWEEN CHILD AND ADULT

Statutory Rape

Nonviolent intercourse (vaginal, anal, or oral penetration) with a child may occur after a long period of preliminary seduction by an adult without the child necessarily experiencing this as a violent attack. With younger children, oral or anal intercourse is perhaps more frequently attempted than vaginal intercourse, but there are few reports on how this escalation was perceived by the child, whether gradual seduction really could make anal and vaginal intercourse less painful in the beginning.

The legal age of statutory sexual consent in the United States varies widely: age 7 in one state; age 10 in three states; age 12 in nine states; age 13 to 16 years in twenty-three states; age 17 in Iowa; and age 18 in fourteen states. Men are liable to charges of statutory rape if they become sexually involved with females under those ages in those states, even though their female partners approve. Penalties range from one year imprisonment to death.

It is our belief that, even with consent, intercourse with its quality of urgency for the adult partner must have a very different significance for the prepubertal child than the fondling and masturbation so much more apt to be found in molestation or in the exploratory sexual play of children. Of necessity, the need for privacy and secrecy is also greater, and this places the child in isolation in at least one aspect of his/her life.

SEXUAL INTERCOURSE BETWEEN CHILD AND ADULT

Forcible Rape

Rape of children and adolescents is viewed with particular anger by most societies, and the penalties for convicted offenders are usually more severe than for rape of adults. Vaginal penetration should be viewed as no more or less damaging an aggressive act than anal penetration (sodomy) or oral-genital acts which may be forced on either boy or girl victims. The physical trauma and the emotional damage may be quite similar and demand the same amount and quality of services. The degree of physical damage to the child is related to the size of the child vis-à-vis that of the attacker, to the violence of the attack, and to the amount and kind of other physical violence inflicted at the same time.

Rape has occurred with victims ranging from a few months in age through all the years of childhood. It is relatively uncommon in the very early years, but oral-genital or anal-genital rape may occur in children before school age.

Rape of children can occur within the family setting (see Chapter 4 on incest) or a boyfriend of the mother or a family friend left alone with the child may be the offender. Also frequent is the rape of a child by someone who takes advantage of access to the unprotected child in her/his own home or neighborhood area or temporarily entices the child into an isolated area or a car. Among older children and adolescents, increased freedom of movement and exposure to unprotected settings increase the possibility for rape to occur. This is particularly true of young adolescent girls who now are allowed more freedom and are less supervised than used to be customary. Older children are also seen as less "off limits," less vulnerable, to some rapists.

The degree of force required for submission may be minimal or limited to threats of harm. Coercive rape may involve only verbal threats which derive their strength from the comparative size and strength of the rapist or his position of authority and power in relation to the child (if he is a father, a teacher, or a doctor). The verbal threat may seem very real to the child who sees no alternative but submission possible. Or rape may be accompanied by threat with a weapon, such as a knife, or by physical assault so severe that the rape itself seems a minor part of the trauma. Even a young adolescent may be so frightened by a sudden assault that, beyond an attempt to flee and tearful pleas during submission if threatened with serious harm, resistance is not even considered. The overwhelming nature of forcible sexual assault to most children must be kept in mind because, in some legal jurisdictions, rape is legally defined only when there is evidence of strenuous physical resistance on the part of the victim, even if the victim is still a child of 12.

Rape by a peer or slightly older adolescent may be particularly hard to report by the victim because many adults view such occurrences as more easily avoided or resisted. Yet again, the individual circumstances must be carefully considered. The feelings of fear, helplessness, and violation may be exactly the same, and the aftereffects may be no less severe—only complicated by issues of self-doubt and confusion.

Gang Rape

In recent years, reports of gang rapes have increased strikingly. These have involved children as young as age 4 and as many rapists as 14. Often male and, on occasion, female witnesses do nothing to stop these very violent acts. Under United States law, these witnesses are not legally culpable. This is in sharp contrast to virtually all Western European countries where being present at a felonious act is taken as an act of complicity and is subject to punishment. It is curious that while in our law anyone is considered an accessory who helps in a felonious conspiracy or is involved in any financial crime, such as bank robbery, our "bystander" laws do not oblige citizens to intervene in rape assault if they do not wish to do so or feel that they cannot safely do so. They are "accessories" only if they are physically involved in the gang rape.

A serious aspect of these episodes is the violence to the victim. Frequently, oral sex and rectal as well as vaginal penetration is forced upon the victim by a large number of attackers, and what may have been primarily a sexual approach quickly turns into a very dangerous attack. Victims require the best possible crisis support and usually prolonged therapy.

Gang rape is particularly traumatic both physically and emotionally. The degrading, dehumanizing characteristics of such an episode are especially hard to cope with for both boy and girl victims. If the offenders are close in age—teenagers—the effects may be even more devastating because the victim may feel both degraded and singled out for the abuse. It is important to note that gang rapes under special conditions such as captivity or those that a victim is afraid to report, may be repeated.

Rape is usually an offense committed by a male adolescent or young man. One half of the rapes in the United States are committed by men under 25 years of age, and three-fourths, by men under 30 years of age. Four main reasons are often given for rape: (1) general hostility against all women or displaced onto women; (2) the influence of alcohol or drugs as an inhibition releaser (over half of rapists had been under the influence of alcohol or drugs); (3) sociopathic personality, which causes the offender to be aggressive and assaultive on occasion toward anyone, with the sexual assault simply one more means of inflicting harm; and (4) the use of sexual attack as a defense against fears of homosexuality or sexual inadequacy. Any combination of these reasons might be operative with the offender. It should be noted that homosexual assault of young boys may often be committed by men with a heterosexual life style.

Child rapists are not a uniform group, but they do share a total disregard for control of violent impulses toward their victims. While it is now often stated that adult rape is nonsexual and an expression of violent anger toward women, we feel that the sexual element in childhood rape is often at least an initial motivation. Rape of children and adults often includes sodomy.

Penetration of the anal sphincter requires penile erection implying, at a minimum, a fusion of aggressive and sexual impulses,
if not primary sexual motivation. The child rapist is seeking an
outlet for sexual impulses and, whatever the causes are that prevent him from seeking out and seducing (or even raping) an adult
woman, those causes may make a comparatively defenseless child
seem an appropriate sex object to him, no matter how unwilling
the child may be. Such rape, if violent enough, can be a life-and-
death matter. The immediate effect of such abuse is hurt—physical pain, fear, helplessness. If the threats include, as they usually
do, a threatening prohibition against telling about the offender or
the incident, the child is also left fearful of seeking help. Rage
against the attacker may be present early but probably goes unex-
pressed, or it may appear later, when the child is safe. Some children do not tell anyone about the rape because of the fear of retaliation (or in boys, apparently, also because of intense shame),
and the rape may accidentally be discovered later, if ever. At times
severe physical assault may be the presenting complaint, and the
rape discovered on physical examination. Even then, the child
may be fearful of telling about the offender and may need specific
reassurance before he/she is able to do so.

John S., a 23-year-old unemployed boy friend of a divorced, middle-class mother, was babysitting for her two daughters, aged 6
and 14. He first began to sexually assault the 14-year-old girl,
then raped her despite her efforts to resist by screaming, hitting,
and biting. While she ran for help to distant neighbors, he raped
the 6-year-old and fled. When captured, he told the police that
he had had two beers and remembered nothing of the events.
The children both required hospital care for emotional as well
as medical reasons. The 6-year-old had a 1-inch vaginal tear
which was repaired. The older child had a hymenal tear and
bruises. Both had semen in their vaginas, and both required antibiotics to prevent gonorrhea with which the attacker was af-
flicted.

Loving and supportive nursing and, later, psychiatric care was given to both victims, who seemed to view the event as a "bad accident." The mother had reason to feel guilty: she had known of her friend's inability to handle any alcohol without becoming violent. The psychiatric diagnosis of the perpetrator indicated he had a violent, sociopathic personality, not likely to change at any time. He remains in prison for an indeterminate sentence, but he is a model prisoner to date and will eventually gain parole.

MALE VICTIMS OF SEXUAL ASSAULT

Evidence is accumulating that sexual assault of male children occurs much more frequently than has been reported; 12 percent to 15 percent of all rape victims are male. Studies have usually indicated that the vast majority—if not all, during the early teen-age years—of sexual assaults are against girl victims. However, there is now reason to believe that older boys are assaulted as well, but that they do not report the attack to anyone. Indeed, as many boys as girls may be vulnerable to sexual abuse.

Male victims of sexual assault most frequently have been subjected to fellatio (oral-genital contact) or sodomy (anal-genital contact). While physical injuries are uncommon, the victim may have resisted and may require emergency care for trauma. The experience is, of course, a most frightening one, especially to children, because it is generally totally unexpected and often accompanied by serious threats. Contrary to public opinion, sexual assault of males is at least as often perpetrated by heterosexual as by homosexual offenders.

Whether the victim is a young male or a young female, rape is an act of aggressive sexual domination which the victim feels powerless to prevent, usually because of fear of injury. Yet being taken unaware or being ineffectual in fighting back leaves the young male with serious doubts about his self-esteem and his masculine identity. Feelings that he should have been able to defend himself or that there must have been some reason for choosing him as a victim, although irrational, may be strong enough to prevent his reporting the rape. Instead, he may continue to suffer shame and doubts about his normality in silence.

Many victims have concerns that the aggressive act will somehow make them follow homosexual practices in the future, and they require much and repeated reassurance. Certain victims do not want to have their parents know of the event, and, if necessary, the doctor must exercise utmost discretion, providing needed physical and psychological care in a confidential manner. It is, however, far preferable to involve the parents, and always the police, to help put a stop to any repeated assault so often feared by the victim. Rarely is this kind of assault an isolated event for the offender, and there may be literally hundreds of victims of a single perpetrator in a given metropolitan area.

Here is an example of a very common, and often unreported form of abuse which involves forcible sexual attacks on a boy.

As a 14-year-old schoolboy, *Jerry* was forced into the driveway of a home while walking along a fairly busy city street. His assailant, a man in his 30s, wielded a knife and threatened him with harm if he did not perform oral sexual acts with him in the shadow of the building. Jerry was left suddenly, with his genitalia exposed, when the assailant, who had threatened to perform sodomy as well, was scared off by a passing car. The victim was unable to move at all for several minutes, and he was found in a state of shock by a passerby, who took him to the hospital for emergency care.

The police were called and participated, along with his parents, in his recounting of the event. It is likely that the entire episode occurred over just a few minutes. The assailant was a suspect known to police as a perpetrator of similar attacks in the same neighborhood but, in the absence of "proof beyond a reasonable doubt," he had been released and not charged by the police in three prior suspected attacks. With Jerry's detailed description, he was apprehended, tried, convicted, and jailed for three years.

Jerry seemed to have great strength and at first showed no obvious signs of unusual distress: he reacted like someone who has had a lucky escape in an automobile accident, his parents were supportive, and his return to school was uneventful. He received no physical trauma, but was treated for the possibility of a gonorrheal infection with antibiotics and remained well. (His assailant was shown to have been actively infected when he was arrested later the same day.) But Jerry was far from well. During weekly sessions he stressed that aside from the fear for his life which he had experienced and the fact that he had put up no defense ("Am I a coward?"), he also had real fears of now being well on the way toward being "unmanly," dirty, and damaged in some way. He wondered frequently if he would ever be able to tell anyone of his attack and how likely it might be that he would now become homosexual, a thought he had never considered before. His relationship with a girl of his own age, which had been a tender and loving social relationship, seemed to him spoiled, and he broke off any contact. His parents, too, were superficially supportive, but also blamed him in some way for the event. "What was he doing in that part of town anyway?" In truth, both they and the boy felt that he was somehow to blame.

After six counseling sessions, with the parents and with the victim alone, all three were seen together once more, and all the issues were discussed for a final time. During the interval, Jerry had told his girlfriend all about the attack and received no rebuff, only loving concern. He felt far more secure about himself, and his life returned to normal state. His parents, too, were able to direct their anger to the attacker and to show patience and understanding during minor and normal adolescent arguments without bringing up this event as if it were the cause of their disputes. Now, seven years later, Jerry is at university and doing well. He hopes to marry his long-time girlfriend when they both graduate from professional schools. They have lived together for the past year and are sexually well adjusted. His recall of the attack is hazy, and he dismisses it as "just one of those things that can happen." Jerry was fortunate to receive supportive help promptly.

A vastly less happy outcome is the case of *Ross* who was arrested for driving without a license at age 15 and held overnight in a general holding cell of a prison for adult offenders before coming before the court the next morning. His father had declined to post bail for him "to teach him a lesson." Ross was not separated from older prisoners because of overcrowding, despite the existing rules of the police receiving unit, and was gang-raped by four older inmates. He committed suicide before sunrise.

CHILD PROSTITUTION AND PORNOGRAPHY

Prostitution

While both child prostitution and child pronography often occur with the active consent of the guardian/parent(s) who directly benefit financially from the activities, in many instances runaway children and adolescents simply find life at home intolerable and look for an easier and more rewarding life. Very often the family life from which they come is disintegrating or has offered them little affection or attention. Neglect or rejection has given them very little self-esteem but a great hunger for attention and approval. If their school work has been poor and if they have no work experience, these youngsters have no skills with which to support themselves, and they often see their sexual potential as their only value.

Runaways who left home because of sexual exploitation or other abuse fall ready prey, especially in major cities, to prostitution rings which promise support, security, and affection, but soon lead fairly directly to prostitution from which escape becomes very difficult. Youngsters may be promised shelter, food, good clothing, and other luxuries, as well as much emotional support, by their procurers. They are often quickly identified at metropolitan bus stops by knowledgeable pimps ("ponce," in the United Kingdom) who specialize in recruiting young male and female adolescents into these pursuits.

The reason for the escape from home may have been the sexual or physical abuse these children were subjected to there, and incest is not an uncommon history when these youngsters finally come to the attention of society through arrests or outreach groups. A significant number of both young male and female prostitutes have suffered forcible sexual acts, either within or without the family, or they have been taught that there is a direct relationship between sex and the material rewards which accompany an easy life. These often quite naïve youngsters can also quickly be made into drug addicts and become first completely dependent on and then fearful of their "protectors." They rarely escape unless very direct action is taken by the police and the family, once the child is found. Indeed, they soon identify with their own small subculture and may resist efforts at rehabilitation.

Some children involved in prostitution do so while still living at home. Prepubertal children may be involved in "sex rings" with several other friends, organized by one or more men who meet with them regularly and exchange gifts, money, or special activities for individual sexual contacts. The adult offenders often have some plausible reason for contacts with the group, leading a sports activity or being a family friend, for example. Peer group pressure, as well as threats and the children's own fears, keep them bound in the secret activity, unknown to their parents.

Adolescents may also become involved in prostitution while still living at home, after initiation by a friend or relative. Occasionally they are forced into prostitution by the parents who keep the proceeds. Although most children who prostitute while at home suffer the same difficulties which have caused others to run away, a few are decided by the lure of "easy money" and a promiscuous environment. Other children have, in effect, been "on the street" as their social milieu from an early age, and prostitution may simply be an additional survival technique in a harsh environment.

Child Pornography

Child pornography as a form of child abuse may be particularly pernicious because it is rarely based on any real relationship with the offender. Occasionally an adult may persuade a child to allow two of them to be photographed by a videocamera, for example, during sexual activity, as part of an ongoing sexual relationship; but ordinarily pornography is filmed for a commercial market, using children, perhaps with strange or different partners. One of the hallmarks of pornography is the tendency to emphasize the deviant as well as the obviously erotic, and children may therefore be asked to perform unusual sexual behaviors for photographing: group sex, sadomasochistic rituals, bestiality, or other deviant sex may be acted out, at least in pretense.

The methods by which children are recruited vary, including persuasion by promises of money or gifts, seduction by an adult and later introduction to the group, outright deception as when the child is told the acts will be "only pretend" and then the rape is performed, and the "selling" of the child's services by a parent or guardian. Some children become so greedy for the money they are paid that they perform eagerly. It might be assumed that some children may be given alcohol or drugs at times to make them willing, but no specific incidence information is available on this point.

Child pornography is not only used for the excitation of adult consumers, it may be used by some of these consumers in the seduction of potential child victims. Pornographic pictures are carefully left out where they will be seen, and the child is encouraged to copy the behavior. Or videotapes or movies may be shown to the child with the dual purpose of rousing sexual excitation and assuaging fear or guilt. Pornography has also been used by fathers in promoting incest. Telling a child that forbidden behaviors are not bad may seem more convincing if they are pictured openly, with flattering captions.

Middle-aged pedophiles tend to build large collections of these child pornography videotapes and films, and there is a ready exchange between such collectors. Presumably the "storage" of such material assures a future supply for those men who fear that they may have a more difficult time in actively practicing their compulsion and can then rely on purchased collected material. The compulsive quality of the hoarding, however, makes this explanation seem inadequate.

While it is thought that the bulk of mass produced child pornography material comes from Holland, Denmark, and the United States, in that order, the customers are located worldwide, with the most numerous customers found in Germany and here in the United States.

The broader implications of child pornography are not the constitutional rights of a relatively few and well-to-do customers but the pervasive view in the Western world that young children are legitimate sex objects for adults. An increasing focus on ever younger fashion models in explicit sexual roles in public advertising has been coming to the fore in recent years, often in "respectable" magazines. Described by the advertising industry as "legitimate kiddie porn," this is to be condemned.

Very young adolescent girls may be photographed as prepubescent virginal girls demonstrating that they are very eager for all kinds of sex. Older adolescents may be involved occasionally in that pseudo-child-pornography which is legal. More often they are involved in male or female adult pornography which has, in the past decade, had an increasing emphasis on deviant sex, especially violent and sadomasochistic situations. A few of these adolescent models become very successful financially, and many hope to make their way to a real movie career via pornographic films.

Traditionally, there is a close connection between pornography and prostitution; being involved in one makes it difficult to resist involvement in the other. Organized crime, which exploits both of these forms of sexual abuse, makes them dangerous indeed for many children and teenagers. But petty criminals, working on a small scale, may be just as dangerous to the individual adolescent, who is often exposed to violence and crime through pornography and prostitution.

CHAPTER THREE

THE NATURE OF
INTRAFAMILIAL ABUSE:
INCEST

In discussing sexual abuse, there is a tendency to treat incest as a completely different subject. In one way this has value, for sexual abuse by a parent does threaten the most important relationships the young child possesses and may have profound effects on development. It also does not occur in a healthy family, and there are, therefore, other serious difficulties for the child in growing up, most often the lack of a mature, warmly loving and concerned mother and father. The same lack of parental protection and close family ties may also be present when sexual abuse involves more distant relatives, acquaintances, or strangers, but the meanings of incest for individual development are special. The physical form incest takes, however, is similar to sexual abuse by anyone else, from exhibitionism to molestation to regular intercourse to violent rape. Incest violates one of the most tenaciously maintained taboos in most societies. It also deprives the child of the essence of his/her role in the family vis-à-vis the parents, that they will meet the child's needs for nurture and protection until the child is mature enough to seek out his/her own relationships.

When discussing any close personal relationships among family members, it is crucial that the reader not fall into the misunderstanding that there is anything abnormal about love, cuddling of infants, and expressions of affection by kisses and hugs between parents and their children. These are, indeed, highly desirable because they are the signs of close concern and love between family members. The question has become relevant, however, where the line should be drawn between what is normal behavior and what is harmful to the child and the family. It is, at times, a fine line. Most parents have by instinct a good feeling of what is "right" as they judge it from their own upbringing, from their expectation of normal sexual modesty developing in childhood, and from an understanding that what is appropriate for a small child might be highly inappropriate for an older one. For example, most fathers do enjoy having their baby of either sex with them in the bath and having them safely experience playing in warm water in a happy and asexual setting. This would not be true if the daughter were to bathe with her father at age 3, to say nothing of age 8.

It is our impression that incest may have been increasing in the United States in recent years, perhaps because of the great changes in family life: rising divorce rates, birth control, abortion, increasing tolerance about sexuality in general, and a more tolerant view of sexual acts between nonrelated household members who come from divorced or previously separated homes. This is particularly true of brother-sister incest between stepchildren who are living as a family but are not related; we believe that cultural attitudes about this group of adolescents are rapidly becoming more casual. In some states, marriages between these unrelated siblings are no longer illegal.

Father-daughter and stepfather-daughter incest account for approximately three-quarters of *reported* incest cases. Girls involved with fathers or stepfathers during preadolescence or very early adolescence are often the oldest daughters. Mother-son, mother-daughter, and brother-sister incest account for most of the remaining one-quarter of reports, though sibling incest is rarely reported and is probably a far more common part of the total sexual-abuse picture than current statistics indicate. It is also important to realize that many cases are never reported or included in statistics, especially in more well-to-do families, which can seek help through other means such as private psychiatry and have not necessarily been included in statistical sources. This is especially true if the "victim" did not seek help until much later, as an adult, as often happens when the relationship is a more unusual one such as that between mother-in-law/son-in-law or father-in-law and daughter-in-law. Reporting of father-daughter incest probably happens most often, because the daughter precipitates a crisis when the situation becomes intolerable to her, as opposed to sibling incest, for example, where the maturing of the siblings may change both partners and, therefore, the nature of the relationship, spontaneously.

Father-daughter incest is usually nonviolent. However, in preadolescence and early adolescence, the association between physical abuse and sexual exploitation is sometimes striking, and it is not uncommon for the adolescent girls we see as runaways or with physical injuries to admit in treatment to suffering from both forms of abuse. We do find men with psychopathic personalities and indiscriminate sexuality who view children as objects, and these men are often also violent. But most fathers incestuously involved with their daughters are introverted personalities who tend to be socially isolated and family oriented.

One noteworthy and largely unmentioned relationship between fathers and daughters and mothers and sons which does not involve any physical or technical incestuous behavior is, rather, a type of symbiotic or mutually dependent state. The growing child and one parent each finds the other the most important person in his/her life, a relationship that often strains the parents' marriage and tends to delay or to make it impossible to form a lasting relationship with anyone else by the maturing child. The young adults' marriages tend to fail, and fail again, or they never attempt marriage. Homosexual relationships, if they occur, are sometimes more successful. Friends may comment on the restricted life and total devotion of daughter-father or son-mother to the virtual exclusion of all others. Clearly, there has been an untoward effect on the child (by most measures) as a result of the too bonded and exclusive relationship. It is not incest, but it does have some of the very same effects as technical incest upon the child's life. She or he fails to grow independently and to make her or his own developmental choices as adolescence progresses, and thus this kind of relationship may be just as crippling. The incestuous nature of the relationship is never recognized on a conscious level by anyone involved.

It is likely that in intensive treatment (which, of course, is not usually indicated) one might find that underlying the openly admirable parent-child relationship is an unresolved Oedipal wish by the daughter to replace the mother, with the father's unconscious agreement. The same situation applies to the devoted son and mother. Neither parent nor child would consciously ever tolerate such thoughts, and it is often the coincidental circumstances which support the relationship. The death of the mother, an early breakdown of the marital relationship if an extramarital affair is unacceptable to the father, or the sharing by the father and daughter in a narcissistic way of a particular talent or interest may serve to endow their relationship with special value. One might think of it as a kind of nonsexual incest. If the child would not otherwise be able to experience such closeness, it may bring great benefit to both partners. Indeed, in earlier times when young women had almost no respectable way to earn a living in order to live independently, the young woman who was not fortunate enough to marry might find such a relationship great consolation. Unfortunately, it often brings the greater benefit to the parent at the expense of the child's maturation. Such intense and exclusive relationships also occur between fathers and sons and mothers and daughters, but they are far more rare. Parents are called "possessive" by others in these cases, but it is a mutual and shared relationship of two people.

Writers and some judges have, for the most part, stressed unduly the seductive nature of young girls involved sexually with fathers or brothers as opposed to the more important participatory role played by mothers. Our experience suggests that while all young girls tend to experiment in seduction a little bit, and safely, within the family, that kind of normal behavior does not explain incest, which is rarely initiated by the child. In the usual family, the father responds to his flirtatious daughter with appreciation of her attractions, but he makes a clear distinction that she is a little girl. If he says jokingly, "You're going to be as pretty as your mother when you grow up," he keeps his daughter firmly in her place as *not* yet competitive with her mother while implying encouragement for her to identify with the mother as a model.

In trying to understand how incest can occur, we must remember that it is a complicated subject and that there is no one simple family pattern that fits every case. Sociological and cultural factors do matter, and the intergenerational family history, with its bringing together of characters and events, also matters. There are isolated communities or subcultures in which incest is accepted readily. In these families, little shame or incentive to change may be found.

We must emphasize again that our knowledge of incest, especially its incidence, tends to come from legal reports or institutional reports. Such reports tend to be weighted in terms of the kinds of cases considered legally significant, such those in which an adolescent daughter has complained. They also tend to be weighted in terms of where the information is given. Incest in most lower socioeconomic groups is reported to public agencies and becomes part of their reporting statistics. Most privately managed cases come from more well-to-do clients who are able to avoid the legal or community-service systems. This is usually less true for extrafamilial sexual abuse, where every family has less wish to protect the offenders.

In general, there may be two prototypical kinds of families in which the more common kinds of incest occur. One kind of incestuous family is the multiproblem, or "chaotic" family, in which problems have gone on from one generation to the next.

Although most of them may be of lower socioeconomic status because poor work habits and chronic social aberration may make them disabled educationally or unable to earn a living, this is not necessarily true. Emotional deprivation, neglect, lack of ability to form lasting relationships, substance abuse, and poor impulse control may occur at any economic level, including the very wealthy. Violence and difficulties with the law may be part of family life, and frequently there are few relationships which remain constant and intact. Children, both boys and girls, may be exposed to incest by a biological father, a stepfather, a boyfriend of the mother, or by several different people, including the mother herself. Incest in some families is carried on fairly openly through all generations, especially by the male members who support each other in the practice.

Sexual abuse may be accompanied by neglect and physical abuse. The mother is often unable to protect herself or her children because she has never herself known enough of happy family life to know how to achieve and preserve it. In some of these families, sexual abuse is only one of the problems, and although sometimes the mother acts swiftly and well to protect her children and control the offender, at other times the mother is too preoccupied with her many problems to realize that incest is occurring or feels too helpless, too fearful of the loss of a relationship she depends on, to risk intervention. In these families, the child may learn that there is really no one to trust for protection.

The other prototypical incest family seems on the surface to be much more stable, and often this family is financially and socially middle-class. The marriage may have remained outwardly stable, although neither spouse may feel really happy in the relationship. The father often works regularly and successfully, and the family tends to be quiet, socially isolated, and self-contained. The father may be very authoritarian, with a rigid, very respectable life-style but no close friendships. His wife is either immature, dependent, and passive, or, sometimes, independent, assertive, and critical of him. Neither parent is apt to have had warm nurturance in his/her own childhood, and both are apt to have grown up needy, deprived but also unable to give affection easily. Neither parent meets the other's needs for love, for affectionate closeness, or for a satisfying sexual relationship. Often the mother is seen as disinterested in sex and distant and unloving with husband and children. Indeed, both parents may be sexually immature, unable to recognize or meet the other's needs and looking for someone to give them warmth and affection. Study of the marital relationship in all incest families indicates that most parents have never attained a mature sexual relationship with the closeness, mutual sensitivity, spontaneity, and skill which would make this aspect of their marriage anything but a disappointment. Sometimes the mother moves outside the family and becomes promiscuous, or, more often, she gets some companionship and a life of her own through work. The father is reluctant to seek sexual companionship outside the home with another adult woman. Together, the parents maintain the shell of the marriage. At some point the daughter, usually the oldest one, is encouraged to take over as the mother willingly abdicates to her more and more of the household chores and the care of the other children as well as the special place as favorite companion of the father. It has been stated, and we believe it likely, that the father is most apt to turn for sex to a daughter with whom he does not have a firm early parent-child attachment. Perceiving the girl less strongly as a daughter makes it easier to perceive her as a sexual companion. Gradually the daughter finds most of her affection coming from the father.

INCEST AT AN EARLY AGE

Children at age 2 and 3 are not at all modest. But at the height of the phallic phase of development, they become curious about and very proud of their growing bodies. At this time they begin to learn modesty, as a natural part of their social training in the home. If, instead, a girl is encouraged to be "sexy" by the father, this training and the child's own developmental tendencies (including the unconscious impulses of the Oedipal period) reinforce one another in a more powerful way than at a later age. The father may gently fondle his daughter, or she may sit in her father's lap while both engage in somewhat stimulating movement. Or, gradually, specific genital fondling occurs, and eventually mutual masturbation. Similar behavior may occur between father and son. Or the father may prolong a bedtime good-night kiss and gradually develop a ritual which again leads to touching or masturbation. As time goes by and nothing is said, the introduction of oral-genital sex or sexual intercourse may occur.

The gradual progression of the sexual activity is usually accompanied by more affection and special inducements to the child. There may be special treats of candy or presents, special privileges and relaxation of discipline, or other evidences of favoritism. Or the child may be threatened with punishment or banishment if she/he tells. Or, with the very young child, she/he may simply be involved gradually as a willing partner in what becomes for her/him an exciting secret pastime, with no other adult sufficiently involved in the child's life to be aware or to provide any major competing interest. Guilt in the young child is often virtually absent because the activity is requested by the father who is the arbiter of right and wrong, and because the secrecy is often enjoined on the premise that others might be "jealous of our nice times and spoil them." If the daughter receives most of her parental affection and attention from the father through these sexual activities, there is real danger that she may perceive nurturance and affection as obtainable only through sexual means. She may completely miss the usual development of a nurturing relationship which is based on respect for her needs as a developing individual, a distortion which can skew all her intimate relationships thereafter.

The preschool child is also at special risk of becoming overwhelmed by the physical stimulation of sexual activity, provided it is kept pleasant and not painful. This is particularly true when sexual behavior has been taught to the child as the way to receive affection and approval. The sexualization gains primacy because affection is provided by the father and not by the absent or disinterested mother.

This reality reinforces the unconscious Oedipal fantasy of the young preschool girl, for example, who, in fantasy, wishes to compete and replace her mother in her father's affections. It is the inevitable recognition that this fantasy cannot come true that causes the normal child (boy or girl) by age 6 to give up these sexual strivings, to repress the sexual impulses, and to settle for identification with the parent of the same sex. This customary solution of the Oedipal conflict frees the energy of sexual interests for sublimated interests, especially the great learning spurt that comes during the latency or elementary school, years. Although the psychoanalytic theory of the Oedipal conflict and its resolution, resulting in a latency period in which sexual impulses are dormant, is not universally accepted, the behavior characteristics of normal preschool and elementary school-age children in our culture fit the expected pattern. It should be noted that the partial repression of sexual activity and the intense concentration on learning and peer activities characteristic of the latency period have very important benefits for the child in our culture.

A child who remains sexually preoccupied has great difficulty in learning how to seek affection in more appropriate ways. Some children, under these circumstances, are totally unacceptable in preschools or daycare facilities or in many foster homes because they immediately and regularly try to involve others in their sexual interest. For the child, this behavior is natural and has been approved by at least one very important adult and her/his preoccupation with sexual pleasure is at first a much more powerful stimulus than the need to please strange adults in untried ways.

A very pretty 5-year-old child, *Johanna* was first seen as a result of report to a local county Social Service Department by a male neighbor of the parents who described an event that had been very shocking to him and his wife. While playing at their home with their 6-year-old boy, Johanna had undressed herself, begun to undress the boy, and told him to lie on top of her. He was scared and called his mother.

When one of us examined this youngster, it was plain that she had in many ways the traits of an experienced prostitute. She would almost immediately climb on the physician's lap and attempt to masturbate him while asking for candy; she kissed and caressed his hands and, even in the presence of a nurse or her mother, she tried to be seductive in a superficially adult way. She was bright and very social with other children of either sex, and had been in preschool for one year. Inquiry revealed that she had, in fact, exhibited similar behavior there but nothing had been done except that her parents had been asked to remove her. Both parents stated that they had no idea what caused this behavior, but, in time, it became clear that the father had trained this only child to behave as she did and that the mother was in dread of her husband's physical violence towards her and did not "know where to get help and not lose him."

Johanna was placed in a special therapeutic playschool for each morning and also in foster care, while both parents were seen by two social workers from the local department. It is not surprising that the first two foster-care placements were of short duration. In the first home, the foster mother discovered Johanna sexually fondling an older boy in the family after just two days in care, while in the next home, that of a childless couple, she tried to masturbate the foster father in front of neighbors, embarrassing the couple who felt that they just could not cope. Luckily, a very patient and understanding older clergyman and his wife were able to tolerate Johanna's behavior for a period of two years, and in conjunction with her school experience, they were able to teach her modesty and acceptable public behavior. While training in modesty is largely parent-determined, it is so routine (for boys as well as girls) as to be taken for granted; retraining young children in socially required behavior is very much harder once the child has had systematic rewards for immodesty at a young age, as was the case with Johanna.

Treatment for the family failed, primarily because the father was a psychopathic personality, unwilling and unable to participate in treatment, and the mother chose to live with her husband, leaving Johanna in foster care. It was not possible to reconstitute the family safely, and therefore parental rights were terminated. The parents moved to another state, and there was no further contact with them.

Treatment for Johanna involved many issues, the most important being the loss of her parents. Feelings of loss and sadness, coupled with anger at all those responsible for the change, including, eventually, her parents, had to be recognized. Very painful for a child like Johanna was her lack of self-esteem and her assumption that the loss of her parents was due to her own badness. This assumption was reinforced by general rejection because of her behavior. It is difficult to understand the sexualized behavior aroused in young children by continued premature sexual stimulation, and most laypeople tend to assume that the child is abnormal and innately at fault. Suddenly the behavior that had given Johanna parental approval and her father's affection made her unacceptable to everyone else, yet she had never been taught any other way to seek attention, friendliness, or affection. The combination of parental loss and a need for total revision of her relationships with everyone else were formidable treatment problems for Johanna, requiring much time and patience on everyone's part. Gradually a more appropriate nurturing and loving relationship developed between the foster parents and Johanna, and Johanna became more able to be interested in the usual latency-age activities.

The foster parents adopted her when she was 9, and her therapist still sees her from time to time. Johanna is now 10 years old and an average school performer. She seems sexually more mature than usual for her age, seductive, using makeup, despite the fact that she as yet shows no evidence of puberty. Her ambition is to be a high-school cheerleader and later an airline flight attendant. She is honest, polite, and has many good friends. It is indeed difficult for Johanna not to rely still on some signs of "sex-iness" as a way of getting approval, a signal that she probably does not yet feel adequately valued by peers. It is likely that she will continue to have difficulty with these issues in adolescence and may need treatment again at that time.

VICTIMS OF INCEST IN EARLY SCHOOL YEARS AND EARLY ADOLESCENCE

The very fact that incest activities continue to take place over a long period of time and involve unusual overt behavior on the part of the child emphasizes the absence of closeness and lack of concern on the part of the mother for her daughter. Possibly the mother sees such behavior as normal because she, herself, went through the same thing and she tends to sexualize relationships as a matter of course. Occasionally the mother is absent for some overriding reason, such as a severe and chronic illness. Sometimes she must work nights and her husband days so that the family can manage on two inadequate incomes without paying for sit-ters. But sometimes the mother *chooses* to work to escape from home and her marital relationship, or she leaves home regularly to pursue her own interests without much attention to her chil-dren. She may even be at home but unresponsive when her daugh-ter approaches her.

If she is aware of a special relationship between father and daughter, the mother may have no capacity for empathy with her daughter's plight, or she may even be jealous. She may not be capable of a more mature mothering relationship or able to place her daughter's needs above her own. or, with the unhappy ex-perience of an incestuous relationship behind her as the example of how love and dependency needs are met, she may not be able to maintain an adult sexual relationship with her husband. She may not be able to deal with the fact of incest because it would threaten the insecure marriage that she cannot improve on her own.

In effect, there may be here the same kind of role reversal we see in other forms of child abuse: the mother looks to her daughter to meet her needs for protection of her marriage at the expense of the daughter's own development. The primary concern for parents and child becomes the maintenance of the status quo because the only alternative seems to be a dissolution of the family and none of them feels strong enough to face being alone. The daughter may become the de facto housewife and take care of home and siblings as well. Further, she is often scornful of the neglectful mother and proud of her own ability to manage and to please, at what great personal cost she does not yet realize. It is not hard to see how a very loving and dependent relationship between father and daughter may result first in acceptable degrees of caressing, and later in increasingly intimate forms of physical contact.

In the silent agreement among husband, wife, and daughter, each plays a role, and each is generally free of overt guilt or anger unless a crisis occurs. One of these crises is discovery. Another is normal adolescent rebellion against denial of access to boyfriends or anger at the molestation of a younger sister. The daughter, of course, is robbed of her developmentally appropriate sexuality, and she is often caught in a dilemma: if she ends a now-embarrassing affair in order to live a more usual life with her peers, she will forfeit the family security that she believes her compliance has assured her, her mother, and her siblings. This is a terrible burden for these immature girls to carry—and relief may not come until they leave home and try to build a new life apart.

The older preadolescent and adolescent girl who is entrapped in incest may still have the special role of favored child as a reward. She may be exempt from some of the household rules, or may be given presents, such as clothes. Some girls are even paid money for sexual favors and soon learn to barter. She may feel herself favored, not only over her siblings but also over her mother, and she may enjoy her position, uneasy though a victory in the subtle competition with her mother is. On the other hand, she may find herself as she gets older replacing her mother far beyond her wish to do so, becoming responsible for babysitting, housework, and cooking in addition to providing for her father's sexual needs. The father may become very demanding and require that she perform all these household tasks for which she receives no real reward, much less praise. Soon she finds that she is not even free like her siblings to spend time with other friends in social activities. What seemed at first to be a favored position has become household drudgery. If her father also gets jealous of possible boyfriends and forbids dating, or if he is very strict about dating rules, the daughter's feeling of exploitation becomes very strong, indeed. It is often at this point that a teen-age girl tries to liberate herself by running away, by becoming promiscuous, or by reporting what has been going on.

Any forcible sexual abuse is frightening and often physically very painful; incestuous relationships usually do not give the victim any pronounced sexual pleasure. Orgasmic experiences do occur in some very young, stimulated children, and such experiences can occur at any age. On the other hand, most children and adolescents experience no sexual arousal, or do so only in the early, affectionate stages of a gentle incestuous relationship. Even then, feelings of fear, shame, desire to please, and passivity dominate, and victims generally do not have orgasmic experiences.

Incestuous rape is, of course, perceived as a violent attack by the child who may be any age (even an infant) and may come to attention as an example either of violent sexual abuse or, often, of physical abuse. Unless mother and child are totally cowed by threats from the father, such violent episodes are apt to come to the attention of the authorities very quickly. Sometimes incestuous rape is really a retaliation against the wife following a major family argument, with the child made a victim to vent the husband's rage against his wife. Prolonged drinking may precede the rape.

There are many girls for whom incest is not a gentle seduction, but a threatening, frightening experience throughout. No pretext at affection is made, and the girl maintains silence and submits because of beatings or the fear of them. Her father or stepfather may be abusive, drunk or both. Threats of violence may keep her mother and siblings cowed as well, with everyone afraid to report the man out of fear. Such episodes may be single disasters or fairly frequent occurrences over a period of years.

There are also occasional families in which the incest is part of a sexually promiscuous life-style on the part of the parents. These husbands and wives believe that any kind of sex is good and "healthy" and that children should be brought up liberated, to enjoy any kind of sex without restriction. In a sense, these parents wish to return to a mythical uncomplicated sexual freedom which humankind is assumed to have enjoyed before social rules came into being to spoil the natural joy of primitive people. The anthropological studies of Malinowski and Mead do indicate no sexual latency period occurs in some primitive societies and that the children show a steady progression in sexual interest and activity, including all types of sexual intercourse with one another during what we know as a latency period. However, all anthropologists seem to agree that once puberty, with the potential for childbearing, approaches, special rites initiate the child into the serious world of the adult. In the adult world, the rules governing sexual behavior vary among these primitive societies, but they are rigid and very strictly enforced.

Our experience with these "free sex" families indicates that parents quite often resist treatment vigorously, having elaborately rationalized their behavior. The children may also angrily defy any interference, and protect their parents, whom they believe to be in the right, completely.

One such family illustrates both the resistance to treatment and the pathology to be found. The family consisted of a father, with his third wife, and his four teen-age children by a previous marriage. The father's youngest daughter, aged 13, had had two friends who had complained when the father fondled their breasts as well as his daughter's. In the history elicited, the father had earlier had incestuous relations eventually leading to intercourse over a long period of time with his older daughters, aged 17 and 18, had regularly fondled all four children, and had on two occasions arranged a vaguely described group-sex experience with the whole family, including his wife.

When protective services were involved, the younger children were placed in foster care because the parents were already separated and seeking divorce. The father agreed to treatment, but tried to make the condition for treatment that his children be returned home to live with him. The 17- and 18-year-old daughters had already left school, were living independently, and had become promiscuous, but they were very protective of their father and resentful of any outside intervention. The third child, a boy of 15, was also very resentful of any change and wish to live with his father with more freedom; he was bitterly resentful of the ordinary rules in the foster home. The boy was diagnosed as having a character disorder, as was his 17-year-old sister. She had been a runaway and was seriously depressed as well. Only the youngest of the four children felt the need for protection and wanted to be placed away from home, preferably with relatives.

Throughout the consultation the father was challenging, not only denying the right of the court to investigate his family's sexual behavior, but also clearly denying any possible harm to his children. The father was a successful, intelligent man of some charm who had chosen wives who were unable to mother his children and had himself been the only stable figure in the family. Unfortunately the affection and warmth he did provide his children was offered within a sexual context. The importance of his attention, whatever the cost to them in all other areas of their lives, was attested to by their loyalty to him in spite of their unhappy relationships with peers, and the evidences of feelings of emotional deprivation in their psychological testing.

Clearly in this family it was not only the sexual abuse, but also the absence of a stable mother figure, which accounted for much of the children's difficulty.

This history illustrates the necessity, in ascribing pathological importance to one pervasive kind of family behavior like incest, to recognize that it does not ordinarily occur in an intact healthy family.

Discovery of incest may be initiated by the child's truancy, delinquent behavior, running away from home, sharing facts with a friend, reporting psychosomatic or hysterical illness to a perceptive physician, pregnancy, or reporting the incest to the police.

If the girl runs away, she is lucky if she is quickly picked up by the authorities and placed in a juvenile facility for evaluation. At that point the incest should be discovered, and she and her family may receive help. If she is not picked up when running away, she is apt to be at the mercy of the predatory people of the streets and exposed to further exploitation. A teenager who has run away from her family is frightened and lonely and may respond quickly to anyone who seems to show concern for her and an interest in helping her. Hungry for affection and some kind of security, she is the kind of girl who can be readily picked up by a pimp. He doesn't at first expose her to prostitution, but gives her affection and takes care of her, only later introducing prostitution as her obligation. The importance of her relationship to the pimp and her willingness to turn over her earnings to him in exchange for his "protection" (which may include physical abuse, drug supplies, and very little actual affection) reveal how poor her self-image is and how desperately she clings to a superficial semblance of caretaking. In one study of how prostitutes feel about their pimps, one describes clinging, against all the evidence of his having other girls working for him, to the idea that she is the only important one, the only loved one, while the others are "business." It is not surprising that so many prostitutes were exposed to incest or early sexual abuse, for the absence of a loving caretaker and the exploitation of their sexual potential as their only asset of value were part of their lives from their early days.

There are other teenagers who do not leave home and who continue to submit to incest until they leave to marry or get a job or go to college. Some of these girls have accepted the role reversal with their parents in a very earnest way. From being the "little mother" or "father's big girl," they grow into adolescence, taking over most of the responsibilities of the house and children. If competent, such a girl may see her parents as unable to manage without her (especially the mother of whom she may be contemptuous), and may become fairly content in being rather "bossy" and running the house. She may continue this role if she can through adulthood, savoring the authority of being the "big mother" and choosing a husband, if she does, who will not challenge her role. She may well avoid sex altogether as an adult. Some girls who have grown up with incest in their past are never able to face dating with any degree of comfort and either avoid sexual relationships altogether or become eventually homosexual. For the girl who marries and has children but is comfortable only when avoiding sex, the stage may be set for the repetition of incest in her own family.

The girl who has, as a preadolescent, been able to avoid guilt about the incest because of the clear encouragement of her father and lack of response from her mother, may have great difficulty if she begins to feel pleasure in intercourse. She can then no longer feel that she participates as a "chore," that she does this for her father and not for herself. The intense guilt roused may force her to take some kind of action to stop the relationship, including reporting to the authorities, running away, or attempting suicide.

While the average age of incestuous activity involves the victim at around 8 to 9 years, the oldest of five daughters of Mr. B, *Jeanie*, was 7 years old when incest began.

Mr. B, a skilled mechanic, was the father of five daughters, ages 16, 14, 11, 9 and 7. The oldest, Jeanie, told her teacher about the fact that her father had been sexually involved with her since she was 7 years of age, first by genital fondling and mutual masturbation, then by oral sex, followed at age 10 by sexual intercourse which she found painful and worrisome. Her mother did not believe her and washed her mouth out with soap. Much involved in this close knit, devout, and outwardly harmonious family, Jeanie feared the social disgrace to her father and the break-up of the family which her mother explained to her.

Jeanie confessed these events to her priest, who encouraged her to come to our Center for help. She came once, gave a wrong name and address, and asked about a "friend," directing discussion to fears of pregnancy and what would happen if her story came to the attention of anybody who by law is required to report incest to both the social services department and the police. After she left and failed to return the following day as planned, it became clear that she had falsely identified herself. She later told of her problem to a teacher who reported to the local city hospital, and this led to intensive social work and medical evaluation. When the father readily agreed to go into "family therapy" on a weekly basis for six months in another institution without, however, admitting his commission of incest, the district attorney decided to waive criminal actions and leave the case in the juvenile court for disposition. Because the father remained in the home, Jeanie refused to remain there and was placed in a foster group home. Within two weeks of taking part in group sessions with her entire family and a therapist, she suffered a severe psychotic breakdown. She entered our adolescent psychiatric in-patient service in an acute state of disorientation and delusions, not drug-induced.

Thus, once again Jeanie came to our attention. With supportive hospital care, she made a rapid recovery from what may have been an acute hysterical state or an episode of atypical psychosis. Shortly after seeing one of us at this time, she discovered that her father was having frequent intercourse with her 15-year-old sister. After a second review by the child protective service and the juvenile court, the second daughter was also removed to foster care, and she, in turn, within three months, suffered a psychotic reaction identical to that which we had seen in her sister. She, too, responded to supportive care in a psychiatric hospital within a month. Both girls then refused to continue "family therapy" at the "official" treatment group and received individual therapy by our unit.

When the officially arranged six months of planned therapy at the first institution had terminated, the court referred the family to a local mental health clinic, but the family did not avail themselves of this. Both older girls are convinced that all the children, in turn, will be molested, but the system has not been willing to date to intervene, except for an occasional visit to the home by a social worker and a regular health check-up on each child. The father was described in all contacts with authority as a kindly, dependable, and "very cooperative person, a family man and provider who hopes that his older children will soon be returned to the family fold.

Physical and psychiatric evaluation of the two oldest girls revealed that the histories they gave were indeed true and little is known about the other children as yet, although the physician following their health care will be alert to anything untoward occurring."

These quotes, which actually come from official documents, reveal the failure of a well-organized system to provide adequate care and protection for the children or adequate diagnosis of the parents. The failure of treatment to reunite this family indicates the importance of truly effective treatment of all members, as contrasted with "going through the motions." The father's refusal to acknowledge his own guilt may have been a clear indication that he was not prepared to accept responsibility for meaningful change and should have been recognized as such at the beginning of treatment planning. (See also Chapter 5, pages 98–106.)

MASKED SEXUAL ABUSE

Over the past thirty years we have seen a number of children whose presenting complaints suggested nothing at all about sexual abuse. But tactful direct questioning revealed the true nature of the problems these children had. Such masked instances of sexual abuse are seen by physicians who deal with infants, preschoolers, and early adolescents for real medical complaints.

> One instance was *Sandra*, who was admitted to our hospital at 14 years of age paralyzed in both legs but with no other neurologic findings and without any preceding illness. Her physicians were concerned about some rare disorder, but, in fact, she suffered from an hysterical paralysis connected with an incestuous relationship with her father which had been going on for three years. She improved almost at once, and recovered fully within three days once she could verbalize her experiences in a safe and supportive place, in this case the hospital. She literally "could not go any further."

Hysterical symptoms are very real to patients: they are not malingering, they truly cannot see or hear, or they really do have an absence of feeling in both hands (glove paresthesia). These anatomically impossible conditions in acute form show a profound emotional disturbance which can be due to sexual abuse. Some symptoms of masked child sexual abuse include abdominal pains, air swallowing, overbreathing leading to tingling and then spasms of the hands, depression with sleep disturbances, over- or undereating, school performance changes, suicide attempts, truancy, and running away, drug overdose, and pregnancy in the very young adolescent of 12 or 13. There may be nonsuspected venereal diseases found on routine tests, injuries to the vagina or rectum, lesions of the penis, or vaginal discharge.

In a recent study comparing 50 masked cases of sexual abuse to a similar group of 31 children who presented with overt complaint of sexual abuse, it was found that the masked group was younger then the overt group and that the greater number of boys were found in the masked group while the overt group had far more girls. The duration of abuse in the masked group was 2.7 years.

In this study, all cases of sibling incest occurred in the masked group, and all of the perpetrators were family members who, with one exception, were males. Identification of the perpetrator was more difficult in the masked group with 13 out of 50 never identified with certainty. Five noncomplaining siblings of identified victims were also found to have been sexually abused. The young adolescent mothers in the group were found to be incest victims who gave birth to infants with unusual genetic disorders (Hunter). Clearly the physician has a unique opportunity for early intervention when a "masked" case presents if he or she regularly considers this possibility whenever a puzzling physical set of complaints brings a youngster to his or her care. Amazingly, many physicians will go to any length not to make this diagnosis.

MOTHER-SON INCEST

While far less common, mother-son, stepmother-stepson, or grandmother-grandson incest seem to be far more damaging to the male victim than is the case for father/stepfather-and-daughter incest. We do not know why this is so. It could well be that a closeness of relationship begins from birth and goes right through childhood and adolescence without normal individuation and corresponding closeness and opportunity for identification with a father. This leads to confusion of what a son's role and what masculinity are.

A minor, common, and far less dangerous form of these close relationships between mother and son is now becoming more common because over 50 percent of all marriages end in divorce within ten years. Thus, an increasing number of boys live alone with their mothers and become a source of comfort and closeness which may, at times, come to substitute for the companionship previously experienced in marriage. This is, to a degree, quite normal, and it does no harm to help children understand the need to pull together what is left of a normal family life by showing more affection. But divorced parents also must understand and ensure that the child's own developmental needs are met. Because mothers still tend to receive custody of children, regardless of the sex of the child, the problem occurs more frequently for them. By retaining her maternal role, and by not considering the child as "the man of the house," by not taking a boy to bed for comfort, by trying to provide or allow adult male friendship for her son, a mother can prevent what could become a delicate and difficult problem.

People are more ready to see possible sexual implications in the questionable behavior of fathers with their daughters than of mothers with their sons. When a school-aged daughter sleeps in the same bed as her father, an immediate question might arise concerning at least an unconscious sexual aspect to their relationship. Yet the mother who allows her boy to sleep in her bed may be thought to "infantilize" him but not to be acting on unconscious incestuous impulses. One study indicates that when this sleeping arrangement occurs with either parent and child of the opposite sex there are apt to be marital problems, and that the situation is sexually stimulating to the child. The idea of mother-son incest is generally more abhorrent (and also much more rare) than father-daughter incest. How much of this difference relates to our need to protect the concept of motherhood as an impervious relationship and how much relates to our concept of the differences in normal sexuality between men and women (with men "naturally" and "appropriately" more sexual) is not at all clear. Some feminists believe that the latter explanation is true, the frequency of father-daughter incest indicating that it is seen as more acceptable and more consistent with masculine rights in a patriarchal society and that mother-son incest is seen as an infringement both on the son's masculinity and on patriarchal rights. Whatever the historical reasons, the difference in incidence, in significance to others, and apparently in effects on the participants has been marked. For example, a very serious situation exists in the case of Gerard.

Gerard is a 24-year-old virtuoso concert pianist who had been seen because of recurrent and intermittently disabling hysterical paralysis of his right hand, various psychosomatic symptoms including insomnia, anorexia, and a very strict vegetarian diet which included only vegetables and nuts. He drank only water and refused vitamin supplements. He had been evaluated by a psychiatrist who confirmed the physician's impression that Gerard suffered from chronic depression and severe anxieties with phobic elements and who had advised him to enter a hospital setting for therapy. While the young man seemed eager to find out what caused these symptoms which threatened to destroy his concert career, his 45-year-old divorced mother firmly refused such a course and never wished him to speak to anyone unless she was present.

When his physical condition deteriorated, she did allow hospitalization in a general medical setting, but refused to talk to the psychiatrist. Her son's manager, however, persuaded him to speak to his physician at length, and over a two-week period it became clear that Gerard had been sleeping with his mother all his life. Indeed, the immediate cause of his parents' divorce had been the fact that he slept between them each night until his father filed for custody on the grounds that his mother was unfit to raise him. Nevertheless, the judge awarded the boy, then 15, to the mother, stating that mothers have a natural close feeling for their children and that there was nothing abnormal about sharing one's parents' bed ("I have done so," the judge said). Overt sexual relations progressed from mutual genital fondling to weekly intercourse. His mother followed Gerard on all his concert tours, and as he became progressively more mentally ill, she exhibited marked paranoid behavior toward all of his contacts.

At age 24, while still able to perform, Gerard also showed signs of schizophrenic behavior, and he has been in a state hospital for the insane for the past thirteen years. His prognosis is said to be poor. His mother, in a chronic psychotic state, lives in the family home. The father totally dropped out of this family picture once the divorce and custody battle were over.

This case shows that mother-son incest can be devastating to the victim, and this has been our general experience with a very small sample. The passive role of Gerald's father over a fifteen-year span is a most important feature, and one can only speculate what might have happened if he had, from the first, taken firm steps to stop what was clearly a totally abnormal family constellation.

An example of grandmother-grandson incest is the case of *Robert*. Robert was seen at age 16 for jaundice. He was addicted to heroin, and also sold heroin to fellow high school students. A bright and above-average student, Robert had no obvious problems until age 10 when his parents divorced and neither parent seemed to want him. His paternal grandmother, who was extremely wealthy, had been most eager to keep him in his home city and in the family home, and she did so. We can only assume that all of this was a very traumatic situation for him and that his subsequent problems (including the incest) presumably derived from his double loss along with a preceding pathological family life.

Robert's jaundice was found in the hospital to be due to serum hepatitis caused by contaminated needles, and he was very frightened by his appearance and the thought that he might soon die. In a week's time he revealed to one of us that he was sleeping with his grandmother each night, occasionally having intercourse, but mostly being fondled. He was repelled by these activities, mostly because she was "ugly and sixty." He had had no other sexual experiences with either sex, and had no friends.

Both parents were called back into the city from distant parts of the country, and both failed to believe the history shared with them in a general way, although they did believe that the grandmother might have provided all the cash needed for any activity Robert would wish. Despite the fact that this case was reported to both the police and the social services department, the grandmother's lawyers were able to convince all agencies that the boy was a chronic liar and that the prominence of this family made the history unbelievable. In light of these facts and because the boy wished not to return to his grandmother's house, we arranged for a placement with a young family consisting of a psychiatrist father, a nurse mother, and two young children with whom Robert at once became very friendly and attached.

Psychological tests (TAT and Rorschach) revealed an extremely anxious, depressed, and fearful youngster with no aggressive or overtly angry manifestations. Robert's external behavior, while still overconfident and bragging, became more acceptable, and he made friends and remained free of any evidence of further drug abuse for eight months. His family paid the foster home fees, but when the foster family moved to another state and all the members of the foster family urged him to come with them, he decided instead to move back into his grandmother's home. Within two weeks Robert was truant from school, was arrested for possession and selling of drugs, and seemed ill nourished. He was very worried about his health and again said that his grandmother made him sleep in her bed.

At this time the police interviewed the grandmother who would not discuss the facts and said that her grandson needed only to join her own religious sect to be well again. The discussion held with her by the physician suggested that she was likely to be a substance abuser (primarily alcohol and cocaine) and not competent. A court order to hear the case in juvenile court was filed by the social services department on Robert's behalf, but he disappeared. He has never been heard from by anyone within his family, but a school friend said that he had died of an overdose of heroin in a distant state two years later. This could not be confirmed.

HOMOSEXUAL INCEST

Incest between father and son, mother and daughter, or stepparents with children of the same sex has been considered rare, but it is now being reported more frequently. Very few cases of mother-daughter incest have been reported, and of these, a few have been described as part of a chaotic family life in which multiple kinds of incest occurred among several generations, or as part of a kind of episodic multiple partner "orgy" of brief nature. The other rare cases are limited to an occasional relationship of a daughter with a mother who had homosexual tendencies.

Incest between father and son does happen more often than between mother and daughter, and it is our impression that (although so seldom reported) it is not rare. The father may be homosexual, bisexual, primarily heterosexual, or a pedophile. Incest may occur with the child at any time from preschool years to early adolescence; it may be brief, or it may continue over a long period of time, as in father-daughter incest. Of the cases described, it has often been noted that a father may initiate with his son the same sexual activities his father performed with him and at the same age. One reason why father-son incest has been assumed to be so rare is that boys are very reluctant to report it and may do so only to a psychotherapist many years later.

Leonard is an example of how serious the results of homosexual incest can be for the child. At 14 years old, Leonard had been subjected to sexual abuse, including sodomy and fellatio, by his father for six years. In recent years, Leonard had tried to interest his father in alternative sexual pursuits, such as female prostitutes, to no avail, but he had never openly defied his father or expressed any anger to him.

When seen for evaluation, Leonard was a very tense, guarded boy who even in his pseudomature appearance showed how much he identified with his successful businessman father. He denied problems and stated that life was better since his parents had separated and there were fewer arguments. He avoided problems by avoiding people, especially his peers at school of whom he often disapproved. He said he was comfortable in avoiding feelings and preventing fights by compliance which was easier. He denied any difficulty about the sexual abuse but refused to talk about it. He tried to control the interview by changing the subject if uncomfortable; occasionally he became confused instead. Leonard described being restless, "like sharks who never sleep," his only real admission of the extent of his emotional turmoil. Psychological testing confirmed the impression that Leonard was barely "keeping the lid on" strong feelings of anxiety, vulnerability, and intense anger by avoiding interactions through isolation and by denial of his problems.

Leonard's father was also seen at the Center, and he described his own sex experiences as beginning with an older boy when he was 9, and continuing in the same relationship for five years. Following this, he had numerous homosexual and some heterosexual experiences. One year after his marriage to Leonard's mother he resumed homosexual relationships. Except for his marriage of fifteen years, all his relationships throughout his life were poor in quality and brief; he controlled them by terminating them. Mr. Smith was a successful businessman but had no real friends. He had no guilt about his relationship with Leonard and no recognition of Leonard's needs. As an adult, he enjoyed introducing sex to adolescent boys, "turning them on for the first time."

Leonard was in a precarious emotional state, in great need of long-term treatment once he was relieved of the stress in his intolerable family situation. It was felt that it would take a long time for him to trust any therapist and feel secure enough to begin to deal directly with his feelings. Careful monitoring of environmental stress would be important during this period, to make sure Leonard was not overwhelmed. How successful treatment would be for Leonard's father is not yet known; treatment in a group of male incest offenders was being offered to him with the option of individual psychotherapy available.

SIBLING INCEST

Sibling sexual contact may be so frequent and so "innocent" in very young children—the proud exposure of the nude body at 2 or 3, the mutual exploration, genital touching, and "playing doctor" at 4 and 5—that it may seem difficult to define what later becomes abnormal sexual activity. Whether bathing together, sleeping together, or just playing, children not uncommonly share sexual fantasies and perhaps stimulate each other or masturbate together. Siblings have more opportunity, if close in age, to do so than friends, and they are apt to feel no more guilt than they would about doing these activities on their own. Such play may occur between siblings of the same sex or siblings of the opposite sex and rarely progress to any attempt at intercourse. Unless the activity is discovered and the parental reaction severely punitive and shaming, or unless it becomes more than a passing interest, the casual sexual exploration between same-age young siblings may not have serious consequences with the present-day, more liberal cultural attitudes.

This, of course, varies with individual children. With somewhat older siblings, the same general attitude of sharing discovered information may be the basis for less guilt than in most other situations. However, by the time the children are in late latency (6 to 10 years) or preadolescence, their increased social awareness makes sexual activity more guilt provoking. During the latency years, children gradually begin to become more modest, and in most families modesty tends to become acute as the first signs of puberty appear. Family customs do vary, and when the parents appear nude or discuss sexual matters in front of the children openly, the children are apt to be more casual as well. However, self-consciousness at the onset of puberty may well be present even in the most "liberated" of families unless the child is teased or shamed for it by the rest of the family.

By this time, any nudity or sexual contact among siblings such as genital touching has usually disappeared. When it does occur, it takes place secretly and probably with feelings of guilt over a forbidden activity. Although children often masturbate separately with varying degrees of guilt, masturbation of one another is seen less often as children grow older.

Sibling incest, with genital fondling eventually leading to intercourse, may be homosexual or heterosexual and, again, is accompanied by varying degrees of guilt. It is not infrequent that the siblings are equal partners, particularly if a pattern of incest has been known in the family and the barriers thereby lowered. Only pregnancy or the choice of another partner may interrupt this kind of mutually consenting sibling incest until the children leave home. Statistics on such activities are seriously lacking, as are studies on the participants. The increasing reporting of sibling incest as part of the history of victims of sexual abuse makes it likely that it represents a much higher proportion of intrafamilial incest than is indicated by current statistics.

In the study of masked sexual abuse mentioned earlier (page 66), all children involved in sibling abuse were found in this "masked" group. Clearly, therefore, some children react with anxiety to sibling incest, often converted into physical symptoms. Presumably they also felt guilt as one of the causes of the anxiety. However, because these feelings were expressed in vague behavioral or physical symptoms, the secret of the underlying cause was suspected only after prolonged medical involvement.

Of the many other siblings involved in incest who are not recognized by such perceptive physicians, presumably many may go on having symptoms causing mild disability for years. Retrospective histories from adults who had been involved in sibling incest describe frequent social isolation, depression, and guilt. Symptoms may not become obvious until adulthood, when there may be avoidance of intimate friendship and marriage or sexual dysfunction within marriage.

If the incestuous relationship is carried on between siblings through later adolescence on into adulthood, the consequences, particularly on the potential for successful marriage, are more serious. Crises tend to center around the beginning, ending, or discovery of incestuous relationships, and, rarely, an acute psychosis has been apparently precipitated by the beginning or ending of sibling incest, usually in the young adult. It has also been noted that in some patients who become psychiatrically ill or psychotic in adulthood, a major focus of the emotional disturbance may be the incest which occurred years before. The fact that the incest was terminated long before without overt symptoms which led to the diagnosis does not rule out the persistence of underlying difficulties which may cause renewed problems years later.

Sibling incest may be true sexual abuse when it is forced with threats of bodily harm on a younger child by the older sibling whose "authority" is insufficient to ensure compliance. Usually the older brother (very occasionally, the older sister) insists upon sexual relations consistently over a long period of time with a younger sibling in exactly the same way a father may impose these demands on an unwilling daughter.

If the incest is enforced by an older sibling and the situation resembles father-daughter incest, many of the same effects may be present, with more anger and feelings of helplessness and devaluation. Indeed, in a few families the brother and father both have an incestuous relationship with the girl.

> *Betty*, a 14-year-old girl, was hospitalized with a history of marked weight loss and a diagnosis of anorexia nervosa. Her 16-year-old brother was extremely worried about her deteriorating condition and finally confessed to his father that he had carried on an incestuous relationship with her for four months and he wondered if he had caused her illness. The patient recovered fairly promptly, and both youngsters received individual therapy. Each requested a therapist of his/her own sex. Both remained in the household and have done well.

This example of a good outcome when serious physical and emotional findings led to early discovery would lead any competent physician to suspect the root of the weight problem as not based on an organic disease. While the actual cause of the symptoms could not be guessed, the exploration of the possibility of sexual abuse should have been considered among other possible causes. Regrettably, denial of incest among physicians continues at a very high level even though all their training and diagnostic skills tell them that more information must be elicited, either by gentle and sympathetic interviewing or by obtaining prompt psychiatric consultations. Quite often the diagnosis is delayed, and we have seen suicide attempts later on which uncover the real problem underlying all of the earlier presenting symptoms. But discovery may not occur, and we now see many young adults who, for the first time, are able to face the problems caused by an incestuous relationship during adolescence which was never worked through and which left lasting scars.

Such an example is *Joyce*, a 26-year-old teacher, who had had an incestuous relationship with her older brother for about a year when she was 14 years old. Neither parent knew of this, and she felt deeply ashamed and broke off their sexual activity gradually. After being totally separated from her for six years, her brother followed her to another city where she had been working and going to university for an advanced degree. He settled nearby, and their relationship was that of loving and compatible siblings. He planned to get married. She had a female roommate who often failed to include her in social activities, and she found that this upset her a great deal.

Joyce was a rather unkempt young woman with little regard for her appearance except for being very conscious of her severe facial acne which had been present for 12 years without improvement and which had never been treated. She was also uncertain about her sexual preference. While she was always able to have good friendships with men, she never had any sexual involvement with any.

Over the first two months of individual therapy, Joyce's acne greatly improved with intensive medical treatment and continued medical attention has maintained this improvement for two years. Her clothing choices, hair care, and striking general improvement in outward appearance were paralleled by a more hopeful attitude toward her future, and she began a two-year group therapy session, limited to adult female victims, which met weekly at our Center. During these months she gradually found that her affection for female friends was profound, and she decided that she was a lesbian and planned her future accordingly. She enjoyed her brother's wedding. She raised the subject of their early involvement once, but he refused to discuss it. She is now out of treatment and doing well six years after first being seen. We believe and she believes that early treatment would have greatly changed the course of her life had incest been discovered and treated at 15 rather than 26 years of age.

THE OLDER ADOLESCENT VICTIM

An example of an older adolescent living in a chaotic, extended, and flexible family setting is Annette.

Annette, a 16-year-old girl, was seen because an unrelated household member, a boy of 16, had been treated for gonorrhea and listed her as one of his sexual contacts. She was free of symptoms, but her vaginal and rectal cultures were also positive—for a distinctly *different* strain of the gonococcus organism. The remaining members of the large family were then cultured. Her stepfather's culture was positive for gonorrhea of the same strain as Annette's, as were her 14- and 18-year-old stepsisters'. Throat cultures for the same gonococcus were positive in her 9-year-old stepbrother, as was his anal culture. Her mother was culture negative, as were two cousins and another, younger, stepbrother. While he did not admit it, the stepfather, who had a criminal record, more than likely, by sodomy and vaginal intercourse, infected Annette, who was not clinically ill and who had not been infected by the boy of 16. The stepfather had, further, infected his 9-year-old stepson through fellatio and sodomy, and had caused vaginal infections in the 14- and 18-year-old girls. The Health Department administered curative doses of penicillin to all members found to be infected. The initial report of the 16-year-old boy was not related to the family infection, nor did he have any part in the family's chaotic incestuous life.

PART II

CHAPTER FOUR

LEGAL ASPECTS

Laws relating to sexual abuse of children reflect cultural values and the degree of public concern about sexual behavior. They therefore vary from one country to another, even from one state to another. For example, some European countries do not have special laws for the sexual abuse of children but fit the cases under old laws condemning indecent sexual behavior. In some countries, incest and sexual abuse of children by caretakers lead to severe penalties; in other countries, there is no punishment for incest.

In the United States, the Child Abuse Prevention and Treatment Act of 1974 sought to encourage reporting and investigative action on all forms of child abuse in the separate states and most (46) have responded by setting up state-wide programs. Many of the states also reviewed and codified the laws defining sexual abuse. There is still great variation from one state to another in legal definitions of child abuse and also in the punishment of offenders (see page 35, concerning rape). The laws set up the limits within which the local law enforcement agencies (police and protective services, juvenile and criminal courts) must operate, but interpretation of the laws always depends on the county agencies and judges.

Law enforcement agencies, including juvenile and criminal courts, have very great latitude within the law in their approaches to all kinds of sexual abuse of children. Quite often they can be most helpful in bringing the authority of law (probably the fear of law) to bear on the immediate care of sexually abused children as well as to enforce what is, in fact, involuntary treatment as a condition of escaping immediate criminal prosecution. Where immediate care is needed, police and sheriffs' departments may take a child or children into protective care without more than their judgment of the situation at the time. They may and do bring the assaulted child to hospital emergency services equipped by training to handle properly the medical, surgical, and emotional needs of the victim or victims. The officers can be instrumental in seeing to it that evidence which may be used in possible court action is collected according to proper rules of procedure and also in informing any suspected perpetrator of his legal rights, a need often overlooked in a hospital setting and only available through law enforcement officers. For example, while it is fully proper for the doctor to provide immediate first-rate comprehensive emergency care for the victim, the doctor is best not involved with the suspect, a function reserved to law enforcement personnel and sometimes physically dangerous to physicians.

While a child, or even a group of children, can be taken into protective custody by the police, the courts must be advised, in most jurisdictions within twenty-four hours, for a requested extension of custody of two to three days until a preliminary hearing in juvenile and/or criminal court can bring the problem into the societal arena. There, under the "equal protection" clause of the Fourteenth Amendment, the rights of all family members can be considered by the court. While the ultimate decisions may be months off, adequate protection is afforded to the victim and the victim's family including, in the case of parental incest, the perpetrator. In some states, such as California, law officers and all medical graduates must be tested for basic understanding in the field of child abuse, including sexual abuse, before they can receive a license or certification. Many communities have set up community councils for child protection to diminish "turf" rivalries between all professionals and to have lay participation in matters which are paid for by taxes collected from the community at large. Further, many states are following the legislative lead of the state of Colorado which, five years ago, made mandatory the creation of interdisciplinary community teams for each county reporting more than fifty cases of child abuse a year; of these reported cases, an increasingly great number are now in the sexual abuse field (between 10 and 25 percent).

Finally, in Colorado by law, and in most states by common practice, a lawyer (guardian-ad-litem) is routinely appointed early on for the child to represent his/her best interest in any court hearings, including those dealing with custody, evaluation, and treatment recommendations.

The assumption that only attorneys should function as the "child's lawyer," or guardian-ad-litem, has become increasingly doubtful, in part because of the costs involved, and also because so much of the work involved is not legal in nature. Scottish, Israeli, Swedish, and Danish laws now incorporate this change in concept. Nonlawyer representatives for the child, as a substitute for the attorney, are being successfully tried in Michigan and Washington and elsewhere. There will continue, however, to be some difficult cases in which the child's interests are best served by having expert legal help, at least for court representation, when termination of parental rights are concerned, for example.

In the United States, any case of sexual abuse coming to the attention of society is heard in a civil court (either juvenile court or family court). It should also enter criminal court when police investigation determines that a criminal act has been committed and can be proved beyond a "reasonable doubt." The degree of proof needed in a civil procedure in family court is of a much lower level, requiring only "preponderance of evidence." The one exception to this occurs in those cases where "termination of parental rights" is sought by a child protective services department. For termination, the United States Supreme Court (1982) requires "clear and convincing evidence," a standard which we had always practiced in our institution. In the more usual civil case, the needs of the victim and the family are considered; nobody is on trial, nor is there necessarily a need to identify one offender or prove anything beyond that "the child's environment is unsafe," a very broad category. It is the district attorney in each of our 3,041 counties in the fifty states who decides if he or she has a case that can be proved in criminal court "beyond reasonable doubt."

Being required to appear as a witness in both the juvenile and criminal court cases may be traumatic to the child victim, however. This is especially true in a criminal court case where cross-examination of the victim by a hostile attorney is allowed by the adversary court process.

While "hearsay" evidence is not admitted in criminal cases as a rule, an exception is now emerging in American law practice when a child complains to any third party about sexual abuse; this is now occasionally allowed as admissable evidence. Recently some appeals courts have ruled in either civil or criminal cases that another person may fully testify to the child's complaints, and that this is not "unduly prejudicial and is highly convincing," a giant step forward because it means that the young victim may not have to appear in court and retell these events in public at all. Further, video or audio tapes of victim-police interviews are increasingly used as evidence in court (see Chapter 6).

But not all court appearances need to be avoided nor must they be stressful. Court appearances can be quite therapeutic when they give the victim a feeling of being a real person with rights to be defended by others. In Oregon, for example, a number of programs do allow child court appearances in selected cases when the offender denies everything. With careful instruction and preparation, older children and adolescents do well and feel strengthened in their new role as a person who matters.

Some child-care professionals tend to deny societal duties and feel that the police and other legal professionals should not be involved in questions of child sexual abuse. They view abusive acts toward children as an illness in the offender or solely a symptom of serious family dysfunction. This is far too limited a view of the problem. Advocates of these views miss certain important

points: (1) whatever the background situation, under the laws of all our states, and most countries abroad, sexual abuse of children is always a criminal act (generally a felony); (2) major psychiatric illness in the perpetrator is a relatively uncommon finding in the vast majority of sexual abuse cases, though it may be more common in forcible rape by a sociopathic criminal; and (3) that "therapy" deals with only part of the problem.

To exclude police, district attorneys, and judges from these matters is asking them to forego their sworn duty to enforce the law. This does not mean, happily, that society's legal involvement needs to be heavy handed, nor that it should ever occur without a very close working relationship with others trained in the diagnosis and treatment of these conditions. Remember that law enforcement is available to anyone on a 24-hour-a-day, 7-day-a-week basis. Few social service protective agencies are always ready to take effective protective action at once—the police are. In a good many major centers of population, as in the model program of the Los Angeles Police Department, specially trained police staff who have good working relationships with social workers, physicians, nurses, and selected hospitals are able to provide prompt emergency care of all kinds of sexual abuse cases. The results in these coordinated efforts are spectacularly good, just as they could be devastatingly destructive in those jurisdictions where professional duty lines are drawn strictly, and sometimes with hostility. Collaborative crisis-intervention skills need to be learned, and there are times when it is far safer for the protective services social worker to be accompanied by a police officer or a sheriff into a family situation which might rapidly become violent. In some communities, the police are unquestionably insensitive to the plight of victim and family, and modification of both attitudes and policy need to be made at top administrative levels to encourage cooperation with social services.

Rape crisis centers in some metropolitan areas still have no firm policy about promptly reporting sexual child abuse to the proper liaison in the police force, though they all know that failure to report a suspected felony offense is itself unlawful. The reason given is that, while reporting by parents is encouraged, the intake workers fear the additional trauma caused by police involvement. No thought is given to possible future victims or the need for early and skilled attempts at offender identification. These workers wish to help everyone and, in fact, may help nobody, not even the victim, if they give the message that stopping the offender does not matter very much or is no part of their mission.

Laws concerning sexual abuse outside the family setting usually place nonviolent cases involving children under misdemeanor statutes, while rape and all other violent offenses and incest are felonies and carry longer criminal sentences. If a child, male or female, is transported across state lines for purposes of prostitution, the Mann Act makes this a federal offense to be followed by the Federal Bureau of Investigation (FBI).

What does, in fact, happen to nonviolent child molesters who either plead guilty or are convicted by the courts? About 17 percent of them receive some prison term; 24 percent are assigned to mental institutions for a time; and over 50 percent are placed on probation after conviction. A single offender, for example, who had never been charged though suspected, admitted to over 3,000 offenses before seeking treatment after his first arrest. A major reason for the lack of better disposition, is our inadequate knowledge about effective treatment for sex offenders.

Because of the many changes in laws relating to sexual abuse, one recent fear is that longer sentences due to tougher rape laws may backfire; rapists may be more inclined to kill their victims. Jurors may even be less likely to convict rapists if they know that life imprisonment will certainly result from conviction. Since 1975, more than forty states have changed their rape laws, and twenty have completely rewritten their sex offense statutes, drastically increasing penalties and imposing mandatory sentence requirements.

Fixed and extremely severe penalties do not allow discretion to differentiate between the less severe and the brutal rapes. Both are serious, but some rapists can be rehabilitated if treated adequately and society might be better served by evaluation of the offender. In California (1981) judges have imposed sentences of 118 years, 100 years, 83 years, and 53 years for four separate rape convictions based on the victims' testimony. In Illinois (1981), six young men were convicted of the gang rape of a 15-year-old girl. The first man convicted, aged 25 and the instigator of the attack, received a total of 228 years in prison; 60 years for rape, 60 years for devious sexual assault, 30 years for indecent liberties with a child, 28 years for two counts of robbery, and 50 years for fifty counts of aggravated battery. Some rapists may well decide to murder their victims to prevent their testifying, because this testimony is a major factor leading to conviction.

In many different cases of sexual abuse, a combination of criminal and juvenile court or civil legal involvement can be most beneficial. Particularly in cases of father-daughter incest, interviews, after proper legal cautioning, by a pair (preferably female and male) of police detectives who are not in uniform and preferably in the perpetrator's home, lead to rapid confession in many of our cases. This works especially effectively when it can be pointed out that legal criminal bypass procedures do exist in the county. In such jurisdictions, the district attorney and the child protective service authorities join the perpetrator in signing a contract which includes the requirement of not less than two years of treatment. Certain perpetrators, such as violent offenders, are automatically not eligible for this program, but these, along with those who do not admit to the offense, constitute a minority. The rest, in fact, plead guilty as charged, but they know that the record can be expunged and no open court hearing will be held, thus guaranteeing privacy, preservation of job and social standing, and, in most cases, keeping the family intact while giving the victim maximal protection from future abuse. A video recording of the child's statements to the police often results in a contrite emotional response from the father and willingness to attempt change with supportive help. Persistent incest denial often ends in an

admission of guilt on the very day that the criminal trial is scheduled to begin, if the prosecution does not give up prematurely.

Less forward-looking communities, where pressure of time
on child protective services is very great and the authorities resort
to "three months of family therapy" and the early closing of the
case, have a very high rate of recidivism, depriving the victim of
protection. In short, an alliance between the juvenile court, the
criminal court, the district attorney, child protective services, and
the therapist is the most effective way to provide the required
multifaceted involvement in cases of sexual abuse, especially in
incest. (See Appendix I.)

Divorce and remarriage now frequently bring nonblood related families together, and sexual abuse by a stepparent of a child
victim or between non-blood-related minors pose additional problems for the judicial system. In each case of sexual exploitation
of a child for the gratification of an older person when the child
is unable to understand the action or to give proper consent by
virtue of age and the partners could not legally marry, it is our
belief that legal definitions of incest apply, regardless of blood
relationship.

A model adult criminal diversion program developed jointly
by the District Attorney's office and the El Paso County (Colorado) Department of Social Services now has had some years
of trial with a very good treatment record. Anne B. Topper, an
experienced social worker, has been able to show that, with
a sizable client group and over a period of more than five years'
experience, in only two cases with deferred prosecution have they
had to refer the offender back to the district attorney's office for
criminal prosecution. One man left the city and a warrant for his
arrest was unsuccessfully placed—presumably he had left the
state. The other man did not comply with the prescribed treatment program, was prosecuted, and sent to the penitentiary. His
family, including the female victim, remain in treatment. Note
that the adult diversion program requires a *two-year treatment
plan* in most cases. This differs from most other diversion pro-

grams, including another one in Colorado's larger city where a *three-month treatment plan* is often agreed to by a rather naive court and by those social work program supervisors who wish to "close the case," even knowing that the designated plan for continued care in community based mental health services is unlikely to occur. (The results in the latter community are poor compared to the program in Colorado Springs described in detail in Appendix 1.)

Finally, note that the offender does plead guilty to the charge as an absolute requirement for inclusion in this diversion program, a feature we feel is vital to its success. Guilt once admitted can be accepted and made truly therapeutic with a resulting improvement of self-esteem, and the beginning of insights which lead to successful treatment of the family, the victim and the offender in most cases. Without admission of guilt, little change is possible because denial totally blocks the path toward understanding and often makes the offender feel that he has "fooled the system." Indeed, sometimes he has, to his own and his family's cost. An initial admission of incest may be later retracted, but as long as the diversion program is in effect and the father is in active therapy, control of contacts between father and child may keep the situation stable until the father is able, with the support of his therapist, to understand the reasons for his behavior and to tolerate his guilt.

While, as we said earlier, many mothers early on deny any knowledge, quite often in time they, too, are able to see their own role in the longer lasting incest situations. If they are able to express openly their own feelings of guilt, then attain understanding and self-forgiveness, this should lead toward improvement in the family dysfunction which caused incest to occur in the first place.

From time to time, professionals, and particularly physicians, have been told by attorneys for suspected perpetrators of sexual abuse that they might be on uncertain legal grounds in taking *any* history and gathering other information without first cautioning the person that these facts may be used later, in court, "against" them in a possible future criminal trial—that is, without giving them the "Miranda" warning. A recent decision (1982) in the California Supreme Court held that no health professional needs to tell anybody anything while a patient is being evaluated and a comprehensive diagnosis is being made. This includes the audio- and/or videotaping of interviews with any person involved, and the obtaining of needed X- rays or photographs. All these, and the patient's clinical record, are protected from the concept of illegal seizure. The court in that instance thus affirmed the legal possibility of eventual use of any material obtained in the course of helping a young patient, and it is within the evaluation and treatment permission granted to physicians and hospitals by either the parents, the police, or child protective service agencies. Interpretation of this California concept by other state courts should be considered in obtaining evidence.

Increasingly, sexual abuse is being committed by minors who, under most laws, cannot be tried in adult criminal courts unless the case is "waived" by the juvenile courts to the adult criminal courts. As a result, even very serious and often repeated abuses result in detention upon conviction in a juvenile facility with all sentencing ending with age 18 regardless of diagnostic studies suggesting that it is simply not safe to have the youngster at large. At age 18 life legally seems to begin anew. Adult sex offenders of the most brutal kind are often found to have had many previous trials and convictions which have gone from initial probation to treatment orders which were often totally inadequate or inappropriate to the offense during short-term juvenile detention. The assumption that all young offenders will respond rapidly to treatment is not warranted. Clearly, the judicial system must soon address the early serious offender in childhood and adolescence if tragedies are to be avoided.

CHAPTER FIVE

COMPREHENSIVE FIRST AID AFTER CHILDHOOD SEXUAL ABUSE

EXTRAFAMILIAL SEXUAL ABUSE

It is sadly true that while a one time, extrafamilial incident of sexual abuse causes emotional and, sometimes, physical pain to the victim, an institutional "second rape," as frightening and painful as the first, may inexcusably be added to this trauma through insensitive and intrusive care of the victim. Unless a clearly planned approach is available to all emergency rooms, their nurses and physicians, the private physicians in the community, the police and detective forces who sometimes specialize in this field in large communities, and the child protective services which get involved, the victim is subjected to repeated traumatic examinations and interrogations.

In virtually all reported instances of extrafamilial sexual abuse, the child is promptly brought to a physician, usually in an emergency room, but sometimes in a private practice office where the very first contact is with a nurse. He or she can and should quickly determine how much speed is needed, after calming the victim and the adult who brings the youngster. Whenever possible, the child should have a familiar and trusted person, usually a parent, with him/her at all times. Because in all extrafamilial sexual abuse the police need to play an investigative role, they should be promptly contacted; generally a trained female detective is available for female victims in any middle- or large-sized town or city.

It may well then be the police officer who is the very first person to interview a child victim of sexual abuse if there is no immediate need for medical intervention. Depending on his or her training, sensitivity, and gentleness, this can often be a therapeutic rather than a traumatic experience for the victim. If the police officer has established good rapport with the child, he/she may be able to obtain sufficient information concerning the exact nature and extent of the sexual abuse and about the perpetrator for an initial plan of action to be made. If the brief initial interview is videotaped, or if an unobtrusive professional observer can take notes, this record may provide the district attorney, the Social Services Department, and all others concerned with the basic information needed to apprehend the perpetrator. It is important to get this information accurately and early for if the perpetrator is not successfully apprehended, he usually goes on to victimize other children. Individual child molesters, in one survey, admitted to being responsible for an average of 68 child molestations each.

Sometimes the sexual abuse is reported first to the child protective services and, unless a good liaison has been set up, there may be some delay in reporting to the police while interviewing goes on with the family. In those cases where an offender must be identified, it is in the best interest of the child and the community for the interviewing to be performed early and in such a way that the professional responsibilities of the protective services and the district attorney's office can be met simultaneously, and without subjecting the patient to the harassment of repetitive questioning.

At times each professional group who has a responsibility to discharge for the child, family, or community feels that only someone in that group can ask the questions needed. This can lead to a race between police and social workers to get to the victim first and then to insist on their "professional" rights to get their information first hand, ignoring the child's reaction to all these interrogations.

In any situation where urgency is present, as is often the case, it is very important for a community, no matter how small, to have discussed possible procedures to cope with crises *before* they happen. Any community can designate a multidisciplinary Sexual Abuse Team (most often the Child Protection Team) who is responsible for planning the care of sexual abuse victims in their county. Such plans provide ahead of time for the different kinds of information that each of the following groups needs:

1.   The police and the district attorney's office need to have specific, legally admissible evidence of the facts concerning how the sexual abuse took place, its extent, and the identity (or clues to the identity) of the offender.

2.   The protective services agency wants to have the same information, but with a different degree of accuracy and burden of proof. They are also concerned with immediate decisions concerning the care of the child, the possible disruption of the family, and the need for future treatment.

3.   The physician must examine the child victim immediately if recent rape has occurred to obtain physical evidence for legal prosecution at a later time and to provide medical care for the victim. Less urgent physical evidence of other kinds of sexual abuse can be obtained, in some cases, at a later scheduled time.

The Sexual Abuse Team (or Child Protection Team) should set up a series of priorities of action which will vary according to the circumstances but which will provide the necessary information and treatment at just the right time. Only if the medical, social service, and law enforcement personnel involved understand one another's role in providing service for the child and have agreed upon a cooperative process can the child victim and his/her family receive optimum help and can the legal prosecution of the offender be adequately prepared.

Priorities of action, then, depend upon the type of sexual abuse and the degree of familiarity of the offender to the child.

When exhibitionism (indecent exposure) by a stranger takes place, the top priority is to reassure the child and to obtain information concerning the offender. More intrusive physical contact and more violent behavior of the offender necessitate medical involvement, with the urgency dependent upon injury. If molestation has taken place over a period of time, with no very recent contact and no immediate evidence of injury, the child can be seen within a day or two in the emergency room or the clinic for evaluation of any physical evidence of molestation and for cultures to rule out venereal infection. The closer the relationship of the offender to the child victim or the more evidence of parental neglect in the situation, the more necessary is the rapid involvement of the protective services worker. Law enforcement personnel should also be involved from the beginning, not only to obtain a history but to ensure the proper safeguards of evidence collection and legally correct interrogation of the victim—and the offender if he is identified and available.

Large city hospitals have a routine for rape investigation which includes precise directions for forensic material collection from the victim's clothing and also the skin, throat, and vaginal and rectal regions, as indicated by the type of abuse. If the admitting nurse and/or physician are unfamiliar with these procedures, the help of a detective should be sought first, unless a delay of a half hour would seriously interfere with comprehensive care. The time spent waiting can often be used for giving comfort and reassurance which would, of course, naturally be done in any case of general injuries due to trauma or rectal tears. It is usually better to consider administering painful treatment under a mild general anesthetic than to cause the additional anxiety, pain, and, to the child's mind, reinforcement of the coercive sexual abuse that results from treatment done under local anesthesia (as is used with adult victims). A joint nursing or physician interview can be video- or audiotape recorded. When the police are not available, we try to have a trained and sympathetic team bring out the needed facts quickly; the support provided by a loving family member present throughout greatly aids in making this a less difficult time for a child who has been abused. A few older children prefer privacy during interviews and they should have it.

With children who have suffered sexual abuse, a physician of the same sex often succeeds best in eliciting a history and providing care on the broadest scale; both physical and emotional needs are addressed at once. Knowledgable and sensitive, gentle care, are, however, always more important than the sex of the physician.

Specimens (properly collected in a forensic kit, signed, sealed, and dated) for the presence of sperm are taken from the victim's clothing, throat, and genital and rectal areas for chemical tests performed by the police laboratory. In both female and male youngsters, specially prepared bacteriological cultures for gonorrhea are routinely taken from the victim's throat and genital and rectal areas. When semen can be demonstrated in the laboratory within 24 to 36 hours of the event by chemical tests and the blood groups are determined, a suspect may be totally ruled out or made eligible as the perpetrator. For example, if the blood group is an uncommon one, such as AB (3 percent of the population), it may be a useful forensic finding if the alleged perpetrator has that blood type. It is important to note, however, that semen is found in a minority of cases; its absence is no indication that rape did not occur. Antibiotics are often given for a few days to prevent infection.

The fear of pregnancy is very strong in all victims. In adolescents in whom pregnancy could occur as a result of rape, physicians may utilize a single hormone injection to prevent any chance of it; depending on the circumstances, however, some patients and physicians prefer to check for possible pregnancy and then plan an early abortion if it does occur. The incidence of rape pregnancy in a one-time adolescent rape experience has been reported to be very low (0 percent in one large study), but more recent studies have shown an average of 7 percent incidence, and the range stands at 0 to 10 percent in all reports.

In the event of rape with physical injuries, necessary medical care of the child takes precedence over everything else, but there may be pressure to obtain some information as soon as possbile. An answer to "Who did it?" if the child can readily say, may be used to apprehend quickly a potentially dangerous person. However, hectoring a child who is in shock, pain, and a state of intense fear is not appropriate or effective; patience and a calm atmosphere are more apt to produce a coherent response. Videotaping, if done without commotion by a sympathetic police officer (generally a well-trained female investigator), may suffice for the court hearing and thus make it unnecessary ever to bring the child to court. This initial interview may also be conducted with an unobtrusive observer taking notes, if videotape or audiotape recordings are not available or sufficient. The two persons involved may represent both police and social services, thus ensuring an interview acceptable to both. It is very important that the interviewer be a person skillful and comfortable in talking with children about sexual abuse. The questions should be decided upon before the interview takes place rather than interrupting it to confer while the child waits.

Even in the midst of crisis and confusion, the interviewer can do much to make the child feel better by a simple sensible approach. He/she must introduce himself or herself simply, along with anyone else who is to remain during the interview. To ask the child if the mother (or other friend) should stay too allows for support if needed but for privacy if the child prefers it. Reassurance about physical status and a statement of recognition of the patient's ordeal can follow, and then a clear statement about why some questions are important should precede the discussion of events. A calm, matter-of-fact demeanor, not uncheerful, is usually reassuring. Arguing with the patient about an interview is not helpful; listing of the vital questions, along with the statement, "These are the things we need to know—we can wait until you feel ready to talk about it," helps to avoid problems. (If the child has particular difficulty responding to one person and gets upset, it is wiser to have someone else to whom he/she responds more comfortably do the interview rather than force the issue.)

In any case, until the offender is in custody if he is violent, it is essential to provide the safeguards that will protect the child from further molestation and from the risk of physical attack and protect others from similar abuse. The hospital is a safe place, and every aspect of the initial treatment approach can often be planned in a brief hospital stay and initiated before the child leaves.

INCEST

First aid in incest is most apt to focus on the shock of discovery to the family and the consequent immediate stress on all relationships.

Occasionally incest is discovered as a rape with injury or as an attack of severe physical abuse coincident with sexual abuse. In these situations, the child must be medically treated as in any other case of rape, but the father may be in police custody as the probable offender and the mother's position may at first be unclear. If she is not supportive of the child, a caseworker or some other professional person to whom the child responds may need to act in a mother's protective capacity for the time being. In cases of long-standing incest, family support may be totally lacking. Here professionals may be the child's sole initial advocates.

While the size of the vaginal opening in a prepubertal girl may well be correlated with incest if penetration has occurred, tests used in acute rape are often negative in incest either for injury or for presence of sperm and infection, although urinary tract infections are commonly found along with evidence of genital irritation. These infections, however, are not diagnostic for incest and may have other causes. They do need medical care in any case. It is never "a rape case"; it is always "a hurt youngster" and the hurt is in all areas of the child's life.

Once incest is discovered, many people may become involved, often compounding the abuse by endlessly repeated interviews by police, social workers, physicians, and, at times, attorneys and judges: each can point out that each has a sworn duty to investigate the situation on his own. In fact, it is quite possible to belive one another and to get most, if not all information by a joint, tactful, single interview. When a competent physician is the person who discovers the problem, much thought should be given to an initial and gentle evaluation, often during a brief hospital stay if an injury is involved or an infection is found, even if the symptoms of themselves might not require hospital care. Just one or two days of such care in a sympathetic "safe place" allows the youngster to be reassured about her/his health, to gain support and strength, to have a program outlined that takes into account the child's needs and wishes as much as possible. The brief hospital stay need not compound the pain of fears of family breakup, rejection by those she/he loves, and uncertainty about the immediate and ultimate future. This time is also often a critically useful one for getting the family mobilized around a nonpunitive program that assesses the family's dysfunction and its strengths.

If the private physician feels too angry to deal with sexual abuse in any form, another physician should be quickly found who can cope, and, often with a nurse-physician team, an emergency treatment environment can be quickly provided. Statements as to just how, when, where, and who is involved might be settled then and there. This information suffices for making a team-treatment plan that should include, aside from the child's primary physician contact, the police, a social worker, a nurse, and usually a psychiatrist or psychologist. A video recording or audiotape of the first and only interview, with the youngster's consent, can then be used to make further interviews at a later time unnecessary. The total family is evaluated and the child is safe, either in temporary care outside the home or at home if the perpetrator is reliably moved out for a time while treatment gets under way. Too often the victim is punished twice, first by the abuse and then by removal from home while the offender remains in the family. The child is made to seem the guilty party when she or he is, in fact, the innocent one. Routine, long-term removal of the victim from her/his siblings may be very ill advised, though often more convenient for the social services departments involved.

An example of how several missed opportunities to help a little girl of 7 years is the case of *Sally*. Sally told her teacher at school that her two uncles who lived with the family were "messing with her." She was interviewed by the school social worker using dolls and clearly demonstrated sexual intercourse which she said had been happening frequently to her for several months and to her 3-year-old sister for the past week. The social worker confronted Sally's mother with this information and arranged for an Emergency Department appointment the next day. When Sally came to the hospital the next day, accompanied only by the child protective worker (a different worker), she had bruises on her back and face. She said her mother had beaten her the previous day, saying, "You pulled down your pants for your uncle." Sally was examined by a woman gynecologist, but was totally uncooperative when asked to assume the usual adult position for a gynecological exam (a very exposed position). The doctor decided that there was no definite evidence of trauma to the genital area, but she did not see the vagina or obtain cultures. Shortly after, another woman doctor reassured Sally and requested her to assume the knee-chest position on her side, obtaining the needed cultures and smears for legal testimony. She corroborated the probability of Sally's story, but also found no evidence of recent injury. Sally responded positively to this more reassuring approach with evidence of indiscriminate attachment

to several people, but especially the second doctor. She was also
very fearful, hyperactive, and seductive.

As Sally was being seen, a foster mother (who appeared im-
patient, in a hurry, of poor intelligence, and unsympathetic to
Sally) was waiting to take her directly off to foster placement.

To review, after confiding her problem at school, Sally was
sent home to her mother which precipitated a confrontation. Her
mother may have felt accused of responsibility for the incest and
angrily shifted the blame to Sally. The next day Sally was brought
to the clinic where the first doctor expected Sally to behave like
an adult. When, in panic, she was unwilling to expose herself, the
doctor decided there was no evidence to be had. yet with a little
more reassurance and a more appropriate approach for a girl of
her age, Sally responded cooperatively. Indeed, Sally showed some
of the probable effects of neglect and prolonged sexual abuse for
she was not only fearful, but indiscriminately friendly and seductive. Immediately after the examination, she was hurried off
to an inappropiate foster home.

For Sally the result of seeking help had been punishment and
rejection from her mother, separation from her school and family,
exposure to a series of strange adults all concerned with doing
their own job and not with Sally's feelings, exposure to frightening
examinations, and finally banishment to a foster home. Nowhere,
in all these events, was there one constant person to whom Sally
could turn for comfort, explanation, and reassurance.

EFFECTS ON THE CHILD

The effects of any kind of sexual abuse on children at first examination do, of course, vary enormously depending on the sud-
denness and violence of the occurrence and the capacity of the
child, in terms of age and previous experience, to understand the
sequence of events and to respond to help.

Thus it is important in providing crisis care to such children and their families to recognize that each child is different and that initial overt behavior may not necessarily indicate the severity of the after-effects. But each child needs immediately to have those responsible for providing care show concern for his/her dignity, privacy, and fearfulness, both in their attitudes toward her/him and in treatment.

It is especially worthwhile to note that children react in different ways to traumatic events, particularly in their ability and willingness to talk about it afterward. Very young children, who have little language, are still sometimes able to describe vividly, if not accurately, what happened. "He hurt me on my bottom, right there!"

Young children up to age 5 or 6, at least, are apt to describe traumatic events with considerable accuracy if they talk at all. They may tell what happened very matter-of-factly and in detail. (Although the details which they describe may not all be relevant, a few questions may supply the relevant ones.) They may seem to show little emotion in talking about the events, giving a false impression of being untouched by the experience. They do not seem to have the capacity of older children to use various psychological defenses to "deny" traumatic aspects of the story or to "color" what happened in order to make it easier to cope with.

Evaluation of very young children must be done with care because they are seldom able to defend themselves against overintrusive questioning or against answering questions they simply don't understand. The obligation they feel to please an adult in authority makes it hard not to try to answer even when they feel unable or unwilling to do so, and they may have to resort to silence or "I don't know."

If they feel pressured by the interviewer, young children may try to please or satisfy the adult asking questions. They may then begin to make up answers to what is asked or, especially if the questions are too detailed and leading, acquiesce to what they believe they are expected to say. For this reason, questions must be few, simple, nondirective, and very carefully worded. Questioning should not be persistent when the child does not answer, and the child's comfort with the interviewer can be a guide as to when he/she is unhappy about the content of what he/she is saying.

Young children, on the other hand, may not talk at all, particularly in response to questioning which makes them feel frightened or uneasy. If they have been warned by the family or the offender not to talk, they may be too fearful. Some very young children refuse to talk because they try to avoid the discomfort of remembering. (This is different from denial in that they may be able to remember perfectly well but try hard not to do so.) Often children who have difficulty verbalizing or resistance to talking about unhappy events will play them out, especially in doll-house or puppet play. Repeated play of this kind can be very significant.

The use of anatomically correct dolls has been found very helpful in this respect because the child can then clearly label anatomical parts with his/her own names for them, reducing confusion. Puppets or doll house play often serve the same purpose although the information may be less explicit. Drawings are also very helpful with young children as a way of expressing feelings.

Children who won't talk when "evaluated" may ask questions or reveal startling information at a time which is nonthreatening or reassuring for them, even though it may seem very inappropriate to the caretaker or parent who is caught unprepared in the middle of some routine activity. For this reason, it is worthwhile to help parents or caretakers be prepared for such moments. At least they can take careful note of the statements or questions and calmly give the child an opportunity to talk, rather than cut off the confidence, perhaps permanently, because of their fear of not having the right answer.

Very young children of 2, 3, or 4 may be exposed to sexual approaches by adults, either in sporadic episodes or fairly regularly. Children of this age are often brought to attention for reasons other than the sexual abuse, such as physical abuse or neglect, and only during the course of investigation is the sexual abuse discovered. When the cause for referral is sexual abuse, definite evidence of physical injury from attempted penetration or of irritation of the perineal area along with complaints by the child of discomfort usually exists. In the case of perineal irritation, fondling and masturbatory activity is the more usual complaint, rather than attempted intercourse. Vaginal tears and bleeding from rectal tears are diagnostic of forcible rape; such bleeding may rarely cause death through exsanguination.

Occasionally the sexual abuse takes place when a child visits a father who is estranged from the mother or when a mother is absent and the child is left with mother's boyfriend. Accusations of sexual abuse without much foundation can occur in the process of marital separation or divorce, and it can be difficult to determine the truth (which may be in either direction). There are important aids sometimes. Young children who have been coached tend to repeat a story verbatim, often in adult wording, and they have difficulty in telling the same essential facts in different ways. Young children who consistently give the same facts in detail in different words have an event in mind. Young children who repeatedly play out a series of actions usually have an event in mind also. The older children are (over 5, for example), the more aware they are of the intent of the questioner and the more able they are to dissemble. It is true that young children may produce fantasy, but fantasy rarely reproduces an event in the same essential detail, for it is the feelings involved which matter in fantasy. It has been said that children may play out or tell the story of their own sexual fantasy, making it difficult to tell whether sexual abuse has taken place. We do not believe we have seen anyone falsely accused because of this, or a fantasy described with sufficient detail that it seemed real unless that child had some actual experience on which to base it. Sometimes a child seems to be telling a story with a specific purpose in mind—for example, living with one or other parent—and in these situations it is indeed difficult to know what has really happened. In these cases, however, the child's motivation is apt to be very clear.

Even for those young children whose family life is not already seriously disrupted, the sexual aspects of the abuse are apt to seem much less important to the child at the time of referral than the difficulties the youngster is experiencing in maintaining trusting and loving relationships with the parents. Fears of separation or violence may be urgent, and the confusion concerning sexual seduction or attack may be of secondary importance at the time. Very young children also have a poor knowledge of anatomy, so that their fantasies concerning what has taken place may be far from what an adult expects. Little girls, for example, rarely are aware there is such a thing as a vagina, and, even if they have looked for what they have been told is there, they are very unlikely to have found it. Fantasies about sexual activity, therefore, are much more apt to involve the urinary tract or the rectum, and therefore lead to fantasies about toilet training and continence or oral-anal ideas or ideas about oral impregnation. In little boys, in addition to these worries, the safety of the penis is apt to be the major focus of attention.

Once the initial medical and social investigation is underway, those who must be responsible to the court, usually the child protective services if the parents no longer are, for ensuring the child's future welfare must make tentative but long-term treatment plans. It is very helpful to the family to interpose a minimum number of persons and procedures between the initial contact at reporting and the actual beginning of treatment. The time of crisis is the time when professional help can be used most effectively and when diagnostic information is most available. Whenever possible, it is desirable, then, for the professional personnel who do the evaluations to be available for the long-term treatment as well. Whether that kind of continuity is possible or not, it is also important to begin to let the family know about the kinds of treatment available to them and to prepare them for what should happen. Allowing them to ask questions about court, legal procedures, and treatment facilities, perhaps with a visit, will reduce somewhat the anxiety of waiting.

While we have said that pregnancies as a result of rape are not common, incest pregnancies are far more common. Eleven- and 12-year-old victims have given birth to babies when they, as children, can cope neither with incest nor motherhood. Eventually, if abortion does not take place, and in some recent examples it has not, both children, mother and infant, end up in separate foster care and a real tragedy is made far worse for all concerned. Early consideration of the possibility of pregnancy and rapid enlistment of help in the consequent decision making about abortion so that it is not forced by time considerations are part of the crisis care of incest.

FIRST AID FOR THE FAMILY

It is sometimes the parents who are more overtly upset than the child by extrafamilial sexual abuse and who are in urgent need of someone to talk to. They may be very worried about the physical or psychological effects of the abuse on their child, sometimes with unrealistic fears of irreversible damage. They may be extremely angry at the perpetrator and need to talk about their feelings so that they are less apt to try to act on them and attack the supposed culprit. Sometimes the anger expressed against the culprit may be partly felt toward the child who has perhaps acted unwisely and destroyed the parents' illusions of her/his innocence. Such feelings should be noted but not necessarily be confronted at once. They can form the basis for a follow-up interview or referral. Parents may be feeling extremely guilty with variable degrees of justification, and a matter-of-fact acceptance of the difficulty in foreseeing events may be helpful to them.

When parents are concerned primarily with their own feelings and not about the child's fears the child will need extra support from outside the family in follow-up. However the family responds, any information obtained indicates directions for treatment planning.

FIRST AID FOR THE OFFENDER

Sexual offenders are not necessarily callous persons whose only concern is to avoid the consequences of their behavior. Some offenders may be fairly young adolescents, sometimes peers of the victim. They usually have multiple problems with poor impulse control. But they also may have never shown evidence of problems before. Their sexual behavior may be a shock to themselves as well as others, and they may be overwhelmed by what is happening.

Some child molesters are older, respected members of the community who have a great deal to lose from discovery; a few of them have never before acted on their impulses. A few elderly men who molest children suffer from organic brain disease and need both medical and psychiatric treatment. Many sex offenders are chronic alcoholics and must receive treatment for alcoholism before they can cope with other behavioral difficulties.

Many sex offenders have used massive denial of their problems and rationalization of their sexual behavior. When forced by intervention to recognize how others view their behavior, they become extremely anxious, guilty, and sometimes suicidal.

Therefore, the offender, as well as the victim may be in urgent need of evaluation at the time of apprehension for his own protection during the initial crisis. Other offenders who are hardened recidivists or who are mentally ill need early evaluation in order to determine whether it is safe for them to remain at large. Evidence of escalation of the offense, or of associated violence or accompanying fantasies of violence, are to be taken especially seriously. In addition to concerns for everyone's safety and the necessity for initiating legal procedures, initial evaluation of the offender must begin to assess his potential for treatment. In many instances this may also be relevant to treatment plans for the victim.

REFERENCES

Cantwell, H. D. Vaginal inspection as it relates to child sexual abuse in girls under thirteen. *Child Abuse & Neglect* 7:2, 1983.

Kempe, C. H. Incest and other forms of sexual abuse. In *The Battered Child* (Third Edition), C. H. Kempe and R. E. Helfers (Eds.). University of Chicago Press, Chicago and London, 1980.

Kerns, D. L. Medical assessment of child sexual abuse. In *Sexually Abused Children and their Families*, P. B. Mrazek and C. H. Kempe (Eds.). Pergamon Press, Oxford and New York, 1981.

Rimza, M. E., and Niggeman, E. H. Medical evaluation of sexually abused children: A review of 311 cases. *Pediatrics* 69:8–14, 1982.

Rush, F., *The Best Kept Secret: Sexual Abuse of Children*. Prentice-Hall, Englewood Cliffs, New Jersey, 1980.

Tilelli, J. A., et al. Sexual abuse of children. *New Eng. J. Med.*, 302:318, 1980.

PART III

CHAPTER SIX

EVALUATION AND TREATMENT OF EXTRAFAMILIAL ABUSE

A single episode of sexual abuse performed by a stranger, or even someone outside the circle of family and friends but vaguely known to the child, has an overall effect upon the child quite diffcrent from that of incest. Long-term sexual abuse, however, has effects that may be in some ways very similar. The variables which seem most significant in judging the effect of any sexual abuse are:

1. The nature of the abusive act, particularly with regard to the degree of seduction, coercion, or violence used.
2. The age and vulnerability, developmentally and physically, of the child, and her or his varying degrees of ability to understand and cope with a traumatic or sexual event. Symptoms are as apt to relate to the developmental level of the child and his or her previous experiences as to the kind of sexual abuse.
3. Whether the offender is a stranger, a member of the child's social environment, or a member of the immediate family.
4. The length of time over which abuse takes place, from a fleeting episode to multiple contacts over months, and the degree of child participation.
5. The reaction of the adults to whom the child confides the story.

6.   The consequences of treatment or legal intervention.

When we look at the individual child to determine the effects of abuse and his or her treatment needs, we must start with as complete an assessment of the child's strengths and weaknesses as we can manage. Then we can better assess her or his ability to cope with the abuse. In addition to the history, we need to know other data about the child as an individual—physical health and capabilities, neurological status, and individual temperament. Whatever the age of the child, if there are chronic health problems or speech, hearing, or visual difficulties, the help of other professional facilities needs to be part of any treatment program.

We need to have detailed historical information about the victim's cognitive and intellectual abilities and the state of his/ her progress developmentally. We particularly need to know how successfully the victim has negotiated the developmental aspects of relationships. Did he/she have the healthy enjoyment of a primary relationship with a consistent and nurturing mother? Was the child allowed to enjoy increasing autonomy and mastery over his/her early environment.

Before 3 years of age, children must learn the difference between self and others, must learn "object constancy" (that is, that every person remains consistently that same person with generally the same behavior, no matter where he/she is, i.e., in sight or not). To grasp this concept and be able to retain it over time makes possible the continuity of a relationship, and therefore the development of feeling valued, of being loved. If mother is always mother, no matter where she is, then you can safely count on her to act the same to you, expect certain responses such as nurturance from her, and safely trust and rely on her to be concerned about you, even when she has left you with a sitter-substitute who is supposed to act like her. A corollary of this important developmental step is the gradual development of a firmer sense of one's own self, as important, individual, and unchanging, except as any response to the events of the moment protects and enlarges that self. These fundamental developmental achievements are not always completed successfully. When the mother or parent figure is seldom present, or seldom responsive, or always inconsistent and variable in response (loving one moment, abusive the next with no consistent reason), the child has great difficulty in developing a firm concept of who the mother is, who he or she is, and of what behavior leads to acceptance and success.

Systematic developmental and psychological testing may indicate specific areas of congnitive malfunction, as well as unrecognized abilities and modes of problem solving, and some clues to unconscious and fantasy material.

Psychiatric evaluation in the playroom, or in an informal interview for the older child, should complete our impression of how a child functions. One wants to know from psychiatric evaluation how the child relates to a friendly but strange adult, and how she or he describes in words or play her or his relations with the family and peers. The themes in play, particularly a preoccupation shown in the repetition of a play fantasy, can point to major anxieties in the child. Prevailing moods (pleasure, anxiety, anger, sadness, suspicion, or hopelessness) need to be recognized with evidence of her or his self-image and ability to trust others. The coping style, or use of defenses against stress, needs to be considered not only as to how effective it is within the family, but also how effective or handicapping it will be in a larger school or social environment.

One must look for strengths as well as weaknesses, remembering that behavior ordinarily considered pathological may have been adaptive, even life-saving, in a pathological environment. Such qualities as attention span and impulse control are of importance in treatment planning as well as in current adjustment. Some young sexually abused children behave erratically because they become overwhelmed by their emotions with little recognition of the connection between events and their response. If the parents have been preoccupied with their own reactions and have never given any overt recognition to the existence or importance of the child's feelings, the young child may also have difficulty recognizing or communicating feelings at all. When such lack of attention to feelings is coupled with expectations of total compliance, the child may be left helpless, unable to develop healthy coping mechanisms. Thus interpersonal communication and reality testing may not have been acquired and must be taught in treatment as a concomitant to the encouragement of basic trust.

When such early developmental issues as basic trust, autonomy, and object constancy have not been adequately resolved, the growth of a treatment alliance at any age can be a difficult task. Active sabotage of treatment by the parents may sometimes compound the difficulty. The therapist can begin to deal with these hazards through scrupulous sensitivity to issues of confidentiality and loyalty and by being very consistent, open, and reliable. (See pages 134–140 of this chapter and Appendix 2 for evaluative interview examples.)

SYMPTOMS OFTEN SEEN AFTER SEXUAL ABUSE

It may be helpful to consider the symptoms, shown by sexually abused children in several categories. These then vary in their occurrence or manifestation according to the age and experience of the child. These tentative groupings are based partly on experience and partly on review of the writings of others, and they in no way represent the results of an organized study. One difficulty in describing the symptoms sexually abused children show is the problem of ascribing the etiology to sexual abuse rather than to the general family environment and other experiences of the child. As we have noted, chaotic abusive or neglectful families may cause problems for the child in which the sexual abuse is only one part. It may be necessary at times to assume that the relationship problems the child has at home contribute much to his symptoms in extrafamilial abuse and be a primary cause of difficulty in intrafamilial abuse. Some symptoms are almost always seen; others, seldom.

Vulnerability, Fears, Anxiety

Fears are almost always present to some degree, and they may be specifically related to the possibility of attack or to the consequences of the child's behavior. They may be expressed as nightmares or preoccupation with fantasied reliving of the sexual experiences. They may be vague, expressed as anxiety over being alone, over going out, over going to school, over any contact with men. Sometimes anxiety may be disorganizing, leading to confusion in thinking. A few children present an almost psychotic picture, but their mental status before abuse is usually not known, and although it is possible, it is not often likely that mental disturbance contributed to the occurrence of the sexual abuse.

Feelings of vulnerability, of being unprotected, may be expressed in concerns about being physically damaged, about feeling small or helpless, about not being knowledgeable or important enough to have any control over events. They may be revealed in the child's efforts to protect himself/herself, like the child who begins to take a toy lion to bed.

Anxiety may take a psychosomatic form and be expressed in sleeping difficulties, eating disorders, vague pains or aches, joint symptoms, bedwetting, and so forth. These physical symptoms are often the only ones noted by family or school or physician, and the cause may go unrecognized.

Separation

A major fear at all ages, although expressed differently at different stages of development, is that of the loss of nurturance, of a threat to the relationships with the parents or other loved ones who are important to the child. In preschool children this may be expressed as direct fear of loss of love and in symptoms of oral deprivation. In older children it may be expressed as fear of loss of love and approval, and great sensitivity to any rejection.

All children victimized by sexual abuse probably feel anger, but its direction may be confused if the abuse is not a clear-cut assault. If the sexual abuse is a forcible assault and if the family and professionals learn of it and clearly blame the offender, anger may be expressed by the child openly and freely against the offender. During ongoing sexual abuse or afterward if the child has not reported it or has not been believed, there may be great anger against the offender which the child does not dare express to anyone. There may also be much anger against the parents or adults who do not believe the child and leave him/her feeling betrayed. The anger may be displaced, either expressed in apparent behavior disorders or turned against the self in depression.

Often feelings of helplessness which accompany the anger remain unrelieved. Some children deal with this combination by "identifying with the aggressor," that is, by later on trying to enforce their will on others as someone's will was forced on them, and they may become aggressive and demanding or, as adults, repeat the sexual abuse in the role of offender.

Shame and Guilt

Very young children, or those who accept the assurances of the sexual abuser that the activity is not wrong, may feel no shame or guilt about their own sexual behavior until later, when they become more sophisticated or are reproached by others. Lack of guilt is especially apt to occur when the adult is a parent or parent substitute. The child may feel shame if others know of the sexual behavior and are critical or if he or she develops more awareness of standards of social disapproval, which in our society are particularly strong in sexual matters involving children. In most children, eventually, guilt is an important part of the effects of prolonged sexual abuse. Unrelieved, guilt may be accompanied by anxiety or depression and give rise to secondary symptoms of a neurotic kind.

Loss of self-esteem or *poor self-image* often occur even in young children who somehow feel damaged or different. This is more strongly felt by older children who believe they are "rotten" or "spoiled goods" and, consequently, unlike others. Such feelings can lead to feelings of isolation and loneliness, of being the only one with such a problem, and depression. In many children, especially in younger ones raised in chaotic families, there are problems of identity—not just confusion over sexual role identity, but also of the self as a separate person. This confusion sometimes persists as a serious problem in psychosexual development.

Often *preoccupation and poor cognitive development* or poor school work are also present. Most often the preoccupation is with fantasies or anxiety related to the sexual abuse and its consequences. It is true that many children, following the onset of sexual abuse, begin to have school difficulties. This symptom tends to be present at any age.

Difficulties with impulse control is fairly often found in sexually abused children. Many children seem to have little ability to delay gratification, to be able to resist impulses in order to follow social rules and to consider consequences. In some cases, this difficulty may be related to anxiety or to the loss of restraint and flooding of instinctual impulses learned on sexual contacts. In other cases, it seems likely that the difficulty in impulse control may have predated the sexual abuse and have been part of the child's vulnerability to the event. Poor impulse control does make for behavior problems, another common symptom, particularly if angry feelings are also prominent and readily displaced to such situations as peer interaction.

Some young children who come from a severely disturbed family background show self-destructive impulses as well, and may be acting out their perception of themselves as bad or worthless in this way. It is known that children often find it intolerable to acknowledge or express criticism and anger against the parents they love and need so badly, and that displacement of these impulses even on to the self is preferable to the possibility of losing the parents' love.

Treatment in Exhibitionism

The exhibitionist seeks an effect which is readily obtained from most children—a rapid facial expression of horror or amazement—after which he is usually content to let the child flee. The effect of such an episode on very young children may be primarily puzzlement because they may not recognize the sexual intent of the act. They may not even recognize the adult genitalia as such but assume some kind of deformity or injury in the adult. Most children immediately recognize the behavior as abnormal and "wrong," although the exact way in which it is wrong might not be at all clear. Older children are often frightened because they do recognize the sexual component of the act and feel very much threatened. If they run away, as they usually do, they may feel they were lucky and escaped an assault. Indeed, this may be true. Although most exhibitionists wish only to display themselves, a few, especially if encouraged in any way, might go on to molestation. Exhibition is for some molesters a preliminary way of testing out a child's responses; if the child remains or appears at all interested, the adult may go further.

Such a brief episode may rouse vague fears which are more apt to be dissipated if the child does describe the occurrence to an adult who responds sensibly and supportively. It is helpful if the parent can calmly ask the child what happened, where it occurred, and what the exhibitionist said. It is useful to let the child know that he/she was not responsible for the occurrence, that he/she did the right thing to run away and to tell a grown-up because the offender should be stopped from doing the same thing and frightening other children. The parents should then notify the police, but they can request that any further questioning of the child, if it is necessary, be done in their presence. Once this is done, the parents can reassure the child that the matter is taken care of, can review the rules for walking in isolated areas and talking to strangers, and tell the child to ask any further questions and not to worry about them. A calm, matter-of-fact recognition by the child that all grown-ups are not to be trusted is appropriate. This warning is especially pertinent if the child had followed the adult into a secluded place.

So far as is known, there are no long-term effects from such a brief episode unless the reactions of the family are pathogenic, unless there are further episodes, or unless the child is particularly vulnerable because of some previous experience to being unduly frightened. If the family overreacts in a phobic or histrionic way, dwelling unduly on possible dangers and markedly restricting the child's activities, the child may feel more damaged by the experience than is warranted and remain fearful.

The opportunity to talk about the episode, however, should be available to the child. Just as overemphasizing the dangers of the episode can lead to continued fears, refusing to discuss the episode at all, even to listen to it, may leave the child feeling that something is wrong and that perhaps she/he is somehow responsible. Even an older adolescent, after witnessing an episode of exhibitionism, may feel the need to talk to someone, to express fear or shock or disgust and have someone listen and accept those feelings. If the child is not allowed to do so, it is more difficult to master the episode, to achieve distance and a feeling of control over what happened so as to be able then to put it out of mind.

When the act of exposure is unusually frightening or remains upsetting to a child for a period of time after adequate explanation and reassurance, it is worthwhile to make a psychiatric referral. The exposure itself may have caused exacerbation of other dormant fears from previous forgotten experiences or from sexual fantasies no longer accessible to memory but troubling. The opportunity to recover these fears gradually with someone other than the parents may free the child from prolonged anxiety.

MOLESTATION

When the child molester cajoles, deceives, or threatens the child into allowing fondling or masturbation or into actively participating in these activities, there is a threat to the integrity of the child's body and the privacy of his/her person. It is difficult to generalize about the effects upon the child of these activities, for so much depends upon the vulnerability of the child and the context in which molestation takes place. We can describe variations and extremes; but it must be recognized that each child lives in a different family environment, has had an individual history of experience, and is approached by a different offender. One of the variables is the nature of the sexual abuse, and we have noted the minimal effect exhibitionism should have if there are no "complications." With molestation, which involves physical contact between adult and child, even if it be only fondling, there is an escalation, at least, in the child's feeling of vulnerability. Touching the breasts of the early adolescent girl or the skin under the clothes of the younger child is an invasion of privacy which may be keenly felt by the child as intrusive and may leave the child feeling helpless and frightened.

If the child at this point is allowed to leave and the child tells an adult who takes appropriate action, the episode may be kept comparatively benign. The adult listener, preferrably one of the parents, should remain calm, making clear to the child that the behavior of the adult was wrong, that such activity must not be allowed, that the child did nothing wrong and was right to tell about it immediately. It is then the responsibility of the adult to take steps which insure that the adult offender will be reported and that no repetition will be possible.

If the child feels believed, supported, and protected at this time, there may be little lasting trauma from such an incident. However, even though the molestation involved minimal physical contact, such an episode could become much more traumatic if the adult to whom the child reports the incident refuses to believe the story and denies its possibility or accuses the child of making it up to get the offender in trouble. (If the offender is a respected person such as a teacher, these doubts could well exist). Then the child is left feeling accused of being in the wrong, but worse, feeling unprotected and helpless in dealing with a repetition of the event. If the molestor, as is often the case, lives in the neighborhood, he may well try again, meet with little resistance, and escalate his activities.

If, when exposed to beginning seduction, a child does not tell anyone or is pleased by the attention and apparent affection, she/he can be drawn further into a pattern of fairly regular sexual activity. If the sexual activity progresses to mutual masturbation, a real likelihood exists that frequent sexual stimulation fixes erotic impulses as an important source of pleasure for the child, who may subsequently seek out the offender in order to share this activity. Such children are then in much the same situation as those caught in early incest: their sexual impulses have become stimulated beyond their capacity to control and repress them. They may become preoccuppied with sexual pleasure in an overt way, and on discovery, the parents may view this with great disapproval and blame. In the past, such children were considered to be innately bad, rather than the victims of an adult's use of their bodies.

The adult offender may well not wish to progress beyond a certain point in his relationship with the child. If, however, he does go on to attempt intercourse, the child's response again may vary. The new activity may also become pleasurable, or it may suddenly become painful or frightening. If the molester persists, using force or threats, the activity may become entirely distressing to the child, or there may be great ambivalence. If the distress is sufficient, the child may now report the activity. But fear, guilt, and attraction may all be present in the ambivalent child victim who feels truly isolated in a situation over which he/she has no control and which he/she no longer dares to report. Discovery may never occur, and such a child may occasionally reveal the emotional difficulties resulting from these episodes many years later in psychiatric treatment or in the course of giving a life history for unrelated reasons.

The immediate effect upon the child of a single episode of molestation is a feeling of vulnerability, often with vague fears, confusion, and a temporary withdrawal from outside activity. There may be some nightmares, eating disturbances, and anxiety about being left alone. Depending upon the child's age, there may also be some preoccupation with fantasy concerning the episode in an effort to master the anxiety that it caused. Unless the episode was quite traumatic, such symptoms may disappear fairly soon, and, except for the residual left in repressed memory or in fantasy, perhaps to be reawakened by future events, the child often seems to recover completely. When molestation has continued over time and included participation, however unwilling, on the part of the child, the effects are much longer lasting and pervasive.

For the younger child (under 8 or 10), guilt may at first be primarily confined to the fact that he/she is involved in a secret activity which is especially not to be told to the parents. Even though the adult may offer rationalizations for this ("they might be jealous of the fun we have"), the child is apt to know that somehow the activity is forbidden and wrong. Some children feel no guilt. If the child has poor intelligence, she/he may have difficulty in discriminating. Or the child may have a home background and social environment in which sexual activities are freely discussed and perhaps acted out by the adults around him/ her. In such an environment, the child's awakened interest in sexual matters may not be noticed. Often with these children, the sexual abuse comes to light when they begin to masturbate openly, to try to repeat their sexual experiences with other children, or to solicit sexual attention from adults, i.e., when their own sexual impulses have become very much stimulated by the sexual abuse. This result is a very difficult one for the child because his/her behavior alienates others, arouses disapproval, blame, and loss of sympathy from caretakers and often leads to the assumption that the child may originally have been at fault or at least looking for trouble. Some children whose outlook has been eroticized in this way may quickly respond to the disapproval of the environment and help from a therapist in controlling and suppressing sexual feelings; others may not be able to do so and continue to have great difficulty in control. These children may also be more vulnerable to a repeat of sexual abuse.

The story of the *Smith family* illustrates some of the characteristics of chronic child molestation and difficulties with treatment. Mrs. Smith was identified at age 20 as a mother who might have difficulty when her first baby was born, and she was offered the support of a lay therapist. When her son was 9 months old, she was referred by her lay therapist for a psychiatric interview, and the family became involved with protective services. Mrs. Smith worried about her impulses to hit her baby when he was demanding. She felt herself depressed, unattractive, lonely, and inadequate, but was actually likable and more competent than she realized. She was most concerned about her husband who admitted to her that he was attracted to little girls, but he denied acting on these impulses. He also joined sometimes in the activities of a group of young teenage delinquents. Mrs. Smith herself came from a family where the father was physically abusive, her mother passive and unprotective, and her brother forced incest on her by breaking her arm when she was 10. She eagerly accepted a referral to a home town psychiatrist, but her husband refused an appointment or any psychiatric involvement although this had been strongly urged.

For four years Mrs. Smith kept in touch with her lay therapist, benefited some from treatment, had two more children, and became increasingly fearful about her husband's behavior. The family was under court supervision because of some abuse and neglect. Mr. Smith was physically abusive with his wife, punished the children with a belt, and was unable to keep a job because he was restless or fought with his boss. After several separations, Mrs. Smith filed for a divorce. She found her husband had molested at least the older boy and perhaps the girl as well. He was arrested for molestation of neighborhood children and seen in consultation.

Mr. Smith had also had a depriving and abusive family life, with three stepfathers and a mother who was critical and unloving. As a teenager he had grown angry enough at her to put his fist through walls. He remembered no childhood sexual experiences except one of mutual exposure with a girl at age 9.

Mr. Smith had a personality disorder, with some question of mild neurological impairment, which needed evaluation. He was mildly concerned about his temper. He admitted to having molested 35 or 40 children between the ages of 4 and 12 years old, mostly girls, occasionally on repeated occasions if they agreed. Molestation consisted of mutual genital exposure, masturbation, and occasionally oral-genital contact. Mr. Smith admitted that he had weak adult heterosexual impulses but very strong pedophilic ones. "Sheer impulse takes over, like a second personality." His view of molestation was that it was not really sexual, "more like a ritual." He had tried to control his behavior by staying away from children, but he could not keep that up for long. He felt no guilt about it because he used no force. He felt no empathy for the children, and had no interest in the effects on them.

Because the first recommendation for a jail sentence with treatment was ruled out by the prosecutor, long-term psychiatric hospitalization was recommended because of Mr. Smith's tendency to violence which had not yet been linked to his sexual impulses. Probation conditional on acceptance of intensive treatment was designated as minimal treatment; this was the disposition given by the court, and its inclusion as a possible disposition was undoubtedly a mistake. Mr. Smith soon disappeared, but in two years he was again apprehended for molestation and this time was given a prison sentence. Mrs. Smith, in the meantime, did fairly well, supporting herself and her children on her own.

Over a course of approximately ten years, Mr. Smith was known to have pedophilic impulses, but even after his first apprehension he was not removed from society. With the treatment available to him at that time, it was unlikely that he could successfully avoid acting on his compulsion. He may well continue to be a danger to little children when he is released from prison because of his poor treatment prognosis.

FORCIBLE RAPE

The response of any child to forcible rape is primarily or first to the physical attack with its violence, injury, and resulting helplessness. For most children, forcible rape is experienced as a painful attack, even if there are no other bodily injuries. The older the child, the more may the reactions of the child approach those of an adult rape victim, but for nearly everyone, the aspect of violation, helplessness, vulnerability, and of feeling permanently damaged is present. The degree to which the experience is interpreted in sexual terms then depends upon the age and sophistication of the child.

The young child is apt to see rape as an unprovoked attack, and, not understanding any possible motivation on the part of the offender, often seeks to find the cause in himself/herself. Children do tend to think in terms of punishment when they are hurt, and often they feel responsible, as if they had been somehow bad. This feeling can be reinforced by the repeated questioning which is often necessary to determine the child's degree of participation in the event, especially for court evidence. Any criticism and lack of support from adults reinforces feelings of badness and irrational guilt, and this is particularly apt to happen with the adolescent who has been unwise and placed himself/herself in circumstances where he/she was vulnerable.

EVALUATION OF THE CHILD VICTIM AND THE FAMILY IN SEXUAL ABUSE

It is to be hoped that the initial part of the evaluation of the child who has been sexually abused will take place soon after the incident is reported so that both child and family can receive early help. The initial contacts may be made in an emergency room of a hospital, in a doctor's office, or perhaps in the child's own home (see Chapter 6). We have discussed the desirability of interviews being done by as few persons as possible and by professionals skilled in dealing with children and with sexual abuse. It is rare, however, that the personnel available during the first contact can continue, desirable as that would be, as the child's primary therapist or advocate.

Evaluation of the child and his/her family in most cases of extrafamilial sexual abuse (except for exhibitionism) may require several interviews. They should include some time talking with the child and his/her parents together in order to gain an impression of the nature of their relationship and how the parents are approaching the problem with their child. Not infrequently parents discuss a problem with the doctor in one way (quite calmly and matter-of-factly, for example) and in another way with the child (very anxiously, complaining about their own upset but insensitive to the child's fear and pain). Interviews with the parents are also needed in order to obtain a past history of the child and to understand the environment in which he/she lives.

Some evaluation of the parents is necessary in extrafamilial abuse as well as in incest, because the child will need their help. The parents' response to the sexual abuse, their ability to appraise it realistically and to empathize with the child, and their motivation to provide help should psychotherapy be needed should all be explored. One should know the family background in which the sexual abuse took place, the amount of affection and attention given the children, the amount of supervision customary, and the attitudes of parents toward child-rearing, including discipline and supervision. It is helpful to know the parents' household behavior, their attitudes towards sex, nudity, "adult" television and literature. Family activities as a group and the presence or absence of parents on a regular basis and relations with siblings give an idea of how closely involved family members are with one another.

The parents' past history, their own experiences as children with their parents, can help: what kind of closeness to one or the other parent, what discipline, what neglect, what losses of close relationships did they experience? Parents' own childhood sexual experiences, job histories, difficulties with the law, financial situations, frequency of moving, all give an idea of family stability. Divorces or marital separations or, if the parent is single, the presence of a live-in parent substitute; the presence of family friends and extended family and how often and what kind of activities are enjoyed with them—all of these pieces of information added together give the picture of a warm cohesive family surrounded by supportive friends and relatives or of an isolated, fragmented family which shares almost no joint activities.

Such a history sounds monumental, and in many cases of extrafamilial abuse detail may not be needed, but if there is some rapport established, most of this material flows from a few key questions. Enough information should be obtained to be sure that family problems are not contributing in a major way to the symptoms of the child. Sensitive questions, of course, are best kept to the last, when the parents have been able to recognize genuine interest in them as a family. Clearly, very detailed material cannot be obtained during the screening interview in the emergency room when an initial decision must be made about the child's immediate disposition—one reason why hospitalization for a brief period is so often a help. However, the questions about the circumstances of the sexual abuse usually do give a limited indication of the family's involvement with the child.

There may at times be real questions about the parent's intelligence, mental illness, or ability to parent. More extended evaluation is then required, often with specific psychological testing of parents and child, before any final plan is made which relies upon the parents to provide for the child's protection and rehabilitation.

In evaluating the child victim of sexual abuse, the mode of obtaining information should vary according to the age and expressive abilities of the child, as well as the degree of physical and emotional disturbance at the time of discovery (see Chapter 6, pages 100 and 101, and pages 112 to 114 of this chapter).

When the medical examination and treatment have been completed and a decision made as to where the child is to remain—in the hospital, in a temporary placement, or at home—arrangements can be made for the more leisurely evaluation of the child's difficulties. Priority must be placed on telling the child as clearly as possible what is to happen, so that there is room for flexibility but some feeling of security. The child is apt to respond best to a low-key, comfortable time in a private room which has just a few well-selected toys, including dolls and a few "neutral" objects such as a ball, plasticene, and paper and crayons. Games, puzzles, and complicated toys are not wise choices for diagnostic interviews because they encourage the child to become completely absorbed in an activity which shuts out the therapist or at least allows for the avoidance of conversation. Toys which promote "distancing" of emotion, that is, an opportunity to talk about "make believe" events using dolls, animal families, and puppets, let the child approach some of his/her experiences and feelings without having to admit openly that they apply to him.

During a first interview, it is important to let a child know who you are, why you are seeing him/her, and what your own part in the interview is. It is often easier for the child to understand clearly that you already know that he/she has had some difficult experiences and to describe only enough of what you know so that you do not lead the child in what he/she is to say. It is often helpful to have the parent present before the interview and give you explicit permission to talk with the child about the event. Perhaps the mother can describe briefly what happened so that the child does not have to wonder how much to reveal. If the parent is not available, the protective services worker can do the same thing. Then it is possible to begin the interview by saying, "I am Dr. K., and part of my job is to try to help children with their feelings when something bad has happened to them.

Your mother just said what happened, but I'd like to know how you remember it." A few children begin immediately to talk freely of their experiences. Most, however, will be reticent and one can go on after a brief pause, "First though, I'd like to get to know you a little bit and have you get to know me, too. Maybe you could draw a picture, while we talk. Won't you please draw a picture of your family, everyone in the family, all doing something together the way you usually do?" Then a few questions about age, school, friends, and activities allow the establishment of some relationship before the therapist can come back to the family and ask a little bit about what the family does (as a natural result of looking at the picture). It may then be possible to ask how the family felt about what happened to the child and go on to ask what actually did happen. The child can be invited to reenact the event using the anatomically correct dolls or puppets or animals sets. If he/she refuses completely to discuss the sexual abuse, it is important to accept the refusal and to indicate that you understand how it might be very hard to talk about something which was scary or made him/her feel bad. A question about whether the child has been asked about it a lot and whether he/she worries about getting anyone into trouble lets the child know his/her anxiety is understandable. It is then possible to say that you hope he/she will be able to talk later about some of his/her feelings with you because children do usually feel better when they can talk to someone who can help. Play can then be resumed allowing the child, as always, to lead in the activity.

It may take considerable time for any child to build up trust in a therapist, and this is particularly so when he/she has already felt betrayed by adults. It is important to make clear to law-enforcing agencies that highly specific information may not be forthcoming from your therapeutic contacts with the child, but that an extended evaluation is usually indicated in any case.

The issue of confidentiality is always very important, both in evaluation and treatment, but it may be a cause of major anxiety in sexual abuse in which a "secret" has often been a major problem. For that reason, it is helpful to the child if you can tell him your position—that you must report to court (if this is true) certain kinds of information, and also what kinds of information can be kept completely confidential. For example, if all of the specific information about the abusive incident has been given to other earlier interviewers in the hospital, you need only corroborate this. The feelings the child has about the sexual abuse, about how other people have responded to him, and about his own behavior and present difficulties need only be described in generalities or in terms of his emotional needs. Such material can be cleared with the child before a report is made.

The older child, and particularly the adolescent, may have a much more complicated response to evaluation. He/she may be very much aware of the nuances of interpretation that can be placed upon what he/she says and very sensitive to any potential blame for his/her own behavior or that of the family. Again, an explicit statement of the therapist's intent, of the number of interviews available, and the limits of confidentiality should be made in a straightforward way. With older children, too, it may take a long time for the child to develop trust in the therapist. With older children, we feel that when the child does not readily volunteer information, to share with him/her what you have been openly told helps to clear the air and may somewhat lessen the need for massive denial.

When a child denies the events, attempts to argue about the "truth" are not helpful. Again, it is more important to recognize that the whole episode has been painful for the child and that you are primarily concerned with his/her feelings. For this reason, it is wise not to let a referring agency assume that a psychiatrist will necessarily obtain more information about the abuse than anyone else can.

Some children, especially adolescents, find one-to-one interviewing very painful. They also find it hard to tolerate repeated sessions with an adult long enough to build up trust. Then a decision must be made as to how important individual treatment is. Very often, peer-group therapy or a residential treatment setting for the severely disturbed child may be more appropriate than individual psychotherapy, which could be useful at a later time, or on a flexible basis.

From the evaluation one hopes to learn how the child perceives the sexual abuse—as an attack, as an experience arousing ambivalent feelings, or as an exciting relationship of which others don't approve. Gradually the child will reveal, by word and by action, some of the feelings about the sexual abuse and about herself/himself. Talks with the parents should provide a history of changes in behavior and any specific symptoms, including psychosomatic disorders and unusual behavior with family and peers.

Part of the evaluation should include psychological testing. An intelligence test and achievement tests indicate the child's intelligence and his/her ability to keep up at school. Discrepancies between the two are important, and it is useful to know whether lower than expected achievement in school, if any, was always present (indicating preceding problems), whether it occurred after the onset of sexual abuse, or whether the child's school performance was unaffected by the sexual abuse. Good individual psychological testing gives evidence of how a child copes—of his/her ability to deal with mild stress, to organize and use information, and to overcome impatience or discouragment during the course of a test.

Projective testing is also very helpful. Drawing is an excellent form of projective testing for younger children, as we have already said. Even when the drawing itself is not informative, the child's description of what a drawing means can be very helpful. The Children's Apperception Test or the Thematic Apperception Test (TAT) for adolescents—a series of cards showing pictures of situations known to be evocative of a standard range of emotional responses—can be given. From the stories the child makes up around each picture, one has a glimpse of the child's fantasy life, and this usually gives important clues to conflict areas. The Rorschach, or ink blot Test is similar: the cards presented show vague forms which require additional input from the child's own fantasy production to identify. The Sentence Completion tests have been modified for children by Conger and focus on the child's perception of himself and his relationships as he completes sentences which begin with key phrases.

There are also questionnaires which can be helpful, such as the Connor's Children's Self-Rating Scale. The fact that these tests are presented as standardized questionnaires which are given to thousands of people may give the child a feeling of protection in answering what could be highly charged questions.

Some children in evaluation will be very guarded in play, in talking, and in performing on tests. Yet, even though the picture is primarily that of a defensive, anxious child who fears exposure—of himself/herself, his/her family, (or even the offender), indications of problem areas can usually be noted as important to the child for later in treatment. Many children become more comfortable as evaluation goes on and begin to respond to the interest in their feelings. A few children are totally undefended and lacking in anxiety; if such children are not young preschoolers, this may well indicate either retarded intelligence or a pathological lack of sensitivity to social judgments.

Once the material from the evaluations of the child and of his parents and, if possible, of the offender are gathered, a case conference or child-protection-team conference should be held to determine the treatment needs of both the child and the family. Even in extrafamilial abuse, it is often important to involve the parents in treatment. The family may be reacting with major disorganization to this crisis, which can awaken dormant pathology in either parent, making them unable to cope. They may feel the child is damaged beyond repair, or blame the child for the event because of difficulty in dealing with their own sexual impulses or because blaming the child allows them to avoid any guilt about lack of supervision. It may be very difficult for the parents to cope with the accusation of an offender who is a friend or an authority figure in their social circle, or to tolerate any degree of publicity about sexual matters. If the child is a some-what rebellious adolescent, the parents may focus only on the child's behavior which may have exposed her/him to abuse and not appreciate the shock to the child and his/her need for support. Underlying difficulties in relationship between the adolescent and his/her parents may need to be mitigated in individual and family therapy before long-term improvement in the adolescent's adjustment to sexual abuse can take place.

TREATMENT OF THE PRESCHOOL CHILD

If the family is relatively healthy and responds appropriately and quickly to the discovery of the sexual abuse, the recovery prognosis for the child is hopeful. In these circumstances, exploratory, individual play therapy for the child may be indicated to help the child express his/her feelings about the abuse and to determine whether or not the child has adequate ability to cope with the effects of the abuse and its discovery. Important aspects of therapy are to understand the fantasies of the child concerning what happened and to try to prevent delays or distortions of psychosexual development and the onset of later symptoms. Work with the family should be directed toward helping them understand the child's behavior, how to respond to him/her, and to help the parents with their own anxiety and guilt.

When the family has a chaotic life-style or has been neglectful, evaluation must be made of the parents' capacity to understand and meet the needs of the child. More extensive intervention may be needed, including therapeutic daycare, preschool, or even foster-home placement. More intensive treatment for the parents, aimed at their own difficulties, as well as their need for aid in parenting, may include individual or group psychotherapy, parenting groups, parent-child interaction therapy, treatment for alcohol or drug abuse, and lay therapy.

In keeping with the finding that some of the younger sexually abused children are especially apt to come from more disorganized families, there may be a need for child protective services, court involvement, and perhaps adjudication for dependency and neglect leading to court supervision. In a few cases, termination of parental rights will be the eventual outcome if the parents are unable to respond to treatment sufficiently to care for the child safely. Here the sexual abuse is only a small part of the difficulties the child must face. Early family diagnosis, with a trial of intensive treatment for the parents, is the only way to prevent such a child from remaining in foster care or at risk indefinitely; only by recognizing the likelihood of termination early can adoption become available to the child at an age at which he/she will truly benefit.

When the treatment takes place in a therapeutic preschool, the aim is to provide a safe environment in which the child can build trusting relationships with staff members and peers. The day includes time for free play during which the child can enjoy the pleasure of play, learn social skills with peers, and learn how to communicate feelings and have them respected and understood. At the same time, the environment is also structured to limit overstimulation in play with peers and to encourage the development of cognitive interests and skills in preparation for school and latency age. Individual play therapy is often provided within the school setting so that it may be integrated with the child's ongoing experience from day to day.

In addition to the opportunity to discuss with an adult the feelings he/she has about his/her own sexual experience, each child should have, in individual therapy or in the preschool or therapeutic group, some sex education, with pictures and simple explanations appropriate to the child's age. The opportunity to ask questions at the same time allows the child to correct fantasies about his/her own body or the meaning of his/her experiences which otherwise can distort sexual attitudes, perhaps unconsciously, for the rest of his/her life. Education will not prevent unconscious sexual fantasies, but it does provide an opportunity for their emergence in a setting where they can be corrected or at least recognized.

TREATMENT OF THE SCHOOL-AGE CHILD

For children from 5 to 10 years old, groups may often be preferred as a form of therapy for sexual abuse. A group, meeting once a week, of four to eight children fairly close in age and all having suffered from some form of sexual abuse, may do well with an activity and discussion kind of group in which a male and female therapist help provide models of supportive, trustworthy adults. One of the main benefits of such groups is recognition that other children share their problems and that they are not completely different. Part of the time is spent by such groups in free play or fun activity—to establish appropriate shared pleasure as an important part of their lives. The free play may also provide diagnostic information as to the fantasies and social skills of the individual children. Discussion time may be used to share any problems or feelings the children themselves wish to bring up. It may be used in part by the therapists to discuss events they know to be happening outside the session, such as moving to a new school for one child, and sharing the feelings such an event might arouse. The time is sometimes used to discuss the events of the other parts of the hour, such as repetitive behaviors in free play or at snack time (which for many children brings out themes of oral deprivation, for example). If one child is seductive with the male therapist, he/she would not be singled out, but his/her wish to be close to someone would be recognized and then the question of affection and its appropriate expression discussed later with the group. Thus, one of the goals of such a group would be to have the children learn how adults respond appropriately to their needs, especially for affection and closeness. When the seductive element is no longer present, a hug by either therapist should be comfortable for both adult and child.

Individual psychotherapy with young children sexually abused over a period of time is not often short-term. Most such children have a real distrust of adults, and it takes a long time before the child can forget that the seducer too was friendly, interested, ready to play, and eager to keep secrets. The freedom of the playroom, with the child "in charge" of initiating play, may be anxiety provoking at first. The therapist may initially need to be explicit about the reasons, the goals, and the rules of therapy. The reasons for therapy may be stated as the sexual abuse and the consequent difficulties for the child. It may also be noted that the child has symptoms or behavioral difficulties with which the therapist would like to help.

The treatment goals for the individual child vary depending upon the symptoms. Feelings of vulnerability, specific fears or nonspecific anxiety, confusion, and distrust are apt to be present, and it takes time to relate these feelings to the multiple events that produced them. Anger may be intense; it may be felt for the parents who have, in the child's opinion, let him/her down, or the anger may be undirected. In any case, like the distrust and fear, the feelings may also be directed toward the therapist who must then try gradually to help the child relate them back to the source as the feelings become acceptable and are no longer frightening. Feelings of badness, worthlessness, of not being loved or lovable, or even of not having a clear identity may lead to confused, self-destructive or aggressive behavior which needs to be understood, accepted, and counteracted by expression of concern for the child's welfare by the therapist. The therapist cannot remake the child's environment for him/her, but she/he can help the child to understand his/her own feelings and needs and perhaps find better ways to meet them.

Problems of impulse control are always difficult in therapy. Enforcing limits and insisting on responsibility for behavior become time-consuming with a bright ingenious child. The importance of maintaining a positive working alliance requires patience and perseverance for the therapist. The effort always to try to understand the child's behavior and the therapist's recognition of his/her own predisposition to respond in certain ways can keep the therapist from developing countertransference difficulties in these more trying treatment sessions. Some children who have always seemed to be very passive and compliant may become very negative or controlling during therapy—an effort to transform their own previous feelings of helplessness into mastery. Such behavior can eventually be interpreted and understood by the child.

We have already spoken of the child who is overwhelmed at times by erotic impulses. These children do not at first know any reason to hide their pleasure in sexual stimulation and later find it often difficult to suppress the impulse. It is helpful to separate carefully the erotic feelings from the wish for affection and to encourage the ability to seek out affection from the right persons in an appropriate way. Recognition with the child that public masturbation or other sexual activities are socially prohibited can lead to an alliance between the therapist and child to find ways to cope with sexual impulses without guilt. This is not an easy therapeutic problem, for the child may choose to resort to massive denial and inhibition of all such feelings on into adulthood. Unless the child can be helped to recognize the benefits of sexual impulses when expression is deferred to a later time and learn how to develop and be comfortable with age-appropriate sublimation activity, the all-or-none choices of promiscuity or total avoidance of sex may become his/her fate as an adult.

For most children, erotic body sensations are present and certainly pleasurable, but the prohibition on their open expression by the family, with ample opportunity for other enjoyable play interaction and ample evidence of attention and love from the family, usually makes sexual play less enticing in contrast to activity with others. This difference can be discussed with the child in therapy, allowing him/her free verbal expression and eventual understanding of sexual fantasies and their place in his/her development.

Whatever the specific reaction to the sexual abuse, some of the child's feelings concern his parents and his relationships with them. His/her guilt at keeping a "bad" secret from them, shame at their disapproval of the activity even though they may understand the reasons for his/her participation, and what may become a mutual diminution of trust between parents and child (even though each would deny this) all need to be considered by the therapist.

TREATMENT OF THE ADOLESCENT

Although the adolescent victim of sexual abuse is developmentally more mature and therefore presumably better able to cope with sexual abuse, the adolescent is also in the process of forming his/her sexual identity and is therefore very vulnerable in this aspect of development. The natural wish to be sexually attractive may seem in retrospect abnormal and indicative of guilt, the answer to "Why did he pick on me?" Intense guilt and shame may follow sexual abuse, especially repeated abuse, and social withdrawal, depression, and sometimes suicidal thoughts may be the result. Fears of being permanently damaged physically or of being sexually "abnormal" or morally inferior can all be part of the aftermath for the teenager.

The question of responsibility is much more difficult for the adolescent to cope with, for often it is his/her own defiance of rules, wish for freedom, or impulses toward mild sexual provocation that placed him/her in a situation at risk and made the abuse possible. Protest and efforts at self-protection come too late.

The great concern adolescents have with peer group approval may make it particularly hard to face public knowledge of their experience—or to share it with anyone, even a most trusted friend. Therefore it is important to protect their privacy in every way possible, not an easy task when there may also be pressure to prosecute an offender or a need for family cooperation.

As with school children, teenagers may often need either group or individual therapy, often both. Individual therapy allows privacy during the initial period of shock, and may be needed for more intensive care and closer monitoring of conditions such as severe depression or for the added support of a one-to-one relationship. Group therapy allows the teenager to have the support of peers in feeling less different and alone, encourages the confrontation of some intense feelings by group members who have also experienced them and provides reassurance about the ability to rejoin the mainstream of teenage life. Simultaneous use of group, individual, and perhaps family therapy may be most effective in occasional situations.

TREATMENT OF THE OFFENDER

Treatment of older adolescents or adults who have sexually abused children has not in the past aroused much interest or optimism among psychiatrists. Comparatively little knowledge has been collected systematically. Most of what is known comes from studies conducted in prisons with convicted offenders or from isolated reports of private psychiatric work, primarily psychoanalytic. Most discussion of sexual offenders has tended to be descriptive of their behavior, without many generalizations as to the etiology of their specific sexual behavior. This may well be appropriate, because individuals vary greatly in how and why they develop their sexual preferences. It may be fair to say, however, that most sex offenders have retreated from, deviated from, or not attained the usual "normal" sexual preference for an adult's reciprocal sexual love relationship (primarily genital intercourse) with a consenting adult of the opposite sex. It is important to note that a preference for other forms of sexual fulfillment may occur along with, or as a sometime alternative to, "normal" heterosexual activity. There is considerable evidence that for some offenders, deviant sexual behavior occurs at a time of failure to attain or to maintain a "normal" sexual relationship. We put "normal" in quotation marks in this context because many professionals and laymen believe that other kinds of sexual activity, particularly homosexual activity, are also perfectly normal and only a matter of taste. We shall make no attempt to discuss this issue, except to indicate our assumption that sexual relations between adult and child are not normal in most of our cultures and under our present legal systems.

Another assumption we make, for which there is some evidence, is that most pathological sexual practices have their roots in the experiences of childhood. What these experiences are and how much they might dovetail with the child's own sexual fantasies to produce difficulty is apt to depend on the individual history. The effect is presumably to cause anxiety, aversion, or anger related to adult heterosexual intercourse and the consequent choice of a different (or partial) mode of satisfaction or a different sexual object either as a substitute or a preference. It would, of course, be helpful to know how often the sexually abused child becomes the sexually deviant adult, but beyond a recognition that it does occur, we have no real information on this issue.

Evaluation of the sexually abusive offender should include a psychiatric evaluation, psychological testing, and a physical and neurological examination. Particular areas of concern are the offender's childhood history, including family stability, abuse, neglect, and sexual experiences. The history of previous sexual offenses and antisocial or violent behavior is also particularly important because of frequency of multiple offenses and of escalation into violence over time in some offenders. The mental-status examination and psychiatric history plus psychological testing lead to the psychiatric diagnosis. Such factors as ego strength, ability to relate and to communicate, guilt, depression, motivation to change, all have bearing on treatability and prognosis. Medical and neurological examinations help to reveal or corroborate the presence of any physical or neurological component to the offender's behavior. Alcoholism, drug addiction, epilepsy, mental retardation, the organic brain dysfunction of aging, and serious depression must all be given priority in treatment planning.

In general, specific treatment of most extrafamilial sex offenders has not been very effective, particularly with repeat offenders. The most frequently recommended therapy has been intensive individual psychotherapy or psychoanalysis for those patients who have the capacity to participate adequately. Supportive group psychotherapy may be of benefit for motivated men, particularly for some kinds of rapists.

In recent years, sexual treatment centers have tried combining individual psychotherapy with behavior modification with some reported success. Some pedophiles may respond to aversive and conditioning therapy as a means of decreasing their attraction to preadolescent girls, for example, and increasing their attraction to adult women. This mode of relatively brief treatment is combined with individual insight therapy. How effective such therapy is, over time, is not yet known, and some recidivism has already been described.

Some groups have advocated castration or drug therapy which lowers male sexual hormone levels for men who are compulsive repeaters of sexual offenses. For those who do not show criminal and violent behavior as well, drug therapy may offer relief from sexual cravings and at least some control over their behavior. Its efficacy needs to be tested.

For some sex offenders, particularly those with a history of severe psychiatric illness or tendencies toward violence, psychiatric hospitalization or prison for protection of the public may be the *only* answer at present. Some of these men demonstrate a tendency toward escalation of their violent behavior. The rapist who repeats his offense more than once while out on bail awaiting trial is a common example.

There is clearly a need for research into the backgrounds and histories of sex offenders, as well as into any promising modes of treatment, for they are sometimes as unhappy as their victims. This is especially true for some nonviolent youthful offenders who receive no treatment addressed specifically to their sexual behavior or relationship problems, or who may be treated as adult offenders without more strenuous efforts at rehabilitation appropriate to their years.

It is premature to speak of "cures" for many of the sexual offenses we are describing because they have yet not been sufficiently studied to be well understood, nor have treatment methods often seemed really effective in bringing about permanent change. The rates of recidivism are high, especially in exhibitionism and homosexual pedophilia.

Pedophilia may not be cured, but it is often possible to bring all illegal acts under control, as we saw in the case of Mr. T. There is no sure "cure" for the aggressive sociopath who engages in violent sexual molestation and rape. Until we know how to treat these people, we must be certain that they cannot menace defenseless children. In many cases, imprisonment is the only alternative after conviction, or psychiatric commitment if the molester is judged legally insane and unable to stand trial.

CHAPTER SEVEN

EVALUATION AND TREATMENT OF INTRAFAMILIAL ABUSE— INCEST

While incest has been facetiously called "a family affair," it is perfectly true that it is essential to focus attention on the family as a whole in both evaluation and treatment phases. Incest is a very clear signal of dysfunction within the family structure— family roles are confused and relationships are distorted.

In clarifying how these distortions have come about, however, one immediately becomes aware of the pain and frustration of every individual family member, and the need for understanding and help for each person seems clear. We feel it makes sense not to limit the approach to a family being referred for incest to any rigid pattern of treatment plans, but first to learn as much as possible about how family members function separately and together. When one knows more of their individual histories and current ability to cope outside the family, one can better understand how they have come to be in their present predicament and how well they can make use of treatment. All incestuous fathers do not have the same psychiatric diagnosis or response to society's intervention. This variability is also true of their wives and children. We try to present some of the problems that are usually found and the most frequent situations that we see, but no two families are ever identical. Father-daughter incest is most often discussed because it is more frequently reported and therefore has been better studied thus far. Many of our statements also apply to parent-son incest or older sibling-much younger sibling incest. There are also obvious important differences, some of which are discussed in Chapter 3, and some about which we do not yet know enough to discuss them adequately. In general, homosexual incest is a more difficult treatment problem. (See Appendix II for evaluative interview examples.)

THE FAMILY AS A GROUP AND THE QUESTION OF SEPARATION

Once the fact of incest has been acknowledged, the medical, legal, and social work personnel involved in evaluation must be concerned about the safety of the children while an adequate treatment plan is initiated. In father-child incest, a temporary separation of the father and the victim is usually necessary to prevent further recurrences unless the father is detained in prison. Mere exposure of the problem and the offer of treatment is not apt to change the father's behavior until after major changes have taken place in the family's life, and especially in the father's self-image.

The temporary separation of the family causes distress, and each of the family members is in great need of immediate "first aid." It is part of good evaluation to discuss some of the possible future plans—not just those leading to separation, but the eventual goals of family reunion in more comfortable relationships. It is impossible to be precise about the outcome early, but it is possible to convey the attitude that treatment is not only for the protection of the individual family members but also for protection of the family group whenever possible.

An important part of the initial evaluation of the incest offender is the question of treatability. If at all possible, this is the time to identify, usually by psychiatric or psychological evaluation, the psychopathic individual who, by history and present behavior, shows no motivation or potential for change and who may have had a lifelong pattern of asocial behavior. For these offenders, for some repeat offenders, and for those with psychosis or very serious drug or alcohol addiction, criminal prosecution or psychiatric hospitalization may separate them from the family immediately.

For offenders who will either return home or live apart from the family, we feel that an admission of guilt, preferably with the signing of a contract for deferment of prosecution, is the best insurance against sudden resumption of incest and break-off of treatment. When both parents continue to deny incest in the face of good evidence, the children at risk should usually be taken into protective custody and placed elsewhere.

Once a decision about criminal prosecution is made, the next decision should deal with how separation of father and daughter or son is to take place. In some instances, as soon as incest is discovered the mother insists upon separation and divorce, and treatment must then be provided for each person separately. It should still be provided, at least for the mother and the child victim who will have many disturbing sequelae to cope with. The message given by the mother to her daughter, for example, may be that the father was clearly the guilty party and the daughter a victim, but this is not always the case. A mother may see herself as the injured party and consider the daughter as a rival and betrayer, even after the father is banished. In our view, treatment should be offered to all members of the family, and separation, rather than immediate divorce, suggested before their future life course is settled in order to have both parents fully cognizant of their true feelings once the shock of confrontation is over. If there are several young girls in the family, even if only one has thus far been involved in the incest, we believe it is almost always imperative that the father be temporarily separated from the family. Frequently, a younger daughter simply replaces the older one if the father remains at home. It is not uncommon for all of the daughters to be involved with their father in some kind of sexual activity, perhaps still limited to caressing of younger daughters but gradually progressing to intercourse for the older ones.

Indeed, when any case of incest comes to light, it is necessary to recognize that siblings of both sexes may also have been involved without complaint. Increasingly family histories reveal involvement of multiple family members and sometimes of several generations, both as offenders and victims. Family history, therefore, should be the subject of some questioning at a tactful time.

If the daughter involved in incest is the only likely victim, then the mother and father may decide, even against professional recommendation, to remain together and have the daughter placed in a foster home. Whenever possible, the best arrangement early in treatment would be for the father to live separately but to be in contact with his family in regular specified family activities where the wife is present and there is no opportunity for incestuous advances. This helps to retain the healthier aspects of family relationships, allows the other children to enjoy both parents, and helps to reintroduce the kind of activities which the family hopes to enjoy again at a later time. It may be that at first a victimized daughter is not ready for these joint activities and can join them only when she has made some progress in treatment.

Many mothers, however, find separation from their husbands more difficult to accept than that from their daughters, and they insist that the husband's presence is necessary for the other children; often the mother insists that her husband is innocent. The mother's own dependency needs are paramount, and she feels unable to function without her husband's support. This may be true, even when many of her parenting functions have, in effect, been abdicated and taken over by her victimized daughter, and when the marital relationship itself has little strength as a sexual and parental partnership.

In the early stages, treatment for the mother should focus on helping her to recognize her own feelings more clearly. It has been said, and perhaps rightly, that the mother often feels criticized and pressured by both professionals and friends to divorce her husband in order to appear to be a good mother. She needs to know that such a decision should come only after she has had time to know what her real wishes are and what potential the marriage has for her. She also needs to recognize her feelings toward her child, especially the probable anger and guilt. It will take support and the development of a therapeutic relationship before she can face and acknowledge the guilt she may feel about having been a passive partner—in the marriage and in the incest situation. To develop real empathy for her child may require her recognition of the difficulties in her own background which have prevented her from being able to be protective of her children. Such a therapeutic process takes time. It is to be hoped that the mother will also derive from treatment the recognition that she, too, has rights as an individual which are as important as those of her husband and her child, but that they must not be exercised at the expense of the child.

Treatment which addresses these problems may be individual, with a group of other mothers or married couples, or with her own family. However it is accomplished, the goal of the family becoming a source of love and mutual respect must be attained.

For the father in incest, there is also a period of intense emotional turmoil immediately after discovery. He, too, must finally confront not only his own behavior, but the quality of his marriage and the extent to which his emotional needs are not being met. Like his wife, he may feel intense fear of outside criticism, of social ostracism, and also of losing his job if the situation becomes public knowledge. Worst of all, he may fear losing his entire family, a disaster for those men who have been so closely involved with their families that they have not developed outside friendships. His own feelings of loss, guilt, inadequacy, and anger may all be intense and require the immediate support of a therapist at this time of real crisis. If he can accept this help, admit the responsibility, and accept court-supervised treatment (which can maintain confidentiality to protect his public position), there is real hope for a good outcome. If he denies the incest but offers to accept treatment "for the good of the family," success in treatment is doubtful.

Here one would differentiate between the father who has already signed a diversion program contract for treatment and the father who wishes to control the situation by accepting voluntary treatment; the latter situation is subject to collapse as soon as involvement becomes irksome, and the family is likely to leave the area. With the diversion contract, however, the court requirement provides external support for continuation of treatment, particularly when after a few months it seems discouraging and painful. This external pressure allows the father's therapist to assure the father of the acceptance and support which he needs in order to be able to face the painful facts of his emotional deprivation and the reasons for his committing incest. Once the father can then tolerate his guilt and begin to forgive himself, he is free to remake his relationships within the family. A very similar process takes place for his wife in her treatment.

In addition to the problems of being separated, the parents may resist strongly the financial obligations involved in the need to maintain two households. They often feel that society has unjustifiably interfered in their private lives and is now making unwarranted demands upon them for sacrifice. This is perhaps a good example of the kind of subtle resistance to change seen in families who do not at first acknowledge any real problem. If the child, however, is placed outside the home against the parents' will, child welfare frequently becomes responsible for the cost. A group home for fathers also helps to make possible an affordable separation. In a number of communities, group living arrangements for fathers are now in operation which lowers costs to the family and allows the father to retain gainful employment, provide for the family, and, at the same time, be able to receive initial group therapy along with other admitted offenders.

The child who is separated from her/his family because of incest, rarely sees the change as being exclusively for her/his protection. The victim is much more apt to feel singled out for exile, that she/he is somehow really the one at fault. If she/he had been a better child, somehow the family would not have been subjected to all this trouble and everyone would still be at home.

The child who is very young, with a poorly developed sense of time, may see the separation as permanent. He/she may suffer acutely from feelings of loss of affection and closeness, and from a very real sense of being rejected. The prospect of a return home in a few months may seem unreal, and visits with the family do little to counteract the difficulty of adjustment during the long periods away. The older child, aged 9 to 12, may feel a much more developed sense of guilt tied to the perception that she/he failed in the role assigned within the family. If she/he had accepted the relationship with the father more willingly and been more ready to take on the household responsibilities, the family might have been spared its difficulties.

For the adolescent aged 12 to 18, the separation from the family may be perceived with very different individual responses. For some girls, for example, there is only blessed relief from the hated burden of deception, and their feelings of resentment and of being exploited far outweigh, temporarily, the affection lost. This kind of girl may "blossom" in a friendly foster family. Gradually her wish for her "real" family and a tendency to deny the problems may lead to early efforts to return home. For some other girls, anxiety over the care of younger siblings and abandonment of their responsibilities to parents whom they see as disinterested or incompetent to maintain the household may be paramount. These girls have taken seriously their ability to replace their mothers successfully and have derived much pleasure from taking charge. Some other girls primarily feel a sense of release now that they are free to become semi-independent teenagers with friends and sexual partners of their own age. Some of these may be among the more seriously disturbed teenagers who have never developed the capacity for mutually dependent close relationships and are on their way to becoming promiscuous or exploitative in their turn. Instead of dwelling on the possibilities of reunion with the family, they are much more interested in escaping to "independence."

Sometimes it is immediately clear that no complete family really exists but that the mother with her children lives successively in a series of loosely structured liaisons. At best, the children live in a one-parent family with their mother, plus temporary "stepfathers" whose interest in the children may be casual at best, pathological at worst. In these situations, the primary question in evaluation must be the ability of the mother to parent and a decision as to whether or not the long-term safety of the children requires termination of parental rights. Sometimes a mother who has no husband and lives with a succession of boyfriends who are poor father substitutes may be meeting her own needs for intimacy and financial support at the expense of her children.

If on evaluation there is evidence that she has been chronically and seriously neglectful of the children and has, on occasion, made no effort to protect them from abuse by others, she should be offered a good opportunity for treatment for an adequate but finite time to see if she can become more effective as a parent. Termination of parental rights requires a trial of treatment and "clear and convincing evidence" that the parent is unable to improve in her care of the children before termination can take place and the children can be freed for adoption. The same diagnostic questions, treatment efforts, and court procedures apply when both biological parents are seriously abusive or neglectful of their children and are unwilling or unable to utilize treatment to change.

Or it may be that the "stepfather" who molests the children is not to be a permanent member of the family, and the mother makes this immediately clear by expelling him and focusing on the defense of her children.

In most families, the parents may be very much alienated from or angry with each other, but the thought of divorce is never seriously considered. Therefore, given some hope that the family may eventually be whole, they are motivated to work toward that goal.

EVALUATION OF INDIVIDUAL FAMILY MEMBERS AND CONSULTATION

In addition to seeing the family members together when possible in order to learn how they interact with one another, the individual family members should have as complete an evaluation as can be managed. (The historical information needed and helpful background questionnaires and tests are detailed in Appendix II.) Both parents should have a psychiatric evaluation and a medical examination. The offender should also have neurological examination. Often very useful information is obtained from psychological testing of both parents. Evaluations of this depth are not at all inappropriate when one is to embark on a course of treatment involving several people for long periods of time and at considerable expense. (Evaluation of the child is discussed separately on page 159.)

Having learned a good deal about the family members' strengths and weaknesses and the methods they have evolved to function as a family, it is time for the several professionals contributing information to meet together and try to evolve a treatment plan which fits the family's needs. Such a meeting can appropriately be a regular meeting of the child-protection team, or the sexual-abuse protection team, or whatever body of people has responsibility for implementing the program in the community, including court or legal representatives. With regular communication about progress planned for, the program is most apt to be feasible as well as effective.

THE DIFFERENT TREATMENT MODALITIES AVAILABLE IN INCEST

The kinds of treatment available depend upon community resources, upon limitations set at times by court recommendations or jail sentences, and the financial resources and motivation of the family. Treatment methods are generally divided into group and individual psychotherapy, supportive services, and self-help groups. Several methods may also be used in combination.

The concept of *family therapy* is neither new nor uniquely utilized in treatment of families involved in childhood sexual abuse. Few psychotherapists have failed to have a *family point of view* in their treatment approaches. Pediatricians, of necessity, have dealt with family problems in the family setting since the field began about one hundred years ago. But *famliy therapy* may involve a confusing mixture of approaches, including those of therapists who insist on the presence in the same room of all family members for group treatment for every meeting from the very start. Other, less rigid therapists can allow for a chance of early help in a one-to-one setting with the goal that, later, combinations of family members might meet together from time to time and, if needed, the whole family may be ready for common discussion of the events that lead to sexual abuse and what can be done to stop them. When incest first comes to light, some victims simply cannot tolerate family pressures early on, and those youngsters badly need personal care and support to make certain they know that they are not the guilty parties, that they have not wrecked the family home and finances, and that they have not abandoned their siblings or their parents. Similarly, mothers, siblings, and perpetrators often need a "cooling off" period before they are ready to go forward into group therapy or into organized family therapy.

Family treatment programs are now active in many states and functioning well and at low cost when compared to individual treatment. But those programs are not for all, at least at the start, and a sensitive and skilled professional often can quickly evaluate the suitability of starting with treatment for the family. Dogma must be excluded: families differ profoundly and no quick fix is likely to result in the desired goal of having the victim rehabilitated and the family kept together. Not all families can or should be saved because they may have already, for all practical purposes, shown the impossibility for a safe reunification.

Group psychotherapy, then, can be used for the family as the group unit. One or two appointments with the whole family may be very helpful at the beginning of treatment for evaluating of how family members function together. Family treatment then can be postponed again until the individual members have benefited enough from other modes of treatment to be able to meet successfully as a family. Learning how to listen to one another and how to communicate their real feelings are two of the first and major goals of family group treatment. The therapist's (or cotherapist's) role is to facilitate this process and to monitor the pace and intensity with which it takes place. He or she facilitates communication by encouraging silent members, especially children, to talk at times, by paying attention to nonverbal behavior and emotional states as well as words, and by questioning ambiguous or inappropriate statements, thus helping the family to learn to listen more empathically. He/she monitors the pace of communication by encouraging some members to communicate in the "safety" of the group and by letting some problems remain untouched until the family seems more ready to cope with them. Family therapy can be used regularly or periodically to help family members understand the changes taking place and eventually to make decisions together about their future.

Group psychotherapy can also be a very useful context in which individual family members can share with peer groups the special problems they face. This is particularly useful because incest often seems to those involved a problem which must put them beyond the bounds of human society. It is not only extremely reassuring to discover that others share the same difficulties, it can be enormously encouraging to recognize that others are often working successfully to ameliorate their problems. Therefore groups are organized for fathers, for mothers, for child victims, for siblings, and for married couples—all sharing with their counterparts from other families in the treatment effort to understand, conquer, and recover from incest.

Many of these groups are *self-help groups*, i.e., they are initiated in a community, usually with professional help and often with a national affiliation (see page 176, Parents United). Because they are self-initiated and managed, they encourage self-respect in participants and are much more acceptable to frightened newcomers. The members also provide one another with many practical kinds of help that make treatment and change possible—transportation, cooperative babysitting, and so on. When such groups are not available, a family may need a great deal of practical help, and a lay therapist provided by the community may make the difference between success and failure of more formal treatment. Providing support and encouragement, companionship, transportation, and know-how about community resources, she/he may help the family to keep their lives going during the treatment process.

There are pros and cons to group versus individual psychotherapy. When incest is concerned the group offers a major benefit that no individual therapist can offer so convincingly—the clear demonstration that other fathers, other mothers, other daughters, and other sons have had the same experiences and many of the same feelings. Group members can see that the others are ordinary people and not monsters; most important they quickly receive the message that help is being offered and that change is possible. The support of sharing, at a time where one feels so isolated from the rest of society, can make the difference between despair and a determination to go on. Having others discuss their own experience makes the incest, and the long-standing family difficulties which have accompanied it, take on a new kind of reality which is more manageable and understandable. Being in a group where all have shared the same conflicts makes it easier to accept confrontation and to allow oneself to acknowledge unpalatable truths.

Not everyone can benefit from group therapy, however. Some individuals are unable to function in a group, either because of the severity of their psychiatric illness or because of their inability to accept the limitations of group therapy. It may take a period of time with intensive individual support and the working out with their own therapist of the immediate life decisions before a parent or child is ready to take on a long-term treatment program. Many seriously disturbed patients cannot fit in to the usual psychotherapy group; their behavior preempts the group time or makes group members too anxious to work on their own problems.

Very often the *combination* of individual and group therapy is an ideal one. In individual treatment the psychotherapist can prescribe medication in those few instances where it will be needed. He/she can help the person understand those past experiences and conflicts which are repressed or are too specific to the patient's own life to be discussed at length in the group meetings but which must be dealt with if he/she is to make progress. For example, a member of the fathers' group may not understand the origin of his phobic response to the sexual attributes of an adult female. Once he has been able to take the time in individual therapy to understand this symptom, he can bring his knowledge back to the group and share with them one of the reasons of his marital difficulties and subsequent incest. This kind of individual work can be done simultaneously with the sharing of current life-problems in the group, each therapy enhancing the other.

The flexibility of this kind of combination therapy is desirable for all family members, and it may also be used when the family meets as a group. The family, after the initial evaluation sessions, may have been separated for their treatment efforts. The parents may then meet together in order to reestablish a working-couple-and-parent relationship. When they have their new image as a couple more securely reestablished and working better, they may be ready to include their children and complete the integration of the whole family. Giaretto recommends that mother and daughter need to meet together fairly early in therapy in order to cope with the anger and feelings of betrayal they may have toward each other; without the ability for mother and daughter to confront one another and for the mother to acknowledge the failure of responsibility she shares with her husband, it will be difficult to reunite the family. In incest, a daughter often has more difficulty forgiving her mother's lack of nurturing and protection than she does the father's exploitation. Most daughters are well aware that their mothers knew about the incest and may have refused to believe their complaints or even "set up" the circumstances for it to continue. A daughter's anger at the lack of loving care and protection from the one person who should above all others provide it may be mitigated only partially by her new understanding of the mother's immaturity and her inability to risk the loss of her husband. The daughter feels betrayed and angry, but it takes time to recognize these feelings for, if she expresses them, she fears she may lose her mother entirely.

The mother, for her part, often has little recognition of her own part in this situation, sees her daughter as a successful rival for the husband's love, as a successful competitor for status in the family, and as an unloving, unhelpful, critical child. Such role reversal, with the mother unable to have empathy with her daughter's needs and concerned mainly with her own, occurs most often when the mother herself suffered the same kind of neglect, abuse, and lack of protection as a child. The mother, too, may feel betrayed and angry. She may need to discuss her own childhood in treatment and remember how she felt before she can recognize the role reversal and understand her daughter's feelings enough to approach her.

It takes time for these two to recognize their feelings of hurt and anger and then the protective presence of their therapists to help them express these feelings. If they can do so, and the mother can develop true empathy for her daughter and express her sorrow and regret, then the possibility for forgiveness and reconciliation exists. If the mother and daughter can remake their relationship (no small task), it becomes easier for the family to be reunited and unlikely that incest could recur. A significant number of young adult victims never manage to forgive their mothers, even after prolonged treatment.

It is difficult in most communities to set up programs for a new kind of patient (and few communities have treated any large numbers of families with the problem of incest until very recently). There is apt to be pressure to set up one program into which all families must fit, whatever their capabilities. In the rush to find quick and cheap treatment modalities, programs have been designed which really do little more than offer extended evaluation. Short-term therapy has been praised for the advantages it does offer because of the pressure of a fixed termination date which can lead to the quicker establishment of a therapeutic alliance, the lessening of old defenses with an increased opportunity to explore conflict and search for a new resolution, and the rapid remobilization of coping mechanisms around the new solutions. Some patients can do such work in three or four months, but the limitations are important. Short-term therapy is most useful at a time of crisis, but the goals must be limited to those which can be accomplished in a limited time, the patient must be able to participate quickly and effectively, and the changes in relationships which result must be capable of being maintained. At first this might sound like the ideal mode of treatment for incest families—they are clearly in crisis, the process of evaluation brings out a great deal of material which they might ordinarily not discuss in treatment for a long time, and they are legally forced to realign the relationships within the family. Furthermore, many of these families have functioned well in their work and superficial social contacts. Changes can be accomplished during the initial phase, but the changes are superficial, and compliance with the rules imposed by society is far from meaning that the intrapersonal changes required to maintain a different family structure have been made.

If incest were not so damaging to the child victim and recidivism such a real possibility, it might be more reasonable to accept the three-month treatment limitation provided by many mental health clinics as adequate treatment. In our experience, little real change occurs in less than one to two years. To make a referral to a treatment facility which has a three or four month time limit on treatment means that the family must, in all likelihood, be referred twice after the initial evaluation, leaving everyone, but especially the family, with a feeling of disappointment. Even worse is the use of the short-term treatment mode with the clear implication that this should be enough. If the family is not able to maintain its temporary gains, they will again feel guilt and failure and be less likely to seek further help on their own.

We would prefer to consider the phase of treatment usually subsumed under the title of short-term therapy as an initial realignment phase, one in which the family relationships are being restructured and the pressures that originally set up those maladjustments are accessible for therapeutic work. An open-ended treatment plan, with understanding between family and therapists that treatment may take as long as two years or more for some family members, is more realistic and shows a commitment to help the family which can be reassuring.

The particular combinations of individual and group treatment should be determined as much as possible by the differing needs of the family over time, and as little as possible by the exigencies of personnel availability and the rule of theoretical dogma.

EVALUATION OF THE CHILD

A fairly complete discussion of the evaluation of children who have been sexually abused by extrafamilial offenders was undertaken in Chapter 7 (and see Appendix II). Many of the effects of sexual abuse are the same, no matter who the offender is, and we will not repeat them here. But the fact that a family member, usually the father, is the offender in incest means that all of the child's family relationships, as well as those of other family members with each other, are threatened. No other sexual abuse has so profound an effect on the child's development or on integration of the whole of the child's psychosexual development (physical impulses, oedipal fantasies toward the parents, identification with the parents as a basis for future personal identity, the concept of self-worth and eventual independence, social values, and ideas of right and wrong).

After we look at the individual child and his/her internal resources, it is important to know how that child fits into his/her own incestuous family structure. Any treatment planning for the child must take into account the role the child has filled in the family in the past, the nature of the parent-child bonds, and the wish and capacity of each to accept and use treatment. If the father is sociopathic but will not be prosecuted or will not be accepted for a deferred prosecution treatment program, the child cannot remain with the family during treatment unless the mother elects to exclude the father permanently. If the mother also is seriously neglectful and unable to parent, there may be no family to reconstruct in a healthier manner.

Treatment goals for the child victim of incest imply, of necessity, fairly long-term and intensive treatment, often combining use of some kind of therapeutic daycare or preschool for younger children, or even a residential facility for older children, plus integrated individual therapy. These goals can also be accomplished at times with foster care if the foster patents are capable, sensitive, and willing to participate actively and if the parents themselves receive intensive help and are motivated.

The Preschool Child: Evaluation and Treatment

The problems most often seen in the preschool child exposed to incest relate to the fear of loss of love, often to lack of basic trust, and to their very poor self-image, sometimes with a very weak sense of personal identity. They may have difficulty in recognizing and communicating their emotions. They usually have many unmet needs for affection and nurturance and must be helped to find nonsexual ways of meeting them. In the process they need to learn successful social behavior. They may show cognitive delays which will put them at a disadvantage in school. To meet such far-reaching goals takes a great deal of work, and a therapeutic preschool, plus individual therapy, is certainly not too elaborate a program for this effort, combined with the treatment for the family.

When very young children—those under 5—are exposed to sexual abuse it is more apt to be fondling than the usual form of regular on-going incest, although preliminary episodes of intimate touching and masturbatory activity, and sometimes intercourse (oral and vaginal), may have occurred by 5 or 6. For other children, boys as well as girls, rape can occur at very young ages, and the violation of the body is apt to be the significant part of the experience, not any impression of sexual activity. The younger the child, the greater the discrepancy between the appropriate protective behavior of an adult and the intrusive effect of sexual molestation. In our experience, the younger the child, in general, the more disorganized is his/her life in a family which does not give close supervision and protection to its children.

The very young child may have judged any sexual experience according to whether it was painful or pleasant and according to the context in which the sexual activity occurred. Intrusive activity, that is, any attempts at intercourse of any kind or any invasion of the child's body unless preceded by prolonged gradual seduction—probably seem very frightening, perhaps painful, and even overwhelming, and would certainly be experienced as a coercive assault. Exposure, touching, and masturbatory activity might be perceived either as frightening or as exciting and perhaps very pleasant, depending on the subtlety of the approach—for example, the incorporation of the sexual activity into other "games" and play, or its introduction as part of affectionate behavior—and the sophistication of the child for his/her age. The child might seek repeated episodes of masturbatory activity if the experience were perceived as pleasant or part of an affectionate relationship. Such activity might go on sporadically for a long time within a family before progression to attempts at intercourse occurred. The less sophisticated the child, however, the more apt she/he would be to generalize his/her own responses in such a relationship, and it would be significant if a mother did not take note of explicitly seductive behavior in a 5-year-old daughter, for example. It is important to remember that when the offender is the father or other close family figure, he is also the adult to whom the child looks for guidance in what is right and wrong and who is also apt to be the one who applies discipline. It is therefore understandable that any feeling of guilt the child has about the sexual activity derives largely from oedipal fantasy, from its being kept a secret from the mother, and from whatever knowledge of sexual mores the child already has.

When a therapeutic preschool is not available, special training in the needs and treatment of physically and sexually abused and neglected children for some staff members can make it possible for regular preschools to take in a few of these children, especially if consultation is available on a regular basis and also for crises.

Many children are not able to cope with the multiple relationships and events of the preschool even after a long period of adjustment; others have developed very disruptive behavior or symptoms which do not change in this therapeutic milieu. These children need individual treatment, with a long-term, one-to-one relationship for more intensive work or a placement. Ideally individual treatment can be given on the premises of the school. Individual play therapy can, and is, done on many levels, including the use of school personnel or therapists for brief play periods as an adjunct to the school program at times of crisis or special problems. For the child who has suffered severe sexual abuse, we recommend very skilled personnel.

One particular time for individual therapy is especially important—that is, in serious crisis. For the child who is separated from a parent or from foster parents or who has lost a sibling through placement or abuse, there is a special need for a trusted staff member to be readily and often available to help the child. Sometimes the professional therapist in such circumstances functions primarily as a frequent consultant for the trusted person to whom the child can most easily confide his/her feelings.

The treatment goals of the preschool or the therapeutic day-care center are to provide the child with a consistent, safe, nurturing environment which is sensitive to the responses and needs of the child. Teachers react on a nonverbal level when necessary, and increasingly encourage verbal communication as a tool for understanding and for socialization. Validation of the child's feelings, acceptance of his/her individuality, and help in modifying behavior and negotiating relationships lead to increased self-esteem and social competence. The encouragement of motor and cognitive skills and problem-solving leads to self-confidence; the sharing of play by staff and children leads to pleasure and increased freedom.

Treatment for sexually abused young children must be even more individualized than for adults. The reality compared to the child's perception of what has happened, the willingness he/she has to talk about it or perhaps the total denial of the experience, the significance of the adult offender in the child's life and, equally important, in the life of his/her mother, and the protection and nurturance available in his/her family, all determine treatment goals. The loss of any family life at all can be the prospect in the eyes of some neglected and deprived children to whom sexual abuse is only one more in a series of traumatic events.

For other little children, the disruption of a comparatively "stable" if not healthy family life is very much more upsetting than sexual episodes which were poorly understood and perhaps not perceived as bad. For all children, nurturance and protection are most important, and often these are absent or poorly provided for children who become sexually abused. Treatment needs to focus on those needs first. For the little girl or boy who has learned to be seductive as the way to get attention and affection, the first goal of treatment must be to help him/her to obtain nurturance and attention in more appropriate ways and then, later, to understand and give up the troubling seductive behavior as not socially desirable. For these little girls and boys, the understanding response and appropriate affection that parents and adults show him/her is necessary to bring about their giving up seductive behavior.

The preschool child spends much time in the care of parents or foster parents, and work with them should be coordinated with what is learned about the child in daycare or school. Parents frequently resist parent classes or teaching of parenting techniques unless they are geared to the parents' own concerns, generally in the context of an ongoing group with social benefits or through Parents United (Giaretto). Therapists dealing with parent groups individually need both knowledge of normal child development and psychoanalytic theory and may use some additional theoretical framework, such as transactional analysis and behavior modification. However, all ideas about child care, to be helpful, must be transposed into the individual situation of the parents for their use, and they must always be presented with careful regard to the parents' self-esteem, which can often be very low.

The School-Age Child: Evaluation and Treatment

Diagnostically, the school-age child may still be attempting to cope with the same constellation of difficulties as the younger child, but now those difficulties are modified by wider environmental experience and may become integrated in a somewhat more stable personality structure. If incest has not occurred until the child has reached school age, there is more possibility that the child had a more favorable early developmental course, with the possibility of his/her at least entering the oedipal period. The transformation, however, of oedipal fantasy into reality makes normal progress of psychosexual development at this time virtually impossible, and the usual progress toward latency is apt to be disrupted. The sexually maltreated school child seldom shows specific symptoms which immediately label her/him as abused, and we must look at individual psychiatric and psychological evaluation in addition to the family history in order to plan his/her personal treatment program. Eroticized behavior, a symptom of probable sexual abuse, is the exception. In the school-age child, subtle clinical manifestations may include sudden onset of anxiety, fear, depression, insomnia, conversion hysteria, sudden, massive weight loss or weight gain, sudden school failure, behavior problems, truancy, or running away.

For many sexually abused children who have good intelligence and adequate impulse control, school comes as a pleasant relief. For them it can be a predictable, safe environment in which their abilities and strengths are realistically appreciated and rewarded. For others whose behavior is less acceptable or who are too preoccupied with the problems at home to be able to participate in learning, school seems to confirm their feelings of inadequacy and alienation, and the need for treatment becomes more pressing.

Treatment for the school-age child is often apt to approach the usual models of clinic psychotherapy, although recognition of the child's history would modify the approach to current symptoms. In this age group, family therapy may often be very helpful when combined with group therapy such as that given in Daughters and Sons United (Giaretto). It is our impression that the use of play or activity peer groups for sexually abused children, perhaps in the school or clinic setting, is especially helpful. If parents successfully avoid all involvement and sexual abuse and incest are never admitted or faced by the parents, those children particularly need the extra support of the group while they are in foster care in addition to individual therapy.

During the latency and adolescent years groups often are more successful if they contain children of compatible ages (usually a span of about two years). The commonality of problems for sexually abused children and some balance of members with respect to impulse control and ability to verbalize, enhance group development. Most groups need a quiet social period for reconstitution of the group each time, some kind of focused but shared activity which may be educational or primarily fun, some time to share problems in discussion, and some time for nurturing with shared refreshments. The changes of pace in activities and the proportion of each will vary with the age and goals of the group.

Relationship opportunities during school years are sometimes helpful to sexually maltreated children. School-sponsored activities, such as clubs or sports events, for children who are isolated and have poor self-esteem can help, provided someone of the school staff is aware of this need and can promote the child's successful involvement. Volunteer groups have some potential disadvantages which must be considered before making a referral. If the volunteer is too naive about the child's history and about incest, unreliable in attendance, or unlikely to remain available, the relationship may lead to perceived rejection. Rarely, volunteers could also be potential sexual abusers, especially with a provocative or vulnerable child, and we recommend choice of individual volunteers, rather than "a program" as such. Increasingly schools have been taking a role in providing family evaluations, counseling, individual psychotherapy, or group therapy for children; they may also be able to provide some services in a sexual abuse community program, both in diagnosis and treatment.

Individual play therapy and psychotherapy are apt to be used readily with preadolescent children, if the child and the family can accept a referral, because clinic or private facilities are often available. Traditionally parents are involved in this mode of treatment in order to understand and help their child. With some of these families, treatment may need to be intensive and outreach methods used.

With all children in incest, the treatment efforts involving the child must be coordinated with the rest of the community programs for the family through court supervision. If the individual and family treatment is to be done privately or in a clinic, those therapists must be willing to participate with the court-ordered treatment program in terms of goals, evaluation of progress, and monitoring of treatment participation.

THE ADOLESCENT IN INCEST

Victimized adolescents may come to attention through their own request for help, but very often they attract attention because their behavior is a serious worry. Teenagers who fail school, are truant, run away from home, become delinquent, are depressed or suicidal, become pregnant, or are seriously involved with alcohol or drugs may have a history of sexual and/or other abuse which began in early childhood and still continues. Other teenagers remain quietly, but unhappily, at home, maintaining a silence about incest. Many of these children find it hard to talk about the behavior of their parents, and, even when they are asked, they may not complain, and the interviewer needs to keep this possibility in mind. Often a girl will tell a girlfriend and she, in turn, tells her own mother who then notifies the police, teacher, or child protective services.

Treatment for the adolescent often must address serious psychiatric or behavior problems. The treatment modalities used for other emotionally disturbed teenagers are appropriate, with the recognition that removal of the offender (or, much less desirable, the child) from home is usually the first step. The adolescent may wish to cling to the presence of nonfunctional parents, but may need relief from continued abuse in order to recognize his/her potential for better adjustment. Treatment may include combinations of tutoring and special academic placement, family therapy, group therapy, residential school, foster home, or group home placement, long-term psychiatric therapy, or psychiatric hospitalization. Outreach methods are often necessary.

Many adolescents are statutory offenders, brought to court for noncriminal behavioral offenses such as truancy. This does give an immediate opportunity for court involvement and evaluation of the family as a whole. Whenever such a referral takes place, sexual and or physical abuse or neglect should be factors to be ruled in or out in taking the history.

Although adolescents generally receive treatment appropriate to any teenager, we believe that one aspect merits special attention. We know that adolescence has its own developmental tasks: achieving sexual maturity and appropriate peer relationships, giving up dependence on family, and achieving independent and individual identity. If we remember the developmental tasks of early childhood, it is easy to see that failures in those early developmental steps, especially in receiving nurturance and developing some identity, may now make it difficult to complete the tasks of adolescence. It would therefore seem helpful to know what the adolescent's early experience of being parented was so that we can better understand his/her behavior now. In addition to the emphasis on the sexual history, this recognition of the early history is important because the needs for trust and nurturance may still be a primary issue. Treatment can deal overtly with superficially adult issues of more immediate concern to each victim and her/his siblings, but the unresolved issues of the past should not lead to inappropriate decisions or disrupt treatment because their importance has been overlooked.

While virtually all instances of incest require family treatment along with some individual treatment of all family members, that ideal situation does not often exist. This may be so because there are simply no private or public funds or trained personnel at hand, or because the family simply does not any longer exist. Then treatment must, indeed, be modified to fit the circumstances.

Such a case is exemplified by *Carmen*, age 12, who was referred to our Center over five years ago becaus she had been the victim of sexual abuse regularly by her mother's boyfriend since she was 5 years of age. She had lived either with her grandmother or her mother. Earlier she had been seriously injured when a different boyfriend fractured her femur.

The court involvement around the many incidents of sexual abuse was somewhat short-lived and very traumatic for Carmen. She had been ostracized by her family—mother, aunts, uncles, and so on—all of whom thought she was lying. Her grandmother provided what little nurturing she had, and this was in the form of shelter. However, there was little real affection and few realistic limits set on her behavior by her infirm 70-year-old grandmother.

Carmen had had psychological testing, and little hope was offered for her ability to attach to any therapist due to her specific personality (ego) deficits. Carmen had had little opportunity in her early childhood to develop feelings of love and being loved, or of trust in anyone. Her mother frequently left her, and did not protect her from serious physical injury by one boyfriend and seven years of regular sexual abuse by another boyfriend. Carmen had been able to develop only superficial, shallow relationships with no continuity, so fragile that any trust could quickly and completely become distrust if someone seemed to be against her once more. We found her to be a highly impulsive young girl who made an instant yet very superficial attachment to us. She had a pseudomature manner which would quickly alternate with the behavior and impulsivity of a young child. Her doll play undoubtedly symbolizes how she responded to everyone at that time, including the therapist. When Carmen first came to us, she picked up a doll and hugged it saying, "I love this doll." Seconds later she said, "The doll's eyes hate me . . . this doll hates me . . . I don't like this doll," at which point she threw it to the ground. These statements and interactions symbolized much of what Carmen was to project on her therapist.

Treatment consisted of seeing her in her own social territory. Clearly, an office setting was much too close and threatening for her. Carmen was willing to take walks and drink soft drinks, and during this activity, she began to explore some of her problems. The first goal of therapy was just to establish enough of an alliance so that she could have someone to reach out to as an alternative to acting out—that is, the therapist tried to talk over with her in very concrete terms what would happen as a result of her behavior in any crisis situation and which of the alternatives she would like best. Helping her slow down her own impulsive actions by thinking in this mode first was a second goal, and an important one in light of her highly impulsive style and the trouble she could get into as an attractive yet immature girl in an Hispanic ghetto environment.

Many children who have been severely neglected and abused as children and subjected to a chaotic life have found it intolerable to face their feelings of helplessness, loneliness, fear, and rage. They therefore avoid recognizing painful feelings as much as possible, often by responding with impulsive behavior. The behavior may get them into further trouble, but it temporarily helps them avoid their fear and helplessness, often substituting what seems to them to be control over the situation by action. Because there is so much underlying anxiety, tasks requiring attention and concentration, like school work, may be very difficult.

Children like Carmen are most vulnerable to loss of an important relationship or any sign of rejection which bring back the feelings of loss, fear, anger, and helplessness of childhood. Therefore Carmen's therapist tried hard to be as reliable, consistent and responsive to Carmen's needs as she could be within the carefully defined limits of the relationship. Talking about the limits of the relationship helped Carmen know that her therapist understood her needs, did not want her to be disappointed, and wanted to be trustworthy.

In effect much of what her therapist did for Carmen was what a good mother would have done for her when she was very young—being nurturing, trustworthy, and supportive of Carmen's own development. To do this within the limitations of a therapy relationship is difficult because one never can nor should one try to replace the mother in reality—only in some of the functions from which children like Carmen must benefit to survive.

Carmen had been placed in a special school for "trouble-makers" and was attending on a sporadic basis. She had difficulty sitting and attending in class. Her lay therapist, a 25-year-old woman, worked with her teachers to design a program for her that would set limits and give her a more structured environment. She responded well and began attending school on a more regular basis. A new and important aspect of her life was the opportunity to have a meaningful job, arranged for by the therapist during two consecutive summers. She worked in a neighborhood health clinic, at first with young children age 2 to 4 in a daycare situation where her work was structured and supervised. The second summer she assisted a secretary within the clinic. Both experiences were very successful. She never missed a day and the staff admired her. Running away had been a regular event during school months, but during the summer she ran away from home on only two occasions. The work experience was very therapeutic; it gave her structure, helped her self-esteem, provided a tangible reward in the small amount of money she earned, and made her more realistically aware that there were people who could be appreciative of and helpful to her.

As school began in the fall, some of her old impulsive behavior returned. She was then between 13 and 14 years of age. She rapidly matured sexually and became a very attractive young girl who was approached by numerous men, many of them in constant trouble with the law. It was at this point that she began to get into more trouble, mainly in connection with her male companions. Adolescence always revives the issues of dependency on the parents when the need to separate from them begins. Often unapproved behaviors and new friends are ways to achieve separation—"I do what I want." Carmen was arrested for curfew violation and driving without a license among other minor charges. Her therapist-friend had often wondered if Carmen could survive her own adolescence, or if the therapist would, because she required so many night rescues. When the therapist went on vacation, Carmen left the city as well. Once when the therapist flew to New York for a conference, she discovered that Carmen had hitchhiked to San Diego, the last place the therapist had been for a conference.

After about two-and-a-half to three years of therapy, Carmen had been able to develop a closer relationship than we had originally thought possible. Although her ability to see her therapist as a reliable, consistent, well-meaning person was not complete, she was well on the road toward it. Treatment diminution, while her therapist returned to the nearby university, was difficult for Carmen, and many of her most worrisome impulsive behaviors resurfaced. She was placed in Juvenile Hall on an old and minor charge when she failed a probation appointment. For several months she was in and out of the Hall. However, Carmen made a dramatic escape from the juvenile authorities and was never apprehended. She seemed lost to follow-up for the next two years.

Recently Carmen, now age 17, made contact again with the Center where her therapist had worked and where she knew several of the staff and felt they were friends. She telephoned and wanted to know if her therapist still remembered her. She said that she had recently been to a rock concert and heard a group who were on a record her therapist had given her before she left. She said the concert reminded her of the Center and she wanted to call. She wanted her therapist to know that she was more "together" and not so wild as before and that she wanted to get her record settled at Juvenile Hall. A staff friend connected her with a probation officer and asked that she call back and let us know if there were any snags. She was now permanently living with her grandmother and somehow had avoided pregnancy. (Birth control had been one of her most talked-about subjects.)

Two successful summer jobs and twice weekly visits with a therapist for two years was unlikely to make up for or reverse a problem of sexual, emotional, and physical trauma lasting almost twelve years. However, it was both a beginning and a very important change in her chaotic life, one that began to provide the structure, nurture, and encouragement necessary for any changes. Carmen is now returning to treatment with her original therapist, far more settled after a stormy adolescence, and with a real sense of being in charge of herself. With such support, the outlook for this bright and ambitious youngster is vastly improved, and, while it is too soon to say what she will eventually turn out to do with her life, she now wishes for a "regular" family life, more education, and perhaps to become a nurse.

Sometimes peer group therapy seems to be the treatment mode of choice for children between the ages of 6 and 18. For all of these children, the recognition that they are not as different as they had thought is reassuring. Younger children need to use the group to understand clearly that what happened to them should not have happened, but that it was not their fault. Many teenagers have not only been isolated within the family but have also been very much isolated in their peer group where their unhappy secret has made them feel as if they could not belong. A group of teenage girls will not only need to discuss their feelings about incest and their unhappy family life, they will also want to share their need to enter the teenage social world. Most children, even adolescents, who have been sexually exploited need to have more accurate information on sex and have their questions and worries discussed so they do not continue to have fantasies which distort their future relationships. Children also need to be able to talk about their families, about separation and loss when this has occurred, about natural needs for affection and attention and how they can separate getting affection from sex and their incestuous experiences. Groups which are going to deal with such issues need to be fairly stable over many months in order that individual members can develop trust in the group and their therapists, can learn how to share feelings, and can have time to absorb and react to what they have learned.

EVALUATION AND TREATMENT OF SIBLING INCEST

There is little organized information concerning treatment of sibling incest, perhaps due to a tendency to assume that it has little significance. However, increasing evidence of unrecognized incest among siblings in which psychosomatic or psychological symptoms are of sufficient severity to require medical help indicates that the consequences may be long-term and disabling. We know that in at least a few cases the incest is followed by serious mental disorder.

Certainly adolescents or young adults who are found to be involved in sibling incest, whether heterosexual or homosexual, should be offered evaluation and treatment. If the sibling incest is also a peer relationship, there may be a question as to whether the family should be told or confidentiality preserved if the adolescents wish it. It should be remembered that some sibling incest occurs in families in which all relationships are distant and there is little emotional warmth. Sibling incest may also be part of other forms of incest in the same family, or it may take an abusive form in which an older sibling seduces or coerces a much younger child. Therefore, whether the treatment offered is individual or also involves the rest of the family, whether it is reported or kept confidential, will depend to some extent on the ages of the participants and the nature of their relationship. We have seen cases in which treatment at an earlier age would probably have prevented serious emotional difficulty in the young adult if the problem had been recognized and treated.

LATE TREATMENT OF INCEST

For the young adult who received either inadequate early treatment or no treatment at all as the victim of incest or other sexual abuse in childhood, an average of two years of individual or group treatment not less than once weekly is probably required to make a mature adjustment, to come to terms with the past, and to work through most issues raised by the trauma experiences at a time when normal sexual development should have occurred. These young people may need to explore and evaluate their own preferred sexual roles, their future life styles, and their relationships to all the members of their families.

While these issues are not unique to sexually abused children, it is striking how difficult they can be to resolve. Further, the first year of treatment tends often to be slow and seemingly not very productive, and therapist and patient may be tempted to give up too soon. Here a clear mutual agreement early on may be of great value. The therapist simply says, "Most of these problems take two years to work through, some a shorter time; if you are willing to stay with it, we will too." This also needs to be done in group treatment so that discouragement does not disrupt the group, each member of which tends to develop a relationship of some depth with all the other members. Sometimes that relationship is far from loving, but the "loss" of any member needs to be discussed because intense feelings of anger and rejection may follow the event. It is common to have former group members continue to meet in groups or individually or chat by phone long after formal meetings have been discontinued.

In some communities, few treatment programs exist, and in others, none. Here resources such as the local clergy, information through the media, or a strengthened child protective services with community support are essential. Many members of the clergy do provide counseling services and some have special training; some physicians and nurses can assist in treatment or find community resources which are not well known—retired social workers or psychologists, for example. In some metropolitan inner-city areas, the problems of sexual abuse are submerged in an almost universal despair about all the other ills of that society: poor health care, drug addiction and alcohol abuse, massive un-

employment, and loss of hope about a better future. Still, obviously, we must do our best to provide treatment services as we
face each problem, and, at times, wear blinders about other valid
concerns. "One family at a time" is a better working plan than
"Why even try?"

ONE MODEL COMMUNITY-WIDE GROUP TREATMENT PROGRAM

While there are a great variety of sexual abuse treatment programs
and some have rigid preferences and fixed divisions among various
ways of treatment, most comprehensive programs have far more
in common than they care to admit. Credit for developing and
then making broadly available a good general model of a comprehensive child sexual abuse treatment program goes to Giaretto
who in 1971, along with his wife, gradually developed a model
for Santa Clara County in California. While counseling sexually
abused children and their families for the probation department
of the Santa Clara county courts, Giaretto found himself unable
to handle the twenty-six cases referred during the first year on a
weekly session schedule. He soon expanded services, which were
still under the initiative of the probation department of the courts
rather than originating from the protective services department.
Many agencies soon began to take advantage of this new community-based child sexual abuse treatment program (CSATP)
which, by now, has served well over 2,000 families in this one
county. Of those families judged suitable for treatment and who
have completed the treatment process, about 90 percent have had
the victims reunited with their families, though some families
have broken up due to divorce or treatment failures of all kinds.
There is said to be a very low recidivism rate, only 1 percent, in
the Santa Clara group. Because this model has been spreading
rapidly and with success throughout the United States, much as
Parents Anonymous groups did for the physically abused children

and their families about ten years earlier, we shall detail this program, some features of which can be found in family-oriented, comprehensive programs in many communities, both here and abroad.

The first, or *professional component* includes all the responsible professionals and trained volunteer members of the community, including court designated probation officers, police, social workers, and all other available mental health professionals such as psychologists and psychiatrists. Judges and defense and prosecution attorneys are also included if they want to be. In most communities in the United States, unlike Santa Clara County, the designated agency is the child protective service of the department of social services. Whatever the set-up, the necessity for full interagency cooperation leads to great savings in resources and money and, most important, makes treatment more meaningful and less confusing and frightening to the victims and their families.

The *volunteer component* is an essential part of the Santa Clara County plan, and it has a membership of about fifty at this time. The members are a mix of students in training for marriage, family, and child counseling; some are "graduate" members of the treatment program. In every way, this group is similar to the lay therapist groups, initiated in our Center by Steele in 1960, which have provided so many successful adjunct therapists for families of physically abused and neglected children all over the world.

The *self-help component* consists of a formal organization, Parents United and its adjunct, Daughters and Sons United (PU/DSU). Parents United started with just two mothers in 1971, and rapidly grew to include other mothers, but not fathers, until years later when the first father joined in the weekly group sessions. There are now well over 200 local members, with an average attendance of 125 members, and a fairly regular sequence of events at the weekly meetings which are supplemented by personal therapy or extra attention from volunteer helpers and members of other families. After an initial group meeting, which has some communal significance without being a religious service of any one denomination, group sessions begin. These include a staff member, a trained member of Parents United, plus approximately ten members (or five couples) in each group. There is a men's group, a women's group, a mixed gender group, an orientation group for new members, an adult women's group consisting of those molested as children, a social skills group, and a group for training group leaders.

Giaretto states that he feels strongly that the number and focus of groups should change according to the needs of the membership. Groups tend to start at the same time and stop after eight sessions, after which members are asked to join other groups. It has been estimated that incoming families in crisis receive an average of twenty hours per week of support, a figure which is strikingly similar to that found by Steele to be needed in his early lay therapy experience with Davoren and Alexander twenty years ago when dealing with families of physically abused children. The communal support among the parents is very great and extends into babysitting, shopping help, job finding, locating attorneys who are competent and charge fair fees, and so forth. The important adjunct of Parents United is Daughters and Sons United which has about 150 members who span an age range from 5 to 18 years. The youngest children have play therapy sessions, and there are groups for preadolescent and adolescent girls and boys as well. The combined children's group has its own organization, and it is quite influential in the parents' group.

Treatment dynamics are not very different from those shown to work well with physically abusive parents, with some notable exceptions. If physical abuse often produces anger in all professionals concerned with the incident, sexual abuse of children causes even more rejection of the offender, and often, subtly, of the victim who is not at fault. All members of the family have their own pain and usually need individual care for a time. They can then move, first into one of several group treatment programs and, in time, face family counseling as well as group counseling by PU/DSU. The fact that Giaretto's model is based on a juvenile and criminal court referral and that the courts of his county prefer to direct the admitted perpetrator to engage in treatment until completed and they may also assess several hundred hours of work time for the organization, serves as a powerful incentive for cooperation from the perpetrator and his attorney when they comtemplate the alternatives of criminal prosecution. (See Appendix I for a contract for by-pass of criminal prosecution in Colorado Springs, El Paso County, Colorado, which demands *two years* of supervised treatment and excludes certain offenders.)

EVALUATION OF TREATMENT

It is evident that we still know very little about how to treat the sexual offender and the abused child most effectively. We need better diagnostic studies and more efforts at innovative treatment methods, but, above all, better documentation of what actually happens now. Longitudinal studies in particular might tell us which treatment has a temporary or lasting effect. Longitudinal studies would also teach us more about the natural history of the sexually abused child and the abuser, information we must have to plan effective prevention and treatment.

In any treatment program and any combination of methods, some common, generally accepted, and to us, essential features make for success. Success as here defined does not necessarily mean that the victim of incest returns to the family, regardless of the continued presence of the offender, nor need it mean that the family has stayed together, nor that a superficial appearance of "normality" has returned that satisfies the courts and the protective service workers. It means that the best possible resolution has been achieved for the victim's emotional health now and for the future management of a scarring event which may need years to work through entirely. The essential features of success in incest treatment are: (1) That the offender accepts full responsibility. If his individual treatment has been successful, he will have recognized the reasons for his incest behavior, come to terms with his guilt and forgiven himself sufficiently so that he is free to remake healthy relationships as a husband and father and is on the way to doing so. (2) That the victim's mother also acknowledges her own role in failing to protect the victim and her need to change for the child's benefit and her own. Somewhere along the line both parents must, in clearly spoken words and in actions, assume their responsibility for events now past and prove their desire to work for a good family life. For both parents, this ideally encompasses understanding of the cause of their problems, acceptance of guilt, and then the ability to forgive themselves and the other. It is to be hoped that such a process has encouraged the development of empathy for one another and for their children so that they can rebuild healthier family relationships. (3) That the victim has been able to understand and forgive her/his parents and has a better self-image, is more self-confident and able to verbalize feelings about many topics of concern, some of which are common to all adolescents. Some of these common adolescent problems may include mild, chronic depression, difficulties in making close friendships with children of the same sex, possible experimentation with drugs and alcohol, unsafe, accident-prone automobile driving, and, for girls, contact with brutalizing rather than gentle adolescent boys. While all of the above are seen in many other adolescents as deviant phases of growth and do, with maturity, tend to improve, this is not as often the case with incest victims unless they receive appropriate and long-term support.

As regards the offender's willingness to admit responsibility for incest and then to feel the relief which he promptly experiences when properly supported and encouraged, it is important to realize that a few offenders use a very standard method of deception which works well with the courts and many social workers and psychiatrists. It is often encouraged by their lawyers as well, and may be very difficult to spot at the beginning. Characteristically, such fathers will ask for the treatment program available under the court's supervision as an alternative to prosecution, and, as in the case in Santa Clara County, they may also be sentenced to provide manual work for the organization involved in their family treatment. They then attend the prescribed ten weekly sessions, obtain a court release, and leave the county with their families. This means that they are quite free to continue their sexual abuse elsewhere, even across the county line a few miles away, provided that the family is also willing to return to this mode of family dysfunction. Unfortunately, the family often feels they have little choice because of a combination of economic and emotional bonds. We have seen a very consistent group of such treatment "successes" in time being seen again and again from one of four neighboring jurisdictions in Colorado.

Just as the too-compliant offender may fool us all, so must one beware of the father who becomes so very much encouraged by his success that he reacts to any return of sexual desires for his child, even if no overt acts of incest occur, by going into a suicidal depression. Unlike Alcoholics Anonymous which is gentle with those who relapse and never gives up in providing personal support, some sexual abuse treatment programs are not on the lookout for deepening depression in some of their offenders in treatment, and tragedies during treatment have resulted. There also is a small but significant number of offenders who seriously threaten to kill the victim or her siblings if they tell of the child's plight, and, when she/he does, they carry out the threat.

In sum, the field requires much more than love and understanding. It requires substantial diagnostic and treatment skills which are not limited to any one profession or specialty: A critical and compassionate attitude, combined with precise understanding of the family's dynamics and the emotional and character traits of each individual involved—not an easy task.

TREATMENT SUCCESSES

An example of many family situations where the outcome was excellent for all concerned involved *Judy*, the 14-year-old daughter of an Army sargeant, a highly skilled electronics specialist who lived a very busy and productive life. To outward appearances, this was a closely knit family with a 10-year-old brother and a very devout and socially active mother in a nonsmoking, nondrinking setting but with few friends. Judy's father, however, had been involved in sexual intercourse with her since she was 11. Both she and her father were ashamed and seemed to be unable to stop what became an increasingly great problem to them both when she wanted to date boys her own age. He sought help from us, fearful of legal and professional consequences. From the start his wife hesitated to admit that she had any knowledge of this matter, although Judy had told her just once that it had occurred when she was only 11. The brother seemed unaware until told.

All entered a program which at first gave individual time to each of the four members for two sessions during which they talked freely and emotionally about their desire to keep the family together and to get over a very burdensome situation. Each then entered a weekly group meeting with other similar daughters, sons, fathers, and mothers. At the same time both parents joined a parents group for about a year. Family problems became very much easier, communication between them greatly improved, and Judy's dating and increasing independence was handled well by her parents.

All members of the family have done well in the following four years, and Judy now attends junior college in her small community. These parents have, in turn, helped others involved in incest, have made a few very close friends, and are truly relieved of the great burden which almost had resulted in Judy becoming a runaway at 14. The entire family was seen together before group sessions were started, but each has told us that the first, individual time was particularly important to them.

Another hopeful example of treatment is that of *Leslie* whose difficulties started at age 9. At 14 years old, Leslie was seen on request by the police because her 16-year-old brother, when arrested as a runaway, had told them that his father had an incestuous relationship with his sister. The parents denied the allegation and, initially, so did the patient. But on the second interview she began to discuss her fears about pregnancy and venereal disease. With more reassurance, she went on to describe her five-year sexual involvement since the age of 9 with her father, a 35-year-old computer programmer with a college education. Full sexual intercourse began early on a weekly basis, was painful for some months, and was never sexually stimulating to her.

Leslie was placed in foster care but repeatedly ran away. The father lost his job when he was first arrested, and, while awaiting trial, he attempted suicide. Subsequently, criminal prosecution was deferred, and both parents received joint treatment around their failing marriage and their relationship with their children. Both children elected to remain in different foster homes until graduation from high school. Criminal charges were eventually dropped, and the father resumed employment. The marriage was stabilized. Both children are now in college and seem to be on fairly friendly terms with their parents, though they never remain home overnight. Leslie seems to have forgiven her father but not her mother from whom she hides her feelings. She is shy with men friends but relates well with her college girlfriends. She is now seeking counseling.

The tragic fact is that delay is common between the onset of incest and discovery, often, as in Leslie's case, for as long as five years. Thus it occurs at a critical stage when the early adolescent normally works through sexual orientation and other conflicts. The help of friends of both sexes, all of whom undergo the same developmental steps at about the same time, was denied to Leslie, and this undoubtedly made her recovery difficult and perhaps incomplete. It should be stressed, however, that many incest victims do eventually recover and may emerge strong and well motivated, often hoping to help others. We continue to find an unusually high number of incest victims in the fields of nursing, social work, and medicine, and they are quite clear that their untoward experiences have contributed to their choice of work as helpers and healers.

Such is the case of *Joan*, 1 21-year-old college student with many minor complaints and episodes of insomnia, who told freely of her anger at her father who, having seduced Joan at an early age, was having an incestuous affair with her younger sister when Joan left for college. She was not jealous but rather wanted him stopped. As she said, "I have given my best years to him to keep us together."

Her father, a judge, had begun to stimulate her sexually at bedtime when she was 12, and he commenced regular inter-course with her when she was 14, often six times each week. Her mother knew of these acts from the start, encouraged them subtly at first, and then simply would not discuss the matter. Whenever Joan threatened to leave home, her mother told her that she kept the family together and that her two younger sib-lings would be forever grateful to her for preventing a divorce. The patient had had no boyfriends and few girlfriends, but she was anxious, until she left home, "to have things stay the same."

On discussion, the mother appeared scared and angry, den-ied that her husband, "an important man in this community," could be so ungratefully accused, asked that he not be contacted, and disowned her daughter as a chronic liar. Joan's father ad-mitted, in medical confidence, that his daughter was totally cor-rect and that he was, indeed, involved with his second daughter. He entered therapy with an experienced psychiatrist and has, over the past years, been able to desist from all incestuous re-lationships. His eldest daughter will not see him, and he accepts this. He blames himself fully, is puzzled by his craving for love from his daughters, and, finally, blames himself for his wife's frigidity. He is chronically depressed, on medication, and in re-cent years, a borderline alcoholic.

Joan will enter a medical school next year, and she seems highly motivated and is maturing well. She is engaged to a loving and understanding young man with whom she shared her past experience freely as soon as he proposed marriage. Through much grief, this rather strong young person has matured, and, while she has had a difficult adolescence, she seems to have mastered her past and to be ready to face the future with optimism.

TREATMENT FAILURES

Treatment failures are in many ways more important to analyze than successes. Even without treatment as such, informal help from friends or teachers, and growth itself, does for a number of incest victims result in their reaching an acceptable level of personal healing. The following is not such a case. Treatment was attempted, but failed to help this family.

Pat, the 13-year-old daughter of a financially successful builder, came to a local police station and stated that her father had been sexually involved with her since she was 9 years old. The immediate reason given by her for telling this to her girlfriend's mother who accompanied her was the fact that her father had become unwilling to allow her to go out in the evenings and that she was not allowed to meet boys. Both parents denied the accusation, and the examining woman physician found Pat to be a youngster with no breast or pubic hair development who had not yet menstruated. Her hymen was not intact and the size of her vaginal opening was that of an adult. There were no other findings suggesting recent intercourse, and no venereal infections or injuries.

Pat was placed in a temporary foster home at her request, and she began to have weekend visits with her younger brother and her parents as a group on Sundays for social activities. Her parents would on these occasions ask her to change her story before she "really wrecked the family." Over the next eight months she developed a good relationship with a young and highly sensitive female therapist who also shared social activities with her. Her school performance markedly improved, and she developed friendships with peers of both sexes. Hearing of a criminal charge placed by the district attorney was delayed repeatedly by the father's attorneys, though Pat was willing to undertake a lie detector test. Against our wishes she did so and passed, while her father failed three such tests in a row.

At age 14 she was allowed to go on a weekend camping trip with her family. Only her brother and father appeared, her mother having suddenly and unexpectedly declined to go on the trip as had been stipulated under court rules and by the social services worker. During this trip Pat was again the object of three instances of incest, witnessed by her younger brother who faked sleep. When she again complained of this, the legal machinery began to move, and the father was indicted. As part of the evaluation of the victim, a series of psychological tests were carried out which showed her to feel isolated, inadequate, unprotected, and depressed ("a snail without a shell"). The father was advised by counsel to allow the court to dispose of the case or face a public trial. The mother, who was interviewed several times over two years, stuck to her story of knowing nothing, disbelieving her daughter utterly, but always adding, "If he did this to her, she should not look at a pair of pants ever again."

Pat was finally sent to another state to live with a family headed by an uncle who was the father's brother. At age 16 she became pregnant, and it became known that while the child's father was a school boy, her uncle had repeatedly, but not successfully, tried to have intercourse with her over the year, despite her complaints to her aunt.

She returned to us as a runaway, and, despite the efforts of all who knew her, she accepted her father's offer to bring up her baby whom she did not wish to abort, to finance her college education (she wanted to be a physician and is intellectually able to pursue such a career), and not to interfere with her rights to socialize with her friends of either sex provided she returned home until she was ready for college. Pat talked very calmly of her options. On the one hand, she could be on her own under the care of social service department until she finished high school in a group setting where there would be support for herself and other young mothers and then set out on her own to get a higher education while caring for a baby. On the other hand, she could have fairly large financial resources at her disposal for the years ahead in exchange for the sexual relationship with her father. She chose the latter. She dropped all contact with her previous therapist and friends and now, at age 22, is in college, while still living at home, and her child is largely cared for by her mother. Intermittent contact by phone, initiated by her about once a year, suggests that she feels trapped but willing to pay what it takes to get what she wants. She is much involved in gathering material possessions and also in becoming a physician in another six years. Her father has had many arrests for drunken driving and is unwilling to seek help around his steadily increasing alcoholism. Her younger brother ran away from home at age 16.

Pat made a number of steady friends in treatment between ages 13 and 22, and she is fond of them and stays in touch. But she has clearly been much affected by her experiences, perhaps from early childhood, with an unloving mother and the onset of incest at age 9. These experiences led to a complex and developmentally distorted life, and, currently, incest has been her accepted life-style for thirteen years. Her attempts at independence—going for help to the police and later becoming pregnant—failed to succeed, and her long-term outlook for emotional health is not good. But it is clear that she is not yet finished; she may yet break loose, and she is so very bright that it might be possible for her to find just the right kind of help which we clearly did not succeed in giving.

CHAPTER EIGHT

WHAT HAPPENS TO CHILD AND ADOLESCENT VICTIMS

A single molestation by a stranger, particularly of a nonintrusive, nonviolent kind, as in an encounter with an exhibitionist, may cause only transitory harm to normal children living with secure and reassuring parents. The event still needs to be talked out and explained at an age-appropriate level, and all questions must be answered. Symptoms that persist over weeks or changes noted in school work might require an evaluation of the underlying difficulty.

After any violent molestation or rape, children need a great deal of care. A brief hospital stay, with the mother in attendance, may help to take care of injuries and also to satisfy the legal requirements for criminal evidence in a setting that is sympathetic and supportive. It is far better to take plenty of time and try to do all that is needed under gentle guidance and with the involvement of the family. In any event, a terrifying experience must not be made even worse. Memories of the event and of early treatment remain for a lifetime, and sensitive early care is essential to minimize trauma (see Chapter 5). Follow-up treatment may be needed for some children for months; others seem to recover quickly from the traumatic event.

A few years ago, one of us placed an advertisement in the campus newspaper of a local private university. The text was simple: "If you have been involved in sexual abuse and still have problems in resolving this, call Dr. C. Henry Kempe, University of Colorado Medical Center." I received fifty-four calls in the first twenty-four hours, and we had to stop the ad continuing in order not to be overwhelmed. The enrollment of that institution was approximately 8,000. Two of the students seen by us were, in fact, not sexually abused but wanted to get help with other problems. Twelve students elected not to meet further, and we know nothing of their subsequent course. Eight others did well in single individual sessions with simple reassurance which consisted mostly of answering questions and leaving the door open for further help if needed. Sixteen students, including two males, were sufficiently in need of personal therapy that we arranged referrals to psychiatrists after consultation to make certain that they would be accepted for care. Twelve young women were referred directly for group therapy at the Center. The remaining group contained four women who needed individual work for a period of time (two to four months) before they were ready to join the therapeutic group of young adult women under the leadership of two therapists (Mrs. Helen Alexander, MSW, and Dr. Brandt Steele, psychiatrist). This group met once a week for dinner at our Center, followed by group sessions intended to last just two hours, but often lasting much longer. Conclusions concerning the long-term effect of sexual abuse, derived largely from experience with the group's progress over a two-year period are described by Steele and Alexander. (See the reference in Appendix 6.) The important point to recall is that it generally requires considerable therapy time to do what is needed to work through the disturbing events.

Incest at any age appears to cause major difficulties, particularly in the distortion of development of close, trusting, and dependent relationships. There may not be obvious behavior which points to incest as a cause, and some victims may appear to be normal adults. Our guess would be that an underlying subtle difficulty with intimacy and trust might remain but might never be clinically recognized. The principal exception to the lack of specific symptoms is the not-uncommon situation where a very young girl is trained to be a sexual object, giving and receiving sexual pleasure in order to win approval. These little girls try to make each contact with any adult male an overt sexual event, with genital stimulation sought, supplied, and rewarded. They have, in short, been trained for the profession of prostitution and no other. Nothing is more pathetic and more difficult to manage. These little girls are far too knowing and provocative to be acceptable in most foster or adoptive homes. They are socially disabled until cared for at length by a mature and understanding couple. Fathers involved in this form of early "training incest" may not be curable in our experience. The outlook for the children also is not good, even with treatment, because of the timing and prolonged imprinting nature of this exploitation. These children, both boys and girls, have not had the opportunity to follow a normal course of psychosexual development in which the child's sexual interests are channeled and repressed in favor of the sublimated activities of the latency period.

Incest *during* adolescence is especially traumatic because of the heightened awareness of the adolescent and the active involvement in identity formation and peer group standards. Frigidity, conversion hysteria, promiscuity, alcohol or drug addictions, phobias, suicide attempts, and psychotic behavior are some of the chronic disabilities one sees in some women who have experienced adolescent incest without receiving help. Only in retrospect are these histories obtained, often many years later, the affair having never come to the attention of anyone outside the family.

But boys do much worse than girls! Both mother-son (or grandmother-grandson) and father-son incest leave a boy with such severe emotional insult that normal emotional growth is often blocked. Some of these boys tend to be severely restricted and may be unable to handle stress without becoming psychotic while others may have symptoms but never be recognized as incest victims. Incest, then, can be ruinous for the male, while it can be overcome with or, sometimes, without help by many girls.

In general, professionals agree that early and empathic working through of the complex emotions and distorted relationships may be curative, while late discovery after serious symptoms have appeared is far less satisfactory. The focus of treatment is the family, but sometimes there really is no functional family, and the youngster must try to build an independent life with sympathetic help from others.

In contemporary society, many explain the taboos against incest as having no function other than the prevention of close inbreeding, with its deleterious genetic effects. Where this explanation has been accepted as sufficient, the result has been a weakening of the sanctions that, in the past, protected the relation between adults and children, including stepchildren. Mead felt that where the more broadly based sanctioning system has broken down, the household may become the setting for cross-generational reciprocal seduction and exploitation rather than fulfilling the historic role of protecting the immature and permitting the safe development of the strong affectional ties in a context where sexual relationships within the family are limited to spouses. Home must be a safe place!

We believe that *all* sexual exploitation is harmful and that it must be stopped. This does not imply that criminal sanctions must always follow. Often an expression of public fury and demand for retribution, they do serve to remove a convicted offender from potential victims for a time. At the same time, we feel that the criminal justice system, principally the police and probation departments, must be meaningfully informed and involved in management on a continuing basis, to provide protection, correction, and, sometimes, to insure treatment compliance. What is clear is that often the child needs weeks and months of individual or group psychotherapy to come to terms with the problem and to integrate the sometimes puzzling, sometimes frightening, and sometimes guilt-laden occurrences back into a normally safe environment. Here the growing child or adolescent increasingly assumes charge of his or her personal control over body and mind.

Failure to treat the victim may be a far more serious societal act than failure to punish the perpetrator.

There still is much discussion about how serious and long-lasting the effects of sexual abuse are on the victim. The comparatively few follow-up studies done until very recently tended to show rather equivocal results—partly because of the great differences in criteria for mental health used from one study to another and partly because of the great variety of victims and types of abuse studied. To date, there is no large-scale, well-documented study that can give us information about long-term effects.

There are two other compelling reasons why, even with well-planned studies, it will be difficult to relate specific effects to specific past trauma of sexual abuse. One reason is that sexual abuse tends to give rise to many variable behavioral symptoms which often relate more to the age, the degree of interference with the developmental status of the child victim, and the child's basic strengths and vulnerabilities than to the specific nature of the abuse itself. Even later sexual symptoms may be difficult to relate specifically to sexual abuse with our present state of knowledge about sexual development. The second reason is that very often sexual abuse, and particularly incest, occurs in the context of an environment, or at least a family life, which may well be responsible for serious emotional difficulties before the onset of sexual abuse. For example, incest often occurs in a family in which not only the father receives little affection and sexual intimacy from his wife but in which the daughter may also receive little affection, nurturance, or even attention from her mother. It may become, therefore, difficult to be able to describe accurately the effect of sexual abuse itself in every case, particularly when the family pathology is severe and where the emotional pathology in the child is also severe. However, in other cases the child of a very healthy family is victimized by extrafamilial sexual abuse, or incest occurs in a family where special circumstances make incest possible without severe intrafamilial pathology. Study of these families would be very helpful in evaluating the significance of the sexual abuse itself. At present, our main source of information is the feelings of the victim as described in Treatment (Chapters 6 and 7).

It has already been noted that the symptoms seen after extrafamilial and intrafamilial sexual abuse are often similar, with phobias, feelings of vulnerability, psychosomatic symptoms, difficulties in school performance, plus depression or acting out in adolescence. Symptoms seem to occur in these clusters frequently enough to be considered common. Our experience has emphasized other symptoms as well: low self-esteem and a poor sense of identify with consequent difficulty in relating to others and difficulty in impulse control—often specifically related to sexual or aggressive impulses, sometimes with confusion involving both. Difficulty in paying attention, and in doing school work, preoccupation with fantasy and withdrawal, or severe hyperactivity may be present. Whether or not these represent attempts to ward off anxiety and deal with flooding impulses is not known. Seductive behavior presumably represents a search for affection or excitement. In seductive children, the ability to repress and sublimate sexual interest so as to allow the freedom for learning and peer activity has not developed, and the child is handicapped by the turbulence of his latency years (ages 6 to 10), another example of the loss of childhood resulting from abuse.

Because all these symptoms are so frequently present in the child victims of sexual abuse, it might well be supposed that many children who in years past were not recognized as victims may have suffered similar effects without treatment. It is now clear that many children require fairly long and intensive treatment to ameliorate these symptoms, and success is not always the result. How much of this childhood trauma remains to distort the adult's emotional life is not known, but we believe it to be significant in many children who do not receive treatment.

Some studies reporting no pathology following sexual abuse do not seem very convincing in light of recent work. The early studies of Bender et al. included children with so many pervasive family difficulties that later problems were ascribed to causes other than sexual abuse and no real distinction could be made. The report of Yorukoglu and Kemph describes two children who were said not to be severely damaged by incest with a parent, presumably because neither received a diagnosis of formal psychiatric illness. The boy of 13, involved for two years in incest with his mother, required placement in a detention home and showed behavioral problems, but he responded well to supportive treatment in a psychiatric hospital. The girl of 17 became very anxious when incest of four years' duration with her father began to become pleasurable. She reported the incident, leading to her father's hospitalization as a schizophrenic. Although anxious, she was felt to show no serious effects. Of probable importance is the fact that incest occurred fairly late for both these children. There was some evidence of a more stable childhood and an assumption of normal early psychosexual development. Also present, however, was clear evidence of role reversal in each child's perception of the parent. No long-term follow-up to show the effects on adult adjustment is given.

Indications that long-term effects are likely can be found in those studies of adults with emotional pathology who have a history of childhood sexual abuse. Amy Katan reported on six adult women patients, all of whom had been raped or abused by outsiders in early childhood and suffered from serious emotional disturbances. Westermeier, in describing thirty-two patients in his private practice who had been exposed to varying kinds of incestuous relationships, most of them as children, described problems of sexual dysfunction, depression, neuroses, psychosomatic illness, and psychoses, all of which he felt were related to the incest. Lukianowicz described twenty-six young women in one study who had been victims of father-daughter incest. In six girls, no apparent ill effects were said to be noted and the incest was apparently accepted mainly with embarrassment; five girls developed frigidity and aversion to sex after marriage; eleven girls developed character disorders with promiscuity; and four girls developed acute neuroses, one with acute anxiety and three with depression and suicide attempts. Sloane and Karpinski also found in a study of five cases of incest (between father and daughter or older brother and sister) that at least four out of the five girls had serious personality difficulties, with promiscuity and often antisocial behavior as well.

James and Myerding, in reporting two large studies of adult and adolescent prostitutes responding to a questionnaire, found that the majority of their respondents had experienced early sexual intercourse in a casual context. In the two parts of the study, figures for incest (sexual abuse by fathers, stepfathers, foster fathers) were 25.5 percent and 23 precent. Other studies report higher figures for incest up to 71 percent in the history of runaway girls and 82 percent for juvenile prostitutes of both sexes. These figures are similar to those in studies in which physical abuse and neglect were experienced by a high proportion of children in legal difficulty for serious delinquincy, running away, drug abuse, or prostitution—over 75% in some series. The number of these children also suffering sexual abuse was not ascertained.

In the process of attempting to cope with the treatment needs of children presently being sexually abused, there should be ample opportunity to learn a great deal of the immediate effects of sexual abuse. Longitudinal studies and follow-up studies are now in progress which will undoubtedly corroborate much of what is already known. The current recognition of the importance of sexual abuse and incest is causing questions about sexual abuse to be asked in personal histories now, without their inclusion considered shocking. It may be that many more former victims who will be encouraged to seek help or who will demonstrate that such a trauma can indeed be survived with comparatively little residual pathology will be found in this way.

The high figures of incidence of unreported sexual abuse (especially those for incest) being found in recent studies imply that many victims (1) seek help for symptoms which are never ascribed to sexual abuse, (2) live with handicaps for which they do not seek help, or (3) have through their own coping abilities and un-identified environmental support survived their sexual abuse with minimal emotional damage or, perhaps, with even increased maturity and ego strength. If so, it is vital to recognize the circumstances which made this outcome possible for those individuals. As we learn why these people were less vulnerable, we should also learn how to focus on the recovery potential in other victims and their families.

REFERENCES

Yorukoglu, A., and Kemph, J. P. Children not severely damaged by incest with the parent. *J. Am. Acad. Child Psychiatry* 5:111–124, 1966.

Westermeyer, J. Incest in private practice: A description of patients and incestuous relationships. *J. Clinical Psychiatry* 39:643–648.

Katan, A. Children who were raped. *Psychoanalytic Study of the Child*, 28:208–224, 1973.

Lukianowicz, N. Incest. *Brit. J. of Psychiatry* 120:301–313, 1972.

Sloane, P., and Karpinski, E. Effects of incest on the participants. *Am. J. Orthopsychiatry* 12:666–673, 1942.

James, J., and Myerding, J. Early sexual experience and prostitution. *Am. J. Psychiatry* 134:1381–1385, 1977.

CHAPTER NINE

PREDICTION AND PREVENTION

PREDICTION

Predicting sexual abuse of children is a truly unstudied field. As opposed to the repetitive nature of much physical abuse and neglect from generation to generation, much less is known about predicting child sexual victimization. There are many case reports of multigenerational incest, some over four generations and more. A man abuses his daughters and then his granddaughters, and the grandfather, father, and other brother may all be potential offenders.

For women as victims, too, incest may be found in successive generations, and it is always important to recognize this possibility in the family history. We have noted a teenage mother, who had herself been sexually abused by her father, treat her neglected 3-month-old baby in an inappropriate way during an interview with her. She called him "Lover" several times and kissed him repeatedly on his open mouth. This kind of inappropriate sexualization of a close relationship, in combination with neglectful parenting, may provide a background for future sexual abuse. Certainly, mothers who have experienced sexual abuse in childhood and within the family, have a great opportunity to help their young children recognize what sexual abuse is and at the same time make certain that their children are protected from those they know to be likely offenders. Very often, however, we have

noted that these mothers are apprehensive that their children will
be sexually abused yet feel completely helpless, not even considering how to prevent it. They need help in doing so. Insisting on
separate housing for abusive relatives and allowing only supervised contact is easily accomplished, and this is happening in
some families.

We do know, perhaps because sexually abused very young
children learn early on that rewards go with sexual activities, that
the number of prostitutes who report childhood incest and/or rape
is very high (up to 70 percent). There is no evidence that they
derive sexual pleasure from the activity by which they earn
money for basic needs and luxuries and, they hope, protection
and affection, and many still hope for the "right kind of man," a
role often filled, in their need, by their pimp. A significant number
of these childhood victims who turn to "stripping" or prostitution
have never experienced or observed in others a good heterosexual
relationship. Some of them continue to hope and others are, in
time, aware that they much prefer women and become practicing
lesbians or are bisexual.

PREVENTION

As with physical abuse, methods of primary prevention are being
actively sought. A number of excellent booklets and films designed for younger and older children now exist, as does audiov-
isual material for helping parents and teachers in trying to educate
all children in sensible ways to try to avoid sexual abuse. These
are listed and described in detail at the end of this book (see Appendices 3 and 4). There is now a 24 hour a day, seven days a week,
free telephone line which gives information to anyone on any
child abuse including sexual abuse (lay, victim, neighbor, families, etc.). For professionals particularly in rural areas, who have
few recourses to consultations, this same call will be immediately
patched through to our Denver Center from Los Angeles. This

would apply to physicians, nurses, social workers, police, ministers, lawyers, etc. The number is easy to remember because it
is "FOR A CHILD" 1-800-4 A C H I L D (1-800-422-4453). It is
sponsored by Childhelp USA and our Center and gives local contact while the caller is on the line.

Aside from the many booklets, video tapes, and other educational materials now available for children and parent and
teacher groups, we are encouraged by a rapidly spreading movement of reaching grade-school children through the visits of theater groups for the young. These groups use role-playing examples,
generally trying to "play" situations which allow the children in
the audience to perceive the differences between healthy and normal, warm, affectionate touching within the family and the advances of family members or strangers bent on sexual abuse. Examples can generally very clearly identify with any child's
experience, and the children take an active part in these brief
scenes and discuss them at once. Thus nurturing touching is contrasted with the exploitative touching which is sexual abuse.

Child sexual abuse worries all parents alike, and parents
groups have endorsed several active school programs. While many
school and parent groups have vigorously opposed sex education
in their schools, it is interesting that support for this preventive
school-based program has been overwhelming in some states.
Originating with the Youth Theater of Minneapolis, Minnesota,
it has spread to many states including Kansas, Iowa, and others.
A particularly well-thought-out program exists in Cedar Falls,
Iowa, where a professional theater troupe ("The Touch Program")
presents skits involving the children themselves. Here, and in
other such attempts encouraged by schools, the parents, and their
parent-teacher organizations, the clear difference between nurturing and exploitative touching is demonstrated and talked
about. In this way, even young school children can safely and
securely learn what sexual exploitation within and without the
family is about.

This is an important start, but we are afraid that total and effective prevention will never be possible for abuse in the setting of the nuclear family. The education of adults about the fact that they can safely, and with total confidentiality, count on help and support is needed before they get too deeply involved in sexual abuse such as incest. Those who know that they are in trouble may seek help, just as alcoholics increasingly seek help from Alcoholics Anonymous. Education could thus prevent incest and nonviolent forms of sexual abuse. It is interesting that, in the face of some psychiatric disbelief, priests hearing confession in the Catholic church are faced with just such questions in the context of confessed "sin of thought." And many priests, ministers, and rabbis now have become involved in knowing more specifically where to sent the penitent for help to prevent continuing temptation.

The following example points out the need for better education of the public as well, so that adults will no longer be so naive about offenders who appear harmless. The wife of a child molester was running a licensed preschool facility with the assistance of her husband for whom sexual abuse of many little girls was readily possible. The working mothers who used the school, many of them divorced and dependent on daycare for their preschool children, were all notified of the dangers posed by this man. Some removed their children, based on stories told by their children after school. Amazingly, three mothers refused to believe their children and kept the children in this facility. The licensing authority declined to remove the licence until there was a criminal conviction. But no such criminal charge could be placed because of "lack of proof beyond a reasonable doubt," and to our best information, the abuser continues, a classic example of bureaucratic bungling and legalism which puts the child's welfare below that of any adult. It is usually unwise to employ adolescent male babysitters for female children even though only a very small number of babysitters would place the children at risk.

Clearly, a physician can often, in the course of routine health care, ask a child in whom he suspects the possibility of sexual abuse innocuous questions such as "Does anybody touch you down here?" Examination may discover physical evidence of an enlarged vaginal outlet, hymenal tears, or, at times, infections typical of sexual abuse.

In addition to education about sexual abuse which will make children and their parents able to recognize dangerous situations and teach them how to get help after an abusive experience, we do need to look for ways to prevent sexual abuse from happening. We need to learn a great deal more about the origins of sexual abuse within the offender through research and better psychiatric treatment. We need to know more about the life situations which make a potential offender become an active threat to others— failure of a marriage, for example. We need to know more about what makes some children vulnerable to sexual abuse and others less so. We already assume that often the offender and sometimes the more vulnerable child live in a family that does not provide warmth, affection, and respect in a nonaggressive atmosphere. We have become impressed with the possibility that continuing sexually abusive relationships can be, in part, an indication of a vacuum in the emotional lives of both offender and victim. The offenders inability to have, or tendency to avoid, a satisfactory adult sexual relationship makes the child victim either more desirable or simply more available. The frequent absence of readily available comforting affection and attention of the mother and of the absorbing activities of a close family life may leave a void for the child which is then more readily filled by a sexually oriented relationship with a stranger or family member.

There is no solid evidence that sexual abuse is "good for you"! At least one New York psychiatrist, after a phone survey of women replying to a newspaper appeal, concluded that it was, at least, not very harmful to many and a positive experience to a significant number. Two lay writers, both women, have published accounts of their personal positive experience with incest over many years, although neither has married and each may well have had to defend against difficulty in living with their personal experience. Such reports need detailed investigation to determine whether they represent denial of problems or are, for these people, valid.

A considerable number of young and older adults come to seek help after having been the victims of incest in childhood because of problems in emotional health, marital difficulties, sexual identity questions, and many other complaints. Some of our patients have seen two or more psychiatrists and may not, even in a full year of treatment, have been able to discuss incest until we talked with them about it. How this is possible is not difficult to discover. The patient's obvious blocks in discussing incest even when seeking help from a psychiatrist or psychologist, is easily understood, and it should generally be dealt with by the therapist. Two intelligent young women in our groups said that every time they approached the subject of incest, the therapist steered the conversation away from it and seemed upset. Psychiatrists, too, need to become more confortable with suspecting and discussing incest.

Further, a considerable number of psychiatrists misread Freud's later suggestion that, contrary to his early observation of high incidence of incest in histories of hysterical young women, this must have been largely a kind of normal fantasy in which incest was imagined, the father romantically glorified and mother hated—that is, the oedipal complex. In fact, while there are in most children and their parents conflicting and sometimes disturbing sexual feelings, these are just that, feelings which are not acted upon by anybody. Many psychiatrists, regrettably, doubt that incest is a reality for the disturbed adolescent patient they may see as suicidal or depressed. In one sophisticated city, a number of psychiatrists in charge of adolescent psychiatric in-patient facilities suggested that the stories told by their young teenage patients of incestuous acts occurring on weekend home visits must be "imagined" and only proof of Freud's later thought on oedipal fantasies. They had never undertaken any investigation of the validity of these stories.

We feel that all sexual abuse is a potentially serious emotionally traumatic event. One-time sexual abuse by a stranger, while not without its scars, is far easier to handle than long-standing in-house sexual abuse with a loved person and/or relative continued over time. It is particularly damaging for the preschool child and for the young adolescent; at these two important times both need to fulfill their sexual development in an orderly and sequential way which this misfortune totally disturbs. As adults these victims have a much higher than normal incidence of poor sexual adjustment and difficulties in sexual identify and preference. As teens they are likely to run away from an intolerable situation, become pregnant, get involved in deliquency such as theft and substance abuse (both alcohol and other drugs), engage in teenage prostitution and, as has been the experience for some of our clients, make a significant number of attempts at suicide. Some have, indeed, killed themselves. Other teenagers have had acute psychotic states and hysterial symptoms, often directly related to discovery and the loss of family, when as victims they are isolated from all family contacts by official agencies and the courts. Child abuse is more common in mothers who were incest victims, and, interestingly, not a few women doctors, nurses, and social workers have admitted to having been sexually abused as children and adolescents, saying that these events led to their professional choices.

The best hope at present lies in bringing sexual abuse out of the closet and, as was done with other forms of child abuse, in giving permission for the victims, children and parents alike, as well as the offenders, to know where to get help early on. A community based, well-publicized program is needed in all communities, and the taboo must be discussed openly. In former years a case of tuberculosis in a family or a single alcoholic forefather were regarded as dread family secrets. Now in many societies homosexuality, while not widely admired, is at least known to exist commonly, and attitudes have changed from being very punitive to being at least more understanding and, perhaps, more tolerant and compassionate. This is now occurring in the field of incest to the benefit of the victim and the unhappy family who can have a very good chance of growing together toward a better and more fulfilling family life.

EPILOGUE: VINDICATING THE RIGHTS OF CHILDREN

In 1792, Mary Wollestonecraft wrote tracts to vindicate the rights of women. Now, nearly two hundred years later, children need that task performed for them. Sexually abused children, like children who have been physically or emotionally abused, neglected, or who have suffered from nonorganic failure-to-thrive due to maternal deprivation in infancy or from deprivation dwarfism in the preschool years, are all stunted in their emotional growth, their personal timetable of normal learning, and in the caring, affection, safety, and support that a family and friends can give. They all, in their own way, are hindered or are unsupported and alone to face developmental tasks and so lose essential parts of their childhood. They also lose the joy of discovery, of tenderness, of compassion which form such a vital part of personality development. The scars of child abuse run deep. We do not wish readers to feel that sexual abuse is a field apart—somehow quite separate in its effect from other forms of child abuse—though this is sometimes believed by experts who work only in this field and who fail to see all other kinds of child abuse.

Our children, like our other natural resources, are neither plentiful nor expendable. Most people agree that all children are entitled to a safe home in which to develop fully their inherent capacities. State intervention in family life is rejected in democratic societies on the basis that the natural bonds within the family should not be interfered with unless the child is not receiving needed care and protection. A child caught up in incest, for example, does need active, firm, and constructive intervention by society. The assigned instruments of society are those tax-supported agencies charged with the task delegated by us all: the child protective services, the police, the courts, and health professionals.

But abuses are also the direct responsibility of all citizens. We all are our children's keepers, and when institutions fail to do their job well or are unresponsive to public will, we all have a public and personal duty to intervene and call problems to the attention of all other adults in our communities. Letters to the editors in the daily newspaper, a concerned press, and investigative media, primarily television, can and do a very fine job of education. Recently, there have been a surprising number of such presentations from newspapers and television concerned with the plight of children involved in sexual abuse. The media have also presented understanding views of the troubled families and have managed, by and large, to give a fair overview of the field. They have done so as a matter of public service and not, with a few exceptions, for sensationalism. The courts have worked toward a humane approach to the criminal and civil management of children in need of care and protection brought before them. The police and detective forces in all our major cities now work toward a close relationship with social workers in the child protection service. Physicians, nurses, and lawyers for both the child victim and the perpetrator have begun to work together toward rehabilitation of the family when that can be accomplished.

There are no "quick fixes." Regardless of what combination of treatment methods is employed, long-standing family dysfunction cannot be cured in three to five months; it simply takes longer, and even then there are failures.

Finally, some situations do not allow us to try to keep the family together. In a real sense, the family has ceased to exist when we first got to know it. In every case, each family member still deserves the best we can offer. Sexually abused children are now in the very forefront of research of child abuse studies, and there is a slight danger that the field will become "popular" to the loss of the other needs of children who suffer other forms of deprivation and abuse. Far more important are the facts that research in this field is growing very fast and that better understanding will lead to better methods of prevention and care.

For the young adult whose early sexual abuse never received care or recognition and who does find life difficult, we can provide proper treatment, though the abuse is many years in the past. It is never too late! One wishes to urge adults in this position to seek help freely and not to fail to be open at once about the real reason for seeking help. Their lost rights may still be retrieved as far as possible, and that is often quite far. Happily, many helping professions include just such former victims who are ready to help others in any way they can.

Because of the forces in the community which brought public attention to the plight of the physically abused child about twenty years ago, it is now likely to take far less time to help the sexually abused child. Although many of the cases mentioned in this book are distressing (and some horrifying), the situation for abused children is better now than at any time in history, and one can be hopeful of the future. Huge strides are being made all over the world. We must not be demoralized or fail to keep pushing forward. Ultimately, our children's future and our world's future are one.

PART IV

APPENDICES

APPENDIX 1

A MODEL CRIMINAL DIVERSION PROGRAM*

DESCRIPTION

The Incest Diversion Program was developed by the El Paso County District Attorney's Office and the Department of Social Services, Colorado Springs, Colorado, to:

1. Minimize the number of criminal filings on incestuous fathers;
2. Eliminate the need to have children testifying about sexual assaults committed by their parents;
3. Alleviate, as much as possible, the trauma associated with involvement with the criminal justice system;
4. Allow immediate therapeutic intervention with family members to begin without getting delayed by procedural obstacles.

The Incest Diversion Program has not created a new agency or new services. It represents a combined effort by different existing treatment resources to provide a variety of treatments through a coordinated approach to incestuous families. This means that mental health professionals (public and private) are

---

* The authors are grateful to our friend and colleague, Anne B. Topper, M.S.W., who contributed this model program which we have found to be truly successful over a long period of time.

involved with these cases as well as protective services case-workers.

To enter this program, the client must agree to:

1.   Make payment for any expenses incurred in the therapy;
2.   Make a commitment to attend therapy sessions prescribed;
3.   Make a good faith effort to change.

Item 2 is critical because the client is not allowed to miss therapy appointments without an acceptable excuse, illness or the therapist's vacation, for example. The client also agrees in the Incest Diversion Contract to a full release of any psychosocial information as requested by all of the agencies involved, and the department of social services specifically.

We are requesting that any therapist involved with the Incest Diversion Program be aware that he or she may be asked to attend staffings on the case, may be asked to help formulate treatment plans and, most important, may be involved in determining whether or not the client is following through with the program as outlined by the contract. The therapist will also be requested to report *immediately* any new incidents of sexual assault or other abuse to the caseworker from the department of social services. Immediate reports of the client's noncompliance with the prescribed treatment program must also be made to the monitoring caseworker. Because the criminal justice system has suspended all of its activity on these cases, noncompliance with treatment is an extremely important issue. If the client is out of compliance with the contract, he or she usually feels that he or she has "beat the system," and all genuine effort toward rehabilitation and family restructuring comes to a halt. Obviously, this cannot be allowed. Noncompliance, casual missing of scheduled treatment sessions, and other lapses need to be dealt with promptly.

The department of social services caseworker continues to be responsible for initiating legal action for protection of the child in addition to providing the family with information on ongoing court status, other department services that are available, any staffings, and, generally, any other information that the family may require.

PURPOSE

The Incest Diversion Program offers the nonviolent, first offender (and, on occasion, serial offenders) an opportunity to be diverted from the judicial process if he/she is willing to undergo treatment of his/her problems and to follow through on the programs set up by professional counselors. If admitted into the program, a person must adhere to the planned treatment and family counseling programs *for up to two years*. Failure to complete the program or dismissal for failure to cooperate can lead to the filing of criminal charges by the district attorney. If the program is successfully completed, no criminal charges will be filed. All proceedings are handled in a confidential manner.

Knowledge of the existence of this program helps to overcome reluctance to report incestuous activity. Treatment helps to rebuild a healthy family unit.

ELIGIBILITY

The Incest Diversion Program was established to provide a nonjudicial alternative for nonviolent incest offenders with a recent history of incestuous conduct. Those who use threats or violence against victims or who have a long-standing history of incestuous conduct are handled through the criminal justice system. Only people who are willing to acknowledge their problems and voluntarily submit to the program are accepted.

This program was modeled after the District Attorney's Juvenile Diversion Program, with input from members of the following groups:

1.   District Attorney's office
2.   Department of Social Services

3.   Colorado Springs Police Department
4.   El Paso County Sheriff's Department
5.   Public Defender's Office
6.   Pikes Peak Advocates for Children
          (The representative was a guardian ad litem)

REPORTING

Incest is a form of child abuse which must be reported; failure to report is subject to criminal penalty. One can report incest or child abuse to the following agencies: the department of social services, victim services, or any law enforcement agency.

INCEST DIVERSION PROCEDURES FOR PROTECTIVE SERVICES STAFF

I.   Sex abuse cases are handled as usual in Child Welfare Intake and then transferred to Protective Services.

II.   Case is assigned by one of the two Protective Service Supervisors, and sexual abuse cases are identified on the case tracking form as such. The case tracking form then goes to the Protective Services clerk who in turn automatically sets up initial staffing on **all sexual abuse cases.** The worker is immediately informed of the date of the next staffing for his or her case.

III.   For purposes of conformity and uniformity, we have Child Protective Teams and review of persons in Diversion on the first and third Wednesday of the month; staffings and any emergencies are handled on the second and fourth Wednesdays of the month. If there is a fifth Wednesday in the month, it is a break for everyone, or used, as needed, for an administrative meeting.

IV.   At the staffing a decision is made as to whether a client meets the conditions of the criminal diversion program.

A. If client appears eligible:
   1. The clerk sends a copy of the discussion minutes to the District Attorney's Office, indicating that there are no apparent relevant exclusions applicable to this case.
   2. The date of the next meeting, which is standardized to four weeks on each case, is provided at the staffing.
B. If the client is determined not to be eligible, the caseworker proceeds in the usual fashion by filing a Dependency and Neglect Petition, and so forth. The Protective Services clerk then sends a copy of the staffing notes to the designated clerk in the District Attorney's office.
C. Caseworker's responsibilities:
   1. Worker presents the diversion contract to the client and has him/her sign **the first line only.**
   2. The client decides to request entry to the program or not, knowing that entry to the system constitutes an **admission of responsibility for his/her actions.**
   3. The worker and client arranges for a psychological evaluation of the client.
   4. The worker files a Dependency and Neglect Petition.
   5. The **caseworker** (knowing what date the Child Protective Team will meet) requests the evaluator and/or other involved therapist to attend the next Child Protective Team meeting.

THE CHILD PROTECTIVE TEAM MEETING

I. Input from the District Attorney's Office on prior offenses should be available at this point.
II. A review of the psychological evaluation, the staffing minutes, and any other pertinent information that the case-

worker and/or evaluator and/or therapist may have, is conducted.

III. After discussion, a decision on whether or not to offer the contract is reached.

IV. If the decision is to offer the contract:
   A. The treatment plan is finalized in written form so the client has a copy.
   B. A review date is then set up.
   C. Worker presents the treatment plan to the client.
   D. If client still agrees, he/she signs all the clauses in the contract. (One week is allowed for the caseworker to accomplish this.)
   E. The original contract is returned to the clerks.

V. Processing of the contract.
   A. A copy of the original contract without the Deputy Attorney's signature is made by the clerk and held in the Child Protective Team files.
   B. The Protective Services clerk sends the original copy of the contract to the District Attorney's office.
   C. The contract must be returned from the District Attorney's office with the appropriate Deputy District Attorney's signature.
   D. The clerk makes one copy of the signed contract for Anne Topper, one copy of the signed contract for the Child Protective Team files, one copy of the signed contract for the caseworker's file, and a copy for the client.
   E. The client is informed by the caseworker that the District Attorney's office has signed the contract and that the contract is in force as of the date the District Attorney signed it.

EXCLUSIONS

I. Persons excluded from consideration by District Attorney's office:

A. Persons charged with sexual assault crimes on victims not related to the suspect by blood or marriage or on victims with whom the suspect has resided for twelve months or less.

B. Persons who use physical violence, overt threats, or intimidation which imply or state threats of bodily harm to the victim during or subsequent to the sexual assault.

C. Persons who have been previously convicted of any criminal sexual assault, who are currently charged with any criminal sexual assault, or who have been granted deferred sentencing or deferred prosecution on any criminal sexual assault. (Recently a few serial offenders have been included if they are judged to be good treatment risks.)

D. Persons who have committed criminal sexual assault over an extended period of time on multiple victims to whom the suspect is related by blood, marriage, or adoption; on multiple victims with whom the suspect has resided for more than twelve months; or a combination of such victims.

E. Persons previously accepted into and/or discharged from the Incest Diversion Program.

II. Persons excluded from consideration by the Department of Social Services:

A. Persons who do not desire to participate in the Incest Diversion Program.

B. Persons who are insane as defined in 16-8-101 C.R.S., 1973, as amended or who are certifiable under 27-10-105 or 27-10-106 C.R.S. 1973, as amended.

ADULT DIVERSION AGREEMENT

Name _____ D.O.B. _____

Address _____ Phone _____

Employment _____ Address _____

SSN or Military ID# _____

I, _____ have been advised of my right to speedy prosecution and to have a speedy trial and I hereby waive those rights for a period of two months until the date of _____ for consideration by the Adult Diversion Program. Upon acceptance into the program, I will give an unconditional waiver of those rights.

I, _____ admit responsibility for the situation which brought this matter before the adult Diversion Program, and I understand that such admission will not be used against me in any criminal prosecution, including impeachment, but this will not extend to any new offenses admitted to.

I, _____ agree to give a release to the Adult Diversion Program for medical or psychosocial information from any physicians and counselors whose services are secured as a requirement of this program.

I, _____ agree to participate in any counseling or therapy that is recommended as a requirement of my Adult Diversion Program or any counseling or therapy approved by the Adult Diversion Program and I agree to pay any costs incurred by these requirements.

I, _____ understand that if I fail to cooperate or comply with any requirements or conditions placed upon me by the Adult Diversion Program that I may be removed from the Program and criminal prosecution may be instituted against me.

I, _____ understand that in any proceeding to remove me from the Adult Diversion Program, I will be informed of the recommendation for removal from the Program. I will be notified of the date on which the Child Protection Team will review the recommendation and I may be present to hear the reasons for removal from the Program and I may respond to the Child Protection Team on those reasons.

I, _____ understand that the duration of this Agreement is to be no more than 24 months and that upon successful completion of the Program, that the District Attorney agrees not to prosecute me upon the incident which brought me into the Adult Diversion Program.

I, _____ understand that the date of the signature of the District Attorney's Office will be the effective date of my acceptance into the Program.

I, _____ understand that I will inform the Adult Diversion Program of any change in address or employment.

I, _____ have read this Agreement and understand the statements and requirements it contains and agree to abide by those statements and requirements.

Date	El Paso County Department of Social Services
Date	Participant
Date	Deputy District Attorney

APPENDIX 2

FORMS FOR EVALUATION AND CASE RECORDS FOR SEXUALLY ABUSED CHILDREN AND THEIR FAMILIES

The following forms have been developed by cooperative efforts of the staff of the C. Henry Kempe National Center for Prevention and Treatment of Child Abuse and Neglect. They are those most applicable to the evaluation of the child and his/her family following sexual abuse. Their purpose is to maintain consistent records for learning and, sometimes, for legal requirements, and to insure thoroughness in obtaining needed information.

FLOW CHART

Child's name: _____ Date admitted: _____

Records	Date release signed	Date sent for	Date received
Welfare Summary	_____	_____	_____
Mental Health Evaluation	_____	_____	_____
Health Care	_____	_____	_____
School	_____	_____	_____
Police Records/ Parents	_____	_____	_____
Police Records/ Child	_____	_____	_____
CWS-59 filed	Yes ( ) No ( )	_____	_____

Permission slips signed   **Date**

1. Rx   _____

2. Adolescent Release   _____

3. Information Release   _____

4. Audio-visual   _____

5. Eval. and RX Consent   _____

6 Transportation   _____

Conners Children's Self-Rating Scale _____

Conger Children's Sentence Completion _____

Kinetic Figure Drawing _____

School Forms: a.   Intake _____

                b.   Conners Teacher's Rating Scale _____

                c.   Primary/Secondary Symptom Checklist __

Self-Esteem _____

Parents

    a.   psychosocial history _____

    b.   children's rating scale _____

    c.   pediatric history _____

Other Agencies Working with Family: Phone:

_____   _____

_____   _____

_____   _____

_____   _____

General information

Mother sexually mistreated	YES ( ) NO ( )
Father sexually mistreated	YES ( ) NO ( )
Mother abuses	YES ( ) NO ( )
Father abuses	YES ( ) NO ( )
Mother and father work opposite time shift	YES ( ) NO ( )
Mother lost father	YES ( ) NO ( )
Mother lost mother	YES ( ) NO ( )
Father lost father	YES ( ) NO ( )
Father lost mother	YES ( ) NO ( )

DATA COLLECTION SEXUAL ABUSE PROGRAM* **

Identifying information:

1. Family Name _____   2. Child's Name _____
3. Name of person   4. Date of first Center
   completing   contact with a member
   this form _____   of this family _____

   _____   _____

5. Date of Completion of this form _____

Child:

6. Sex _____   Birthdate _____

7. Child's birth order _____   8. Race _____

9. Age of child at first incidence of sexual abuse _____

10. Number of sexual contacts _____ over period of __
    months and _____ years.

11. Perpetrator's relationship to child _____
_____

* *Note*: 1. With the exception of questions 5, 16, 29, 59, 69, 97, and 107, the
remainder of the form should be completed at intake interview(s).
2. Question 114 is marked to indicate that this question is asked of the child.
It is the only one not included in the Child Section.

** This form was developed by Claudia A. Carroll, PsyD, and William van
Dornick, PhD, with the collaboration of The C. Henry Kempe Center Staff.

12. Length of time sexual abuse has been going on (**only check one**):

_____ One incident only

_____ Three months or less

_____ Longer than three months, up to one year

_____ Longer than one year, up to three years

_____ Longer than three years

_____ Not known

13. Types of sexual abuse which occurred (**check all that apply**):

_____ Intercourse (vaginal)

_____ Intercourse (anal)

_____ Cunnilingus

_____ Fellatio

_____ Use of foreign objects of manual penetration (vaginal)

_____ Use of foreign objects of manual penetration (anal)

_____ Fondling of genitalia

_____ Fondling of breasts

_____ Attempted sexual activity

_____ Other (specify) _____

_____ Not known

14. Means through which compliance of child in sexual abuse was obtained (**check all that apply**):

_____ Physical force

_____ Threat of punishment; threat of physical force

_____ Threat of consequences to family (parent would be jailed or divorced)

_____ Adult authority

_____ Enticements, bribes

_____ Not known

15. Victim's initial perception of sexual abuse (**check all that apply**):

_____ Violent   _____ Stimulating

_____ Scary   _____ Tender

_____ Repulsive   _____ Other _____

_____ Pleasurable   _____

_____ Not known   _____

16. Most severe harm to child of sexual abuse (**check one only**):

   _____ Severe or irreversible developmental physical or psychological impairment

   _____ Moderate or mild developmental physical or psychological impairment

   _____ Impairment not evident at present, but likely to appear in the future

   _____ Child appears unharmed

   _____ Not known

17. Who did child initially tell about the abuse? _____

   _____

18. Why did victim decide to tell at that time? What happened to make the child tell? _____

   _____

19. How long after the telling did an agency become involved?

   _____ weeks   _____ months   _____ years

20. By whom does the victim feel most loved (attached, loyal, cared for, depends on)? (List all major attachments.)

   _____

In items 21 through 26 below, please indicate any special characteristics the child may have had:

	Yes	No	Unknown
21. Product of difficult pregnancy or delivery	____	____	_____
22. Low birth weight	____	____	_____
23. Premature	____	____	_____
24. Born addicted	____	____	_____
25. Unwanted child	____	____	_____
26. Unplanned child	____	____	_____

27. Chronic diseases or handicapping condition _____

_____

_____

28. Is the child provocative sexually or seductive?

Mother's impression _____

Father's impression _____

Evaluator's impression _____

29. Role reversal behaviors in victim (identify) _____

_____

30. School behaviors _____

     Performance _____

31. History of extrafamilial molestation of child (explain) ___

     _____

32. Other sexual activity of child (i.e., masturbation, sexual
     play, sexually active with peers: homosexual,
     heterosexual) _____

     _____

33. Did any other type of abuse/neglect occur in the family
     to victim?

     _____ Emotional: explain type and duration _____

     _____

     _____ Physical: explain type and duration _____

     _____

     _____ Neglect: explain type and duration _____

     _____

34. At the time of first contact with the Center, how many
     out-of-home living arrangements had this child had
     (including voluntary and involuntary placements of one
     day or more) (**check one only**)?

_____ None   _____ 5–9

_____ 1   _____ 10 or more

_____ 2–4   _____ Not known

Mother or surrogate

35. Relationship to victim _____

36. Race _____   Birthdate _____

37. Last grade completed _____

38. Number of vocational training years _____

39. Occupation (list up to three positions—most recent first, and briefly describe duties) _____

    _____

    How long in current position? __ weeks __ months
    __ years

40. Number of job changes in last five years _____

41. Chronic diseases or handicapping conditions _____

    _____

42. Substance abuse: _____ alcohol _____ drugs _____ not
    applicable

    Is this related to sexual abuse?

Mother's impression _____

Father's impression _____

Evaluator's impression _____

43. Married:

_____ No

_____ Yes   How long? _____ months _____ years

Number of previous marriages _____

44. Previous legal involvements:

_____ Arrests   Date _____

Status _____

_____ Criminal Court   Date _____

Status _____

_____ Civil Court   Date _____

Status _____

45. Was mother sexually abused as a child?   __ Yes   __ No

Specifics of age, perpetrator, duration, treatment _____

_____

_____

46. Was mother a parent loss as a child? ___ Yes ___ No

    Type _____ At what age? _____

47. Was mother physically abused or neglected as a child?

    ___ Yes ___ No   Specifics of age, perpetrator, duration,

    treatment: _____

    _____

48. Mother is or has been in therapy:

    _____ Currently   Type _____

    _____ Past   Type _____

49. Was mother's treatment court ordered?

    _____ Yes _____ No

50. Was mother sentenced to jail as a result of this sexual

    abuse?

    _____ Yes _____ No

51. Were criminal charges filed against mother as a result of
    this sexual abuse? _____ Yes _____ No

52. Mother's perception of the quality of the marriage _____

    _____

53. Mother's perception of the quality and frequency of the

    sexual relationship with spouse _____

    _____

54. Mother's account of the alleged sexual abuse _____

    _____

    _____

55. Mother's response to disclosure of incest _____

    _____

56. Mother's explanation at the time she first began
    receiving Center services for sexual abuse (**check one
    only**):

    _____ Accepts responsibility

    _____ States another person was the maltreater (other
          information confirms lack of involvement of this
          client)

    _____ Cites extenuating circumstances

        _____ States sexual abuse was accidental

        _____ States sexual abuse resulted from lack of
              knowledge

        _____ States she was not responsible for behavior
              due to psychological state at time of sexual
              abuse

_____ States sexual abuse was a response to provocation of seduction on the part of the child

_____ States sexual abuse was the result of household situation and pressures beyond her control

_____ Denial or disclaimer

    _____ Declines or refuses to give explanation

    _____ States that no sexual abuse occurred

    _____ States that she has no knowledge of

    _____ States another person was the maltreater (but other information suggests that this mother was in fact involved in abuse or neglect)

_____ Assertion of parental right

    _____ States child deserved sexual abuse as punishment

    _____ States sexual abuse is assertion of legitimate parental rights

    _____ States sexual abuse was an expression of affection

    _____ States sexual abuse was an attempt to educate sexually

_____ Not known

57. Degree to which mother acknowledged harm done to child by sexual abuse (indicate extent of acknowledgement by mother at the time she first began receiving Center services (**check one only**):

_____ Denied or failed to recognize actual or potential abuse

_____ Partially acknowledged or tended to minimize actual or potential harm

_____ Acknowledged actual or potential harm

_____ Not known

58. Initial attitude of mother toward accepting Center services (**check one only**):

_____ Reluctant, nominal compliance

_____ Willing, readily accepts

59. Mother's relative motivation to change self or environment such that abuse (or high risk) does not recur (**check one only**):

_____ More motivated than most other mothers in sexual abuse program

_____ About as motivated as most other mothers in sexual abuse program

_____ Less motivated than most other mothers in sexual abuse program

_____ Not able to assess

In items 60 through 68 below, you are asked to indicate the mother's level of functioning in a number of specified problem areas. Please check **one box only** for each item.

	No problem	Mild or moderate problem	Severe problem	Not known or not applicable
60. Lack of knowledge regarding child development	_____	_____	_____	_____
61. Inaccurate sense of child's needs	_____	_____	_____	_____
62. Excessive need for child to obey commands or comply with parental wishes	_____	_____	_____	_____
63. Inappropriate expectations that the child should care for the adult(s) or otherwise assume adult responsibilities	_____	_____	_____	_____

64. Inability to handle routine child-related, household, and family responsibilties _____ _____ _____ _____

65. Inability to manage anger appropriately _____ _____ _____ _____

66. Presence of sexual dysfunction _____ _____ _____ _____

67. Low self-esteem _____ _____ _____ _____

68. Debilitating psychological disorder _____ _____ _____ _____

69. Clinical judgment of likelihood of future maltreatment by this mother of following categories of abuse:

    S = sexual abuse   P = physical abuse   E = emotional abuse

    _____ Very likely   _____ Very unlikely

    _____ Somewhat likely   _____ Unable to assess

    _____ Somewhat unlikely

70. Was mother involved in any other type of abuse/neglect with victim?

    _____ Emotional.   Explain type and duration _____

    _____

    _____ Physical.   Explain type and duration _____

    _____

    _____ Neglect.   Explain type and duration _____

    _____

71. Has mother ever been involved in extramarital relationship(s)?

    _____ No

    _____ Yes.   When?   What did it mean to her? _____

    _____

Father or surrogate

72. Relationship to victim _____

73. Race _____   Birthdate _____

74. Last grade completed _____

75. Number of vocational training years _____

76. Occupation (list up to three positions, most recent first and briefly describe duties) _____

    _____

77. How long in current position? __ weeks __ months __ years

78. Number of job changes in last five years _____

79. Chronic diseases or handicapping conditions _____

_____

80. Substance abuse: __ alcohol __ drugs __ not applicable

    Is this related to sexual abuse?

    Mother's impression _____

    Father's impression _____

    Evaluator's impression _____

81. Married:

    _____ No

    _____ Yes. How long? _____ months _____ years

    Number of previous marriages _____

82. Previous legal involvements:

    _____ Arrests Date _____

           Status _____

    _____ Criminal Court Date _____

Status _____

___ Civil Court   Date _____

Status _____

83. Was father sexually abused as a child? ___ Yes ___ No

Specifics of age, perpetrator, duration, treatment _____

_____

_____

84. Was father a parent loss as a child? ___ Yes ___ No

Type _____   At what age? _____

85. Was father physically abused or neglected as a child?

_____ Yes _____ No Specifics of age, perpetrator, dura-

tion, treatment _____

86. Father is or has been in therapy:

_____ Currently   Type _____

_____ Past   Type _____

87. Was father's treatment court ordered?
     _____ Yes _____ No

88. Was father sentenced to jail as a result of this sexual
     abuse?
     _____ Yes _____ No

89. Were criminal charges filed against father as a result of this sexual abuse? _____ Yes _____ No

90. Father's perception of the quality of the marriage _____

_____

91. Father's perception of the quality and frequency of the sexual relationship with spouse _____

_____

92. Father's account of the alleged sexual abuse _____

_____

_____

93. Father's response to disclosure of incest _____

_____

94. Father's explanation at the time he first began receiving Center services for sexual abuse (**check one only**):

_____ Accepts responsibility

_____ States another person was the maltreater (other information confirms lack of involvement of this father)

_____ Cites extenuating circumstances

_____ States sexual abuse was accidental

_____ States sexual abuse resulted from lack of knowledge

_____ States he was not responsible for behavior due to psychological state at time of sexual abuse

_____ States sexual abuse was a response to provocation or seduction on the part of the child

_____ States sexual abuse was the result of household situation and pressures beyond his control

_____ Denial or disclaimer

_____ Declines or refuses to give explanation

_____ States that no sexual abuse occurred

_____ States that he has no knowledge of sexual abuse

_____ States another person was the maltreater (but other information suggests that this father was in fact involved in abuse or neglect)

_____ Assertion of parental right

_____ States child deserved sexual abuse as punishment

_____ States sexual abuse is assertion of legitimate parental rights

_____ States sexual abuse was an expression of affection

_____ States sexual abuse was an attempt to educate sexually

_____ Not known

95. Degree to which father acknowledged harm done to child by sexual abuse (indicate extent of acknowledgement by father at the time he first began receiving Center services (**check one only**):

_____ Denied or failed to recognize actual or potential abuse

_____ Partially acknowledged or tended to minimize actual or potential harm

_____ Acknowledged actual or potential harm

_____ Not known

96. Initial attitude of father toward accepting Center services (**check one only**):

_____ Reluctant, nominal compliance

_____ Willing, readily accepts

97. Father's relative motivation to change self or environment such that abuse (or high risk) does not recur (**check one only**):

_____ More motivated than most other fathers in sexual abuse program

_____ About as motivated as most other fathers in sexual
abuse program

_____ Less motivated than most other fathers in sexual
abuse program

_____ Not able to assess

In items 98 through 107 below, you are asked to indicate the
client's level of functioning in a number of specified problem
areas. Please check **one box only** for each item

	No problem	Mild or moderate problem	Severe problem	Not known or not applicable
98. Lack of knowledge re-garding child development	_____	_____	_____	_____
99. Inaccurate sense of child's needs	_____	_____	_____	_____
100. Excessive need for child to obey com-mands or comply with parental wishes	_____	_____	_____	_____

101. Inappropriate expectations that the child should care for the adult(s) or otherwise assume adult responsibilities _____ _____ _____ _____

102. Inability to handle routine child-related, household, and family responsibilities _____ _____ _____ _____

103. Inability to manage anger appropriately _____ _____ _____ _____

104. Presence of sexual dysfunction _____ _____ _____ _____

105. Low self-esteem _____ _____ _____ _____

106. Debilitating psychological disorder _____ _____ _____ _____

107. Clinical judgment of likelihood of future maltreatment

by this father of following categories of abuse:

S = sexual abuse   P = physical abuse   E = emotional
abuse

_____ Very likely   _____ Very unlikely

_____ Somewhat likely   _____ Unable to assess

_____ Somewhat
unlikely

108. Has father ever been involved in extramarital relation-
ship(s)?

     _____ No

     _____ Yes.   When?   What did it mean to him? _____

Family

109. Who has primary responsibility for the household finances (relationship to child)? _____

110. Total household income _____

111. Are members of this household receiving public assistance of any sort? _____ Yes _____ No _____ Not
known

112. Any family member (other than father, mother) reported
for CA/N or sexual abuse to a mandated agency prior to
current report:
Date _____   Relationship to child _____

Specifics _____

_____

113. Household in rural or urban setting?

_____ Rural (community under 5,000) _____ Urban

114. Was there marital collusion in alleged sexual abuse? (Give specifics.)

*Child's impression _____

Mother's impression _____

Father's impression _____

Evaluator's impression _____

115. Was there sibling collusion? (State how siblings could have been aware but failed tell.)

_____

_____

116. Sleeping arrangements in household _____

_____

117. Multiple incest within family (i.e., other siblings, multiple perpetrators)? Explain: _____

_____

* Remember that this question is asked of the child.

In items 118 through 133 you are asked to indicate the family's level of functioning in a number of specified areas. Please check **one box only** for each item.

Attribute of family household

		No problem	Moderate or mild problem	Severe problem	Not known or not applicable
118.	Financial difficulties	_____	_____	_____	_____
119.	Physical violence between adult spouses or partners	_____	_____	_____	_____
120.	Disruptive conflict between adult spouses or partners	_____	_____	_____	_____
121.	Detachment between adult spouses or partners	_____	_____	_____	_____
122.	Sexual dysfunction between adult spouses or partners	_____	_____	_____	_____

123. Physical violence between siblings   _____ _____ _____ _____

124. Disruptive conflict between siblings   _____ _____ _____ _____

125. Disruptive conflict among members of extended family _____ _____ _____ _____

126. Social isolation, lack of extended family   _____ _____ _____ _____

127. Substance abuse on part of adult household member   _____ _____ _____ _____

128. Disrupting mental illness of household member   _____ _____ _____ _____

129. Role reversal between parents and children   _____ _____ _____ _____

130. Parents pow-
     erless over
     children   _____ _____ _____ _____

131. Lack of fam-
     ily cohesion _____ _____ _____ _____

132. Symbiotic
     family
     cohesion   _____ _____ _____ _____

133. Other (spec-
     ify) _____ _____ _____ _____ _____

Items 134 through 141 below refer to family stresses. Please indicate whether each occurred during the time in which abuse or
neglect took place, or up to a year prior to that time. Check **one
box only** for each item.

Stress affecting family household	Occurred	Did not occur	Not known or not applicable
134. Job difficulties, loss of job	_____	_____	_____
135. Disrupting physical illness of household member	_____	_____	_____
136. Death of close family member	_____	_____	_____
137. Divorce or separation	_____	_____	_____

138. Change of resi-
     dence   _____   _____   _____

139. Residence in sub-
     standard housing   _____   _____   _____

140. Pregnancy, new
     baby   _____   _____   _____

141. Other (specify) ___   _____   _____   _____

In items 142 through 146, please indicate any attributes of the
family or household which represent particular strengths which
assist successful clinical treatment. **Check all that apply.**

	Yes	No	Not known
142. Good economic situation (fi-nances, employment)	___	___	_____
143. Good relationship between adult spouses or partners	___	___	_____
144. Strong family cohesion	___	___	_____
145. Supportive network of extended family, friends	___	___	_____
146. Other (specify) _____	___	___	_____

SEXUAL MISTREATMENT PROGRAM

Psychosocial Interview Format for Natural Parents

First Interview: Focuses on Parent

Introduction

Explain that child has been referred for treatment, explain content of referral, and ask for parent's understanding of incident.

Explain purpose of this interview, i.e., obtaining background and understanding of family for treatment.

Recognize parents' feelings; ask for permission to continue with interview.

History of Childhood

1. Parents and siblings
2. Who did they live with
3. Relationships—positive and negative
4. Losses and separations
5. Traumatic events
6. Injuries, self and siblings
   Specifically ask about bruises, broken bones, burns, suffocation, drowning, and by whom
7. Discipline
   Way in which disciplined, i.e., talked to, scolded, shamed, threatened, isolated, grounded, spanked with hands, spanked with object, whipped or beaten
   Was discipline reasonable or unreasonable
   Was parent disciplined more harshly or less harshly than siblings
   Who disciplined
8. Sexual experiences
   Ages, types of experience, by whom, feelings about

Feelings about opposite sex
Feelings about same sex
Sex education
9. Social behavior
See if there is joy, list of pleasure activities
Job history, success
10. Lifelines
Degree of isolation, close friends, frequency of contact
Available avenues of rescue
11. Marital history
12. View of self, "what would you like to change?"
13. Current situation
Family composition
Job
Home
Relationship with social services re child, visiting, court
14. Explanation of treatment program

Second Interview: Focused on Child

Parental Information about Child

1. Pediatric history of child
Health
If applicable, sex education for child, onset of menses, developmental stages, or other milestones
Diet
Sleep
Previous diagnosis
2. Parents' Rating Scale of Child (page 254)
3. Interview about parents' perception of child, use of discipline, areas of difficulty
4. Parents' impression of child's school adjustment and performance
5. Parents' impression of child's peer relationships
6. Obtain releases if necessary
7. Reexplain and reoffer treatment program

CHILDREN'S RATING SCALE

Parent Questionnaire

Behavior Traits

1. Describe (*name of child*). Could you tell me what he's like?

_____

_____

_____

_____

_____

_____

2. What does (*name of child*) like to do?

_____

_____

_____

3. What do you and (*name of child*) enjoy doing together?

_____

_____

_____

4.   What does he/she do well?

_____

_____

_____

5.   At what age has (*name of child*) been the greatest problem to you?

_____

6.   At what age was (*name of child*) the easiest to get along with?

_____

INTERVIEW OUTLINE FOR
CHILDREN AND ADOLESCENTS
(age 5 and up)

Gradual transitions should be made between each area of information.

1. *School*
   Friends—both male and female
   Favorite subjects
   Likes and dislikes
   Preference of what to do for fun

2. *Family*
   a. Siblings—how many, descriptions, relationships with, changes in relationships, likes and dislikes
   b. Parents—where living, descriptions, relationships with, changes in relationships, likes and dislikes
      Parental behavior when angry and how this makes child feel
      Discipline methods and how child feels about these
      Parental signs of affection to child, description and feelings of child

3. *Sexual experiences and development*
   a. Knowledge about and experience with sexual behavior
      When first started to develop
      Who has shown or told them about sexuality
   b. Knowledge of own body
      Feelings in the past
      Feelings now
   c. Masturbation
      How
      When

How often
Feelings about

4. *Losses and separations*
   a. Through death or moves who have they lost
   b. When and what happened
   c. Who helped them deal with feeling

5. *Traumatic events*
   a. Nature
   b. How dealt with

6. *Self and emotional response*
   a. What brings joy? Sadness? Anger?
   b. What like about self
   c. What dislike about self
   d. What would change if they could

7. *Isolation and support*
   a. Who close to
   b. Who can talk to
   c. Who can turn to for help

FORMAT FOR DIAGNOSTIC EVALUATION OF SEXUALLY MALTREATED LATENCY-AGE CHILDREN

Latency-age children entering treatment groups at the C. Henry Kempe National Center for the Prevention and Treatment of Child Abuse and Neglect are diagnostically evaluated prior to their entrance into the group.

Purpose of the Evaluation

The purpose of the evaluation is twofold: (1) to introduce the child to the Center, both to the physical surroundings and to the group leaders; and (2) to obtain diagnostic information about the child, including how the child is able to relate to the examiner, coping styles, level of anxiety, child's role in the family, family relationships, and ability to use group treatment. The evaluation here described consists of an interview, a questionnaire, and a drawing by the child. In some programs, a child psychiatrist may see the child for one or more interviews instead, particularly if individual treatment is also being offered, or if sufficient prior evaluation has not been done for diagnostic purposes. Use of the questionnaires and sentence completion test are helpful in learning about these children as a group for research purposes, as well as in individual planning for them.

Since it is likely that most of the children who will be considered for group membership have been through a variety of examinations, i.e., court appearances, psychological testing, gynecological examinations, police questioning, social work interviews, and so on, a primary goal of the diagnostic evaluation should be to introduce the child in a nonthreatening way to the Center. The child should have the opportunity to see the physical setting and meet the group leaders. This decreases the child's anxiety and facilitates acceptance of the therapeutic group.

Diagnostic information is used to assess the child's need and ability to use group treatment as a therapeutic modality. Children with good ego strengths who do not appear to need further treatment are screened out. Children who are psychotic or are too infantile are also not accepted in the group. Reports of previous evaluations are reviewed, and additional testing, for example, arranged if needed.

Format of the Evaluation

The child is brought to the Center by the foster mother, natural parent, or social worker. The child and mother (or parents) are observed when together and details of their interactions noted throughout the course of evaluation and treatment. Such observations should become part of the child's clinical record because they may be discrepant from, or amplify, history and interview information. The group leader whom the child has already met introduces the evaluator to the child.

The Center is housed in a comfortable old rambling house with a kitchen and since there is a cook on the staff, it provides an ideal environment for nurturance. This nurturing atmosphere is utilized by inviting the child to come into the kitchen for cookies and milk and spending a few minutes to chat. The child is then taken downstairs, shown the audio-video room and the one-way mirror where the camera person will be filming. The child is shown the examination room through the one-way mirror. The evaluator explains the filming and offers to show the child himself/herself on videotape after the evaluation. The child is shown the playroom where the group diagnostic sessions are held, then taken into the examination room. The examination room is set up as shown below:

The child is directed to sit in the chair facing the one-way mirror, and the examiner sits in the chair slightly to the side.

The examiner begins by saying, "This is the room you and I will be in today. Did anyone tell you why you came here today?"

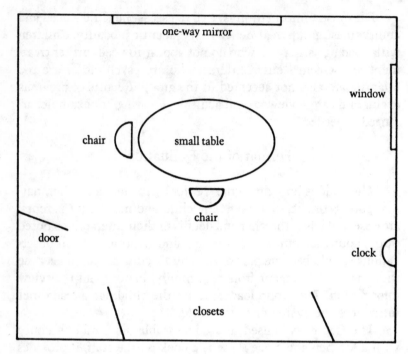

The examiner then reexplains that the child might be coming here for a group with other children and that they would be talking, playing, and eating during the group meetings. The child is reminded of the two group leaders he/she had met previously and is told that in the group the children will talk about their feelings, some of which will be happy and some sad. The examiner explains that before any child goes to the group the leaders and examiner want to have a chance to know the child a little better and for the child to know them better too. The examiner then attempts to elicit some of the child's feelings about coming to the evaluation. Subsequently, the examiner attempts to engage the child in the examination by saying, "You and I will be talking today and drawing some pictures so that I can get to know you a little better. I'm going to need you to help me. I hope you will be willing to do that."

If the child is not ready, some time is given so the child can walk around and explore the room. In cases where the child is extremely anxious, the examiner may open the closet where there is a doll house and allow the child to play during the interview. This is felt to be important in the examination of abused children in order to gain an accurate measure of the child. The rest of the interview may be rescheduled for the second hour if need be. "Assessment conducted under rigorous standardized conditions will tend to produce inordinate anxiety in these children. . . . Evaluation procedures need to be modified in order to maintain cooperation and optimal effort with the abused child."[1]

Once the child is engaged, the examiner may administer the Conger Sentence Completion Test. The child is told, "I'm going to read some sentences to you, and I'd like you to tell me the first thing that you think of." The examiner asks for clarification or elaboration, as well as giving the child ample time between sentences if necessary. The Schaeffer Children's Reports of Parental Behavior are also given, in one form for mother and another for father.

Following the Conger Children's Sentence Completion Test, the child is asked to complete a Kinetic-Family Drawing. The examiner places one sheet of $8\frac{1}{2}'' \times 11''$ paper in front of the child with a #2 pencil with eraser in the center of the paper. The child is asked to draw a picture of "everyone in your family, including you, doing something." The child is given ample opportunity to complete the picture, and then the examiner asks the child to "tell about the picture." If the child is in a foster home, he/she is then asked to draw a picture of the foster family or whichever family he/she has not drawn previously.

The completion of this task ends the first evaluation session. The child is encouraged and thanked for his/her participation,

---

[1] Harold P. Martin and M. Rodeheffer, Problems in developmental assessment. In H. P. Martin (Ed.), *The Abused Child: A Multidisciplinary Approach to Developmental Issues and Treatment.* Cambridge, Massachusetts: Ballinger Publishing Co., 1976, p. 122.

and the examiner explains that the child will come back for one more session in the same room. The timing of the different parts of the evaluation interview, play, questionnaires, and drawings depends upon the child's response, but ordinarily it takes two sessions. The child is again offered a cookie to eat or take with him/her as he/she departs.

APPENDIX 3

EDUCATIONAL MATERIALS ON CHILD SEXUAL ABUSE

A number of excellent publications and audio visual materials useful to children, parents' groups, teachers and professionals are now readily available, and many are most helpful in trying to prevent child sexual abuse by providing children at all age levels and their families and advocates some very well written and produced materials in a field where prevention remains our best hope.

A. MATERIAL FOR CHILDREN AND ADOLESCENTS

Publications

He Told Me not to Tell, Jennifer Fay, 1979. King County Rape Relief, 305 South 43rd Ave., Renton, Washington, 480554. $1.50, 28 pp. A brief booklet informing children at age-appropriate levels about sexual abuse and ways to avoid abuse.

My Very Own Special Body Book, Cary Bassett, 1981. Hawthorne Press, P.O. Box 3910, Redding, California 96049. $2.95 plus shipping and handling. Information about sexual abuse and incest, family roles, and how to protect oneself. Illustrated, to be read to children.

Once I Was a Little Bit Frightened, Joy Williams, 1980. Rape and Crisis Center, P.O. Box 1655, Fargo, N.D. 58107. $3.00 plus $1.00 postage and handling, 15 pp. Illustrated booklet which encourages children to talk about sexual abuse they may be experiencing. Of help to professionals to identify the child who has already experienced abuse, but cryptic and vague for a child who has not.

Red Light, Green Light People, Joy Williams. Rape and Abuse Crisis Center, P.O. Box 1655, Fargo, N.D. 58107. $3.00 plus $1.00 for postage and handling. Coloring book for children which describes child molestation by helping children to think about feelings they have about touch and to recognize the difference between appropriate and inappropriate touch. Also presents information on what a child should do in a threatening situation.

Bubbylonian Encounter, Gene Mackay, Theater for Young America, Inc. NCPCA Kansas Chapter, 214 W. 6th St., Suite 301, Topeka, Kansas 66603. Available by request. Theater script or videotape play for children ages 8–13.

Audiovisual Materials

Speak Up, Say No (filmstrip/color/6 minutes). Krause House, P.O. Box 880, Oregon City, Oregon 97045. $40. Best used with younger children, ages 3–6, this is a presentation which explains, in cartoon format, the problem of child sexual abuse. Based on research which indicates that small children identify more readily with animals than with human models, the film

---

* This title, and all others so marked, is available by reservation, from C. Henry Kempe Center, 1205 Oneida Street, Denver, CO 80220, rental at $12.00, plus mailing.

portrays Penelope Mouse, who is victimized by her Uncle Mouse Sid. Although the cartoon is clear about what sexual abuse is, the rhymed narration seems forced and sing-song, possibly patronizing to children. Youngsters over 8 or 9 will probably find the format silly. The description of the mice's home indicates that Penelope has her own room and even her own telephone and consequently subtly biases the film strip toward the middle and upper classes. Although this segment is intended to encourage children to recognize their privacy needs, there are ways to discuss privacy with children that do not exclude youngsters from less affluent families. The teacher's guide which accompanies this presentation is excellent and does fill in some of the particulars missing from the strip itself. Teachers are encouraged to discuss more specifically what privacy is, things a child might not want to share (including one's body), the kind of feeling which often signals that touch is inappropriate, and what to do in such situations. The guide also helps teachers understand that, unlike Penelope, many sexually abused children are not protected by their parents. It is suggested that teachers have a responsibility to find help for the child and family when they become aware of such cases. The film strip has the advantage of being relatively inexpensive and will be useful in the hands of the sensitive teacher who follows the advice of the teaching guide. If shown in schools, any prevention materials will be best used under the supervision of the school social worker or psychologist who is familiar with the issues involved in sexual abuse or incest.

*Who Do you Tell? (16 mm/color/11 minutes). MTI Teleprograms, Inc., 3710 Commercial Ave., Northbrook, Illinois 60062. $250. Through animation and discussion with children, the film explains how the young viewer can use supportive adults when she/he is confused or threatened by such dangers as a house fire, being lost, family violence, or sexual abuse. In its attempt not to frighten and to touch all bases, the film addresses child molestation only superficially. Teachers or others who use this film should provide additional information to the child and facilitate a more thorough discussion of the problem of sexual abuse. Although produced for children ages 7–12, this film has been used successfully with kindergarten children, and, in fact, may be most appropriate for the younger child.

*No More Secrets (16 mm/color/13 minutes). ODN Productions, Inc., 74 Varick St., Suite 304, New York, N.Y. 10013. (212)431-8923. One of the most tastefully prepared films on sexual abuse for the *grade school audience*. During an afternoon of play, a few friends exchange uneasy confidences about personal experiences they have had with abuse. As they talk among themselves, animated vignettes depict the problems in an explicit but not alarming way. The children speculate about possible solutions, and agree to speak up and seek help from trusted adults. The film gives children the knowledge that some touching is inappropriate and provides the language to help themselves and others work through solutions to a sensitive problem.

*Child Molestation: When to Say No (16 mm/color/13 minutes). Aims Instructional Media Service, Inc., 625 Justin Ave., Glendale, California, 91201. $220. Probably most useful with children *over 8*. In contrast to *Who Do you Tell?* this film discusses sexual abuse directly without sensationalizing or deliberately frightening the audience. Children are shown the kind of adult attention they should reject and why. Four episodes illustrate different children in the least to most threatening of attempted sexual abuse encounters. The actors model techniques for successfully rebuffing advances, and the audience will hopefully incorporate the suggestions for handling the situations and gain the confidence to say, "No." A prominent emphasis is that child molesters are "crazy, sick-in-the-head-weirdos." Although simplistic enough for children to understand, this message potentially contradicts the film's recurrent warning to be wary of everyone. Most children will not classify their own relatives, who might hurt them, as weirdos.

Girls Beware (16 mm/color/12 minutes). DACOM Communications Media, Inc. 626 Justin Ave., Glendale, California 91201, $215.

Boys Beware (16 mm/color/14 minutes) DACOM Communications Media, Inc. 626 Justin Ave., Glendale, CA 91201, $250. Both of these prevention films are suitable for adolescents. These films examine the subtle choices teenagers must make to protect themselves from sexual assault. In addition, the films briefly restate the traditional warnings against hitchhiking and other common risks, without neglecting the more disturbing problem of sexual abuse by relatives and family friends.

Boys Beware depicts three boys in different situations where attempted sexual assaults by adult men take place. Two vignettes illustrate how a stranger might gain a boy's confidence and then attempt to victimize him. The last segment portrays a boy who was sexually approached by his trusted baseball coach and neighbor. The boy decides, after agonizing deliberation, to tell his parents.

Girls Beware demonstrates the dangers of accepting flattery and gifts from much older men at face value. The narrator suggests that normal adult men are not interested in junior-high-school age girls and asks young women to question such attention. The film goes on to look at the possibility of incest. One sequence depicts a girl who is sexually molested by her stepfather; her reactions and attempts to get help are discussed. Examples of people who might be available to help a child abuse victim are listed. Since the first person to whom an incest victim turns may deny or minimize the child's report of sexual abuse, the film is careful to remind teenagers of supportive resources of all kinds.

B. AUDIOVISUAL MATERIAL FOR ADOLESCENTS AND COMMUNITY GROUPS

Child Sexual Abuse: The Untold Secret (Video-cassette/color/30 minutes). The University of Calgary, 2500 University Drive, N.W., Calgary Alberta, Canada T2N 1N4. $250. A Canadian production which describes the many and varied difficulties incest victims face. Five adolescent victims discuss their lives. Each young woman tells about the incest she experienced and the resultant trauma. A description of the girls' families indicates that not all incestuous families are alike and that response to the broken secret, by the family and community, will have a significant effect on the amount of damage the victim suffers. Two counselors provide continuity throughout the film by elaborating on the girls' descriptions and giving general information about sexual abuse. The only flaws in the presentation are technical ones. The monologues of the children and counselors lack spontaneity; the result is a rather monotonous quality overall. Despite this, in light of the excellent information presented, these weaknesses seem insignificant. Use of this program by junior high or high schools or community education groups is highly recommended. It is especially appropriate for identified groups of incest victims.

Shatter the Silence (16 mm/or videocassette/color/29 minutes). S-L Film Productions, P.O. Box 41108, Los Angeles, California 90041. $395. A dramatic portrayal of the adolescence and young adulthood of the incest victim, Marianne. First-person narration delineates the anxiety, confusion between reality and fantasy, and emotional isolation Marianne feels. Although melodramatically presented, the feelings typical of incest victims are accurately recognized. The incest dynamics of family enmeshment, secrecy, and role confusion are also identified. The film is billed as "an educational experience directed towards young people, adults, and professionals." A major fault with the film is the producer's ambitious attempt to reach an overly broad audience—professionals may find the soap opera tone and stilted dialogue unrealistic and simplistic. Adolescent and young adult victims, however, may recognize their own experiences that are similar to those portrayed in the film. The film's subject and tendency toward exaggeration is likely to create anxiety in most audiences. However, a teacher or counselor may suspect that a child who suffers an extreme of feeling while viewing this film could be experiencing an incestuous relationship. The potential of the film to educate young people about resources for family intervention and assistance is not realized. The film's forte is in its ability to spark discussion and allow a young audience to begin exploring ways they might handle their own sexual abuse experience or that of friends.

Don't Get Stuck There (16 mm/14 minutes). Boys Town Center, Boys Town, Nebraska, 68010. Addresses adolescents concerning the types of abuse they may experience and gives them encouragement to seek help rather than to escape through drugs, running away, or suicide.

C. MATERIAL FOR TEACHERS, PARENTS AND LAY PEOPLE

Publications

No More Secrets: Protecting Your Child from Sexual Assault, Caren Adams and Jennifer Fay, 1981. Impact Publishers, P.O. Box 1094 San Louis Obisbo, California. 93406 $3.95., 95 pp. A useful paperback for parents of children under 12 intended to help parents in informing their children at age-appropriate levels about ways to prevent sexual abuse.

The Silent Children, Linda Tschirhart Sanford, 1980. Anchor Press/Doubleday, Garden City, N.Y. $12.95., 367 pp. An excellent book for parents and useful for professionals, particularly teachers. Useful in enhancing children's self-esteem, discouraging sex-role stereotyping, and encouraging parents to teach children respect of their own instincts and feelings. Also included is information about dynamics of sexual abuse and incest, family roles, and the offender, himself, in addition to how to discuss sexual abuse with children and advice from offenders who have been in treatment about how parents can protect their children.

Betrayal of Innocence: Incest and its Devastation, Susan Forward, 1978. Penquin Books, 299 Murray Hill Parkway, East Rutherford, N.J. 07030. Paperback, $3.95, 198 pp. Excellent, easy-to-read book which describes incest from the perspective of a social worker who not only treated hundreds of incest victims and families, but was a victim herself. Illustrates by analysis of case histories the author's understanding of incest dynamics and the issues victims, offenders, and family members often face. Helpful to professionals, lay people, and victims.

Conspiracy of Silence: The Trauma of Incest, Sandra Butler, 1978. New Glide Publications, Inc., 330 Ellis Street, San Francisco, California, 94102. $10.00, 208 pp. Based on hundreds of interviews with victims, aggressors, mothers, and family members, this is sensitive analyses of research of case histories. Damage that can be done by well-intentioned professionals is explored. While directed to a general audience, the research is of interest to experienced and beginning professionals in the field.

BIBLIOGRAPHY

Armstrong, L. *Kiss Daddy Tonight: A Speak-Out on Incest.* Hawthorne, New York, 1978.

Burgess, A. W., et al. (Eds.). *Sexual Assault of Children and Adolescents.* Lexington, Lexington, Mass., 1978.

De Francis, V. *Protecting the Child Victims of Sex Crimes Committed by Adults.* American Humane Association, Children's Division, Denver, Colorado, 1969.

Finkelhor, D. *Sexually Abused Children.* The Free Press, New York, 1979.

Kempe, R. S., and Kempe, C. H. *Child Abuse.* Harvard University Press (The Developing Child Series), Cambridge, Massachusetts, and Fontana Press, London, 1978.

Macdonald, J. M. *Rape: Offenders and their Victims.* Charles C Thomas, Springfield, Ill., 1971.

Masters, R. E. L. (Ed.). *Patterns of Incest.* Basic Books, New York, 1963.

Mrazek, P., and Kempe, C. H. (Eds.). *Sexually Abused Children and Their Families.* Pergamon Press, Oxford, 1981.

National Center on Child Abuse and Neglect. *Special Report Child Sexual Abuse: Incest, Assault and Sexual Exploitation.* U.S. DHHS Pub. No. (OHDS) 79-30166, Washington, D.C., 1978.

Pincus, L., and Dare, C. *Secrets in the Family.* Faber & Faber, London, 1978.

Sanford, L. *A Parent's Guide to the Prevention of Child Sexual Abuse.* Anchor Press/Doubleday, New York, 1980.

Schultz, L. G. (Ed.). *Rape Victimology.* Charles C Thomas, Springfield, Ill., 1975.

Wells, H. M. *The Sensuous Child: Your Child's Birthright to Healthy Sexual Development.* (A guideline for parents). Scarborough, Stein & Day, New York, 1976.

Audiovisual

Incest: The Hidden Crime (16 mm/color/16 minutes). The Media Guild, % Association Film, 7838 San Fernando Road, Sun Valley, California 91352. An excellent documentary produced by CBS New Magazine Series. A journalist introduces the subject of incest, its prevalence, and the modern myths surrounding it. The reporter then begins interviewing incest offender, Chuck, his wife, Sandy, and 12-year-old daughter, Michelle. Each member of the incest triangle discusses his or her feelings about the incest and the history of its occurrence. Clarifying remarks by skilled therapists who treat such families are interspersed throughout the movie to highlight typical individual and family dynamics as well as treatment options. The most disturbing aspect of the film is the interview with Michelle. She vacillates between her intellectual understanding of her father's responsibility for the incest and her fear that her sexual curiosity and questions were to blame. Interviewing a real family makes this a superb educational film. Yet are we again exploiting the child victim by asking her to reveal her feelings to the world? CBS does attempt to soothe our qualms about this by asking Michelle why she agreed to participate; she replies, "So that maybe this won't happen to another girl." This film successfully outlines the major points about incest to the general public as well as the uninitiated professional. Especially important are the practical suggestions about how a family can prevent incest and sexual abuse.

*Incest: The Victim Nobody Believes (Videocassette or 16 mm/color/21 minutes). MTI Teleprograms, Inc., 3710 Commercial Ave., Northbrook, Ill. 60062. $440. This film allows the audience to join the conversation of three women, all sexually abused as children. The women candidly discuss their experiences, and through their interactions this film subtly indicates different stages of resolving the feelings of depression and rage that they have felt. This motion picture is excellent as an impetus for discussion.

D. MATERIAL FOR STUDENTS AND PROFESSIONALS

Publications

The Broken Taboo: Sex in the Family, Blair and Justice, 1979, Human Sciences Press, 72 Fifth Avenue, New York, N.Y. 10011. Paperback, $8.75, 304 pp. Provides basic information

---

* Available by reservation, from C. Henry Kempe Center, 1205 Oneida Street, Denver, Co 80220, rental at $12.00 plus handling.

about incest: the dynamics, causes, consequences, and intervention at the family and societal levels.

Child Sexual Abuse: Incest, Assault, and Sexual Exploitation, Richard Roth, 1978. Superintendent of Documents, U.S. Government Printing Office, Washington, D.C. 20402. DHHS Pub. No. (OHDS) 81-30166. 22 pp. Outlines research findings on child sexual abuse and gives general information about intervention and treatment approaches.

Child Sexual Abuse, The British Association for the Study and Prevention of Child Abuse and Neglect, 1981. John Pickett, 30 Bankfield Lane, Norden, Rochdale, Lanc., England 0L1 5RS. 13 pp. A small pamphlet designed to give a most concise and general overview of the problem in England. Designed for students and those professionals who wish to have an introduction.

Understanding Sexual Child Abuse, Vol. 1, Gary May, 1978. The National Committee for the Prevention of Child Abuse, Suite 510, 111 East Wacker Drive, Chicago, Ill. 60601. $3.00, 31 pp. Basic information of types of incest and sexual abuse and describes research regarding the offender, family, and child victim.

Dealing with Sexual Abuse, Vol. 2, Jo Ensminger, 1978. The National Committee for the Prevention of Child Abuse, Suite 1250, 332 South Michigan Ave., Chicago, Ill. 60604. 33 pp. Brief articles for the professional who has had limited experience in child sexual abuse cases. Information on the legal, medical, social work, psychotherapeutic, and team aspects of sexual abuse treatment are outlined.

Incest: Confronting the Silent Crime, A Manual for Educators, Law Enforcement, Medical, Human Services and Legal Personnel, Linda Muldoon, 1980. Minnesota Program for Victims of Sexual Assault, Documents Division, 117 University Avenue, St. Paul, Minnesota 55155. $5.00. Designed for professionals who investigate or manage sexual abuse or incest cases. Although some of the information is based on Minnesota laws, the information on identification, interviewing techniques, investigation, and intervention is helpful to those outside the state as well.

Audiovisual

*A Time for Caring: The School's Response to the Sexually Abused Child (16 mm/color/28 minutes). Lawren Productions, Inc., % G. B. Media. 333 North Flores Street, Los Angeles, California 90048. $390. An excellent film which focuses on the indicators of sexual abuse and the role and responsibility of school personnel in helping the child. Acknowledging the many responsibilities that teachers currently accept, the film suggests ways that educators can also successfully intervene in sexual abuse cases. Unfortunately, the insightful interviews with actual victims are difficult to understand due to voice-disguising techniques.

Double Jeopardy (16 mm/color/40 minutes). MIT Teleprograms, Inc., 3710 Commercial Avenue, Northbrook, Ill. 60062. $595. A good advocacy film which focuses on the insensitivity shown sexual abuse victims during long, uncoordinated investigation by community agencies and the legal system. This film follows several children through the investigation and trial process. Some receive sensitive and gentle attention from physicians, lawyers, and child advocates, while others are subjected to belittling questions and disbelief. A few scenes are deliberately overdone and amusing, indicating how the professional's anxiety can be unintentionally detrimental to the victim.

*Interviewing the Child Abuse Victim (16 mm/color/25 minutes). MTI Teleprograms, Inc., 3710 Commercial Ave., Northbrook, Ill. 60062. $435. A filmed sequence of narrated interviews of abused and neglected children. Two abused children are examined, and one of the children is interviewed in a play session by a gentle pediatrician. Especially well done is the interview, by a social worker, of a small boy left home much of the day. A teacher's sensitive intervention into the life of a sexually abused girl is exceptional. The narration is unobtrusive yet beneficial by indicating important issues. This is an excellent training resource for lawyers, nurses, police officers, guardians ad litem, or anyone working directly with children.

Sexual Abuse: The Family (16 mm/color/25 minutes). National Audio-Visual Center, U.S.A., Order Section, Washington, D.C. 20409. $150. Introduces professionals to the subject of intrafamilial sexual abuse by presenting the basic psychosocial aspects, community role, and medical interview and examination. A pediatrician, psychologist, and social worker discuss the problem of sexual abuse, the myths surrounding it, and professional intervention. A role-play example indicates potential reactions of family and victim after a sexual abuse incident. Sensitivity to the child is emphasized. Raylene Devine, M.D., (Children's Hospital Medical Center, Washington, D.C.) articulates requirements of the physical examination in a well delineated and useful manner. Despite the important information presented, this film is not a comprehensive, professional overview nor does it achieve a complete, multidisciplinary focus. The film offers relatively sophisticated instruction about the medical interview and examination while only cursorily inspecting the role of other professionals. The actual investigative role of child protection services is almost totally neglected. The physician's role in diagnosis and treatment of families and victims is thus overemphasized at the expense of portraying a multidisciplinary approach. The role-play method of instruction is successful in this film. Although an adult plays the child victim, her responses are credible, and the ethical problem in exploiting an actual victim is avoided. This film would be useful in combination with other films or a presentation by a variety of professionals.

E. ADDITIONAL BOOKS AND CHAPTER REFERENCES PRIMARILY FOR PROFESSIONALS

Books

Allen, C. *Daddy's Girl: A Memoir.* Simon & Schuster, New York, 1980.

Angelou, M. *I Know Why The Caged Bird Sings.* Random House, New York, 1970.

Armstrong, L. *Kiss Daddy Tonight: A Speak-out on Incest.* Hawthorn, New York, 1978.

Bernard, J., and Denson-Gerber, J. *Incest as a Causative Factor in Antisocial Behavior: An Explorative Study.* Odyssey Institute, New York, 1975.

Brady, K. *Father's Days. A True Story of Incest.* Seaview Books, New York, 1979.

Burgess, A. W. (Ed.). *Sexual Assault of Children and Adolescents,* Lexington Books, Lexington, Massachusetts, 1978.

Cook, M., and Howells, K. (Eds.). *Adult Sexual Interest in Children.* Academic Press, London and New York, 1981.

De Francis, V. *Protecting the Child Victims of Sex Crimes Committed by Adults.* American Humane Association, Children's Division, Denver, Colorado, 1969.

Eldred, C., Burgdorf, et al. *National Study of the Incidence and Severity of Child Abuse and Neglect.* No. (OHDS) 81-30325, Government Printing Office, Washington, D.C., September, 1981.

Finkelhor, D. *Sexually Victimized Children.* The Free Press, New York, 1979.

Forward, S., and Buck C. *Betrayal of Innocence: Incest and its Devastation.* Penguin Books, New York, 1978.

Geiser, R. *Hidden Victims,* Beacon Press, Boston, 1979.

Giarretto, H. *Integrated Treatment of Child Sexual Abuse: A Treatment and Training Manual.* Science and Behavior Books, Palo Alto, California, 1982.

Goodwin, J. *Sexual Abuse: Incest Victims and their Families.* Wright PSG, Littleton, Massachusetts, 1982.

Groth, N. (Ed.). *Sexual Assault of Men and Boys.* Plenum, New York, 1982.

Helfer, R. E., and Kempe, C. H. *Child Abuse and Neglect: The Family and the Community.* Ballinger, Cambridge, Massachusetts, 1976.

Herman, J. L. *Father-Daughter Incest.* Harvard University Press, Cambridge, Massachusetts, 1981.

Kempe, C. H., and Helfer, R. E. (Eds.). *Helping the Battered Child and His Family.* Lippincott, Philadelphia, 1972.

Kempe, C. H., and Helfer, R. E. (Eds.). *The Battered Child*, Third Edition. The University of Chicago Press, Chicago and London, 1980.

Kempe, R. S., and Kempe, C. H. *Child Abuse* (Developing Child Series). Harvard University Press-Fontana, Cambridge and London, 1978.

Lloyd, R. *For Money or Love: Boy Prostitution in America.* Vanguard Press, New York, New York, 1976.

Macdonald, J. M. *Rape: Offenders and their Victims.* Charles C Thomas, Springfield, Ill., 1971.

MacFarlane, K., Jones, B., and Jenstrom, L. (Eds.). *Sexual Abuse of Children: Selected Readings.* National Center on Child Abuse and Neglect, OHDS, U.S. DHHS, Washington, D.C., 1980.

Masters, R. E. L. (Ed.). *Patterns of Incest.* Julian-Basic Books, Newport Beach, California, 1963.

Maisch, H. *Incest.* Stein and Day, New York, 1972

McKerrow, W. D., *Protecting the Sexually Abused Child.* American Humane Association, Denver, Colorado, 1973.

Meiselman, K. *Incest: A Psychological Study of Causes and Effects with Treatment.* Jossey/Bass, San Francisco, 1979.

Morris, M. *If I Should Die Before I Wake.* T. B. Tarcher, Boston, 1982.

Mrazek, P., and Kempe, C. H. (Eds.). *Sexually Abused Children and their Families.* Pergamon Press, Oxford, 1981.

Renvoize, J. *Incest: A Family Pattern.* Routledge & Kegan Paul, Boston and London, 1983.

Ricks, C. *Carol's Story.* Tynsdale House, Wheaton, Ill., 1981.

Rossman, P. *Sexual Experience Between Men and Boys.* Associated Press, New York, 1976.

Rush, F. *The Best Kept Secret: Sexual Abuse of Children.* Prentice Hall, Inc., Englewood Cliffs, N.J., 1980.

Schlesinger, B. *Sexual Abuse of Children: A Resource Guide and Annotated Bibliography.* University of Toronto Press, Toronto, 1982.

Schultz, L. G. (Ed.). *Rape Victimology.* Charles C Thomas, Springfield, Ill., 1975.

Sgroi, S. M. *Handbook of Clinical Intervention in Child Sexual Abuse.* Lexington, Lexington, Massachusetts, 1981.

Shore, D., and Conte, J. (Eds.). *Social Work and Child Sexual Abuse,* Haworth Press, New York, 1982.

Chapters of Special Interest

Anson, R. The last porno show. In *The Sexual Victimology of Youth.* Charles C Thomas, Springfield, Ill., 1980.

Constantine, L., The effects of early sexual experiences. In *Children and Sex,* L. L. Constantine and F. M. Martinson (Eds.). Little Brown, Boston, 1981.

Duquette, D. Liberty and lawyers in child protection. In *The Battered Child,* Third Edition, rev., C. H. Kempe and R. E. Helfer (Eds.). University of Chicago Press, Chicago and London, 1980.

Freud, A. A psychoanalyst's view of sexual abuse by parents. In *Sexually Abused Children and their Families,* P. B. Mrazek and C. H. Kempe (Eds.). Pergamon Press, Oxford and New York, 1981.

Giarretto, H. A comprehensive child sexual abuse treatment program. In: *Sexually Abused Children and their Families*, P. B. Mrazek and C. H. Kempe (Eds.). Pergamon Press, Oxford and New York, 1981.

Gottlieb, B. Incest: Therapeutic intervention in a unique form of sexual abuse. In *Rape, Sexual Assault: Management and Intervention*, Carmen Germaine Warner (Ed.). Aspen Publications, Germantown, Maryland, 1980.

Helfer, R. E., and Schmidt, R. The community-based child abuse and neglect program. In *Child Abuse and Neglect: The Family and the Community*, R. E. Helfer and C. H. Kempe (Eds.). Ballinger, Cambridge, Massachusetts, 1976.

Howell, J. N. The role of law enforcement in the prevention, investigation and treatment of child abuse. In *The Battered Child*, Third Edition, rev., C. H. Kempe and R. E. Helfer (Eds.). University of Chicago Press, Chicago and London, 1980.

Kronhausen, E., and Kronhausen, P. Pornography, the psychology of. In *The Encyclopedia of Sexual Behavior*, A. Ellis and Abarbanel (Eds.). Hawthorn Books, New York, 1961.

Mead, M. Incest. In *International Encyclopedia of Social Sciences*, 7:125. Macmillan and The Free Press, New York, 1968.

Mrazek, P. B. Definition and recognition of sexual child abuse: Historical and cultural perspectives. In *Sexuality Abused Children and their Families*, P. B. Mrazek and C. H. Kempe (Eds.). Pergamon Press, Oxford and New York, 1981.

Mrazek, D. A., and Mrazek, P. B. Psychosexual development within the family. In *Sexually Abused Children and their Families*, P. B. Mrazek and C. H. Kempe (Eds.). Pergamon Press, Oxford and New York, 1981.

Mrazek, P. B., The nature of incest: A review of contributing factors. In *Sexually Abused Children and their Families*, P. B. Mrazek and C. H. Kempe (Eds.). Pergamon Press, Oxford and New York, 1981.

Schechter, M. D., and Roberge, L. Sexual exploitation. In *Child Abuse and Neglect: The Family and the Community*, R. E. Helfer and C. H. Kempe (Eds.). Ballinger, Cambridge, Massachusetts, 1976.

Shay, S. W. Community council for child abuse prevention. In *The Battered Child*, Third Edition, rev., C. H. Kempe and R. E. Helfer (Eds.). University of Chicago Press, Chicago and London, 1980.

Steele, B. F., and Alexander, H. Effects of sexual abuse in children. In *Sexually Abused Children and their Families*, P. B. Mrazek and C. H. Kempe (Eds.). Pergamon Press, Oxford and New York, 1981.

Other Publications

Baker, C. Preying on playgrounds: The sexploitation of children in pornography and prostitution. *Pepperdine Law Rev.* 4:809–849, 1978.

Bulkley, J. *Recommendations for Improving Legal Intervention in Intrafamily Child Sexual Abuse Cases*. National Resource Center for Child Advocacy and Protection, American Bar Association, Washington, D.C., 1982.

Burges, G., and McCausland, M. Child sex initiation rings. *Am. J. Orthopsychiatry* 51:110–119, 1981.

Cantwell, H. B. Sexual abuse of children in Denver, 1979: Reviewed with implications for pediatric intervention and possible prevention. *Child Abuse & Neglect, The International Journal.* 5:2, 75–85, 1982.

Cantwell, H. D. Vaginal inspection as it relates to child sexual abuse in girls under thirteen. *Child Abuse & Neglect* 7:2, 171–176, 1983.

Congressional Hearings on Child Pornography and Prostitution. "Pornography and Child Prostitution." United States House of Representatives, Ser. #12, 95th Congress, 1st Session. Government Printing Office, Washington, D.C., 1977. United States Congress, Senate Judiciary Committee, Subcommittee on Juvenile Justice, "Exploitation of Children," Hearing, 97th Congress, 1st Session, November 5, 1981. Government Printing Office, Washington, D.C., 1981. Pp. 1–165.

Davidson, H. *Child Sexual Exploitation: Background and Legal Analysis*, National Legal Resource Center for Child Advocacy and Protection, American Bar Association, Washington, D.C., 1981.

Eldred, C., Burgdorf, et al. *Study Findings: National Study of the Incidence and Severity of Child Abuse and Neglect.* DHHS Publications NO (OHDS) 81-30325. Government Printing Office, Washington, D.C., Sept., 1981.

Nash, D. Legal issues related to child pornography. *Legal Response: Child Advocacy and Protection.* 2:2, 8–9, 1981.

National Center on Child Abuse and Neglect. *Sexual Abuse of Children: Selected Readings.* U.S. Dept. of Health and Human Services, DHHS Pub. No. (OHDS) 78-30161, Washington, D.C., 1980.

National Center on Child Abuse and Neglect, *Special Report Child Sexual Abuse: Incest, Assault and Sexual Exploitation.* US DHHS Pub. No. (OHDS) 79-30166, Washington, D.C., 1978.

Solheim, J. S., and Johnson, E. L. *When a Child Needs You: Emergency Intervention for Law Enforcement Officers.* Kempe National Center Publication, Denver, Colorado, 1983.

Wilson, J. Violence, pornography and social science. *The Public Interest.* Winter, 1971, 45–61.

Publications of

American Humane Society, 5351 S. Roslyn Street, Englewood, Colorado 80111.

C. Henry Kempe National Center for the Prevention and Treatment of Child Abuse and Neglect, 1205 Oneida St., Denver, Colorado 80220.

CHILDHELP-USA, 6463 Independence Ave., Woodland Hills, California 91367.

National Committee for the Prevention of Child Abuse and Neglect, Suite 1250, 332 South Michigan Avenue, Chicago, Illinois 60604.

Parents United, P.O. Box 952, San Jose, California 95108.

INDEX

Achievement Tests, 132
Alcoholics Anonymous, 181, 200
Alexander, H., 178, 189

Bender, L., 193
Bentovim, A., 9

Cantwell, H. B., 15, 17, 108
Castration, 142
Chaotic family, 51, 52, 134
Child Abuse Prevention &
    Treatment Act of 1974, 82
Child Protection Teams, 94
Clergy, 175, 200
Conger, J. J., 133
Courts
    criminal, 82, 84, 89, 176
    family & juvenile, 82, 84, 89,
        167, 168, 206
Criminal diversion program, 89,
    149, 206, appendix 2
Criminal prosecution, 146, 179,
    206, appendix 1

Daughter & Sons United, 165,
    177
Davoren, B., 178
Day care centers, 163
District attorneys, 86, 89, 94

Educational materials, appendix 3

Exhibitionism, 11, 25, 26
    treatment of, 119, 120

Finkelhor, D., 21, 176
Forms
    case records, appendix 2
    evaluation, appendix 2
Freud, A., 278
Freud, S., 202

Giaretto, H., 14, 19, 157, 164,
    176–179
Guardian-ad-litem, 84

Henfler, R. E., 108

Incest, 47–49
    adolescent victim, 79, 167,
        appendix 2
    definition of, 10
    early onset, 53–58, 160–164,
        appendix 2
    evaluation of, 144–152
    family therapy, 153, 168
    father-daughter, 48–51
    fathers group homes, 149
    homosexual, 72–74
    individual therapy, 168
    intelligence, 19–20
    late treatment, 174
    mother-son, 68–72

peer group therapy, 173
racial differences, 19
school age onset, 58–66, 164–
  167, appendix 2
self help groups, 155
sibling, 74–79, 174
socioeconomic status, 18–19
treatment, 153, 187
Indecent exposure, 11, 25
Intelligence tests, 132
Intrafamilial abuse, 47–79

James, J., 196
Judges, 86, see Courts

Karpinski, E., 196
Katan, A., 194
Kempe, C. H., 6, 21, 108
Kempe, R. S., 6
Kemph, J. P., 194
Kerns, D. L., 108

Lay therapists, 178
Legal Aspects, 82–91
Lukianowicz, N., 194
Lynch, M., 9

Mann act, 87
Mead, M., 61, 191
Media, 206
Miranda warning, 91
Molestation, 11, 27, 121–126
Mrazek, P. B., 9
Meyerding, J., 196

National Center on Child Abuse
  & Neglect, 10
Neglect, 52, 134, 205
Niggeman, E. H., 108

Nurses, 175, 203, 206
Nurse-physician team, 99

Parents Anonymous, 176
Parental rights,
  termination of, 84
Parents United, 155, 164, 176–
  178
Pedophilia, 11, 27–34, 143
Physical abuse, 52, 98
Physicians, 94, 96, 99, 175, 201,
  203, 206
Pornography, 12, 44–46
Police, 84, 94, 167, 206
Prediction, 197–204
Prevention, 197–204
Preschool
  therapeutic, 135, 160, 163
Prostitution, 13, 42, 43, 190
Protective services, 94, 167, 175,
  206
Psychological tests, 72, 132, 152
Psychotherapy, 137, 142, 154–
  156, 162, 178

Rabbis, 200
Rape
  crisis centers, 86, 95, 142
  definition, 11
  forcible, 35, 126
  gang, 36–37
  initial interview, 97
  investigation, 95
  physical injury, 98
  pregnancy, 96
  statutory, 11, 34
Residential facilities, 160
Rimza, M. E., 108
Roberge, L., 9
Rush, F., 108
Russell, D. E. H., 18

Schechter, M. D., 9
Schools, 162, 165, 166, 200,
    appendix 3
Sexual abuse
  effects on child, 101
  evaluation, 126
  extrafamilial, 22–46, 106, 107
  first aid, 92–108, 134
  incidence, 13–18
  male victims, 39–42
  masked, 66–68, 76
  siblings, 147
  team, 94
  telephone hot line, 199
  treatment, 134–143
Sexual hormone reduction, 142
Sexual intercourse, 11
Sexual sadism, 12
Sloan, P., 195

Social workers, 92–108, 137, 142,
    154–156, 162, 178, 206
Spouse physical abuse, 52
Steele, B., 178, 189

Theatre groups, 199
Tilelli, J. A., 108
Teachers, 162, 163, 199, 200,
    appendix 3

United States Congress, 21

Volunteer groups, 166

Westermeyer, J., 194
Wollestonecraft, M., 205

Yorukoglu, A., 194